A Close Look at

CLOSE
READING

GRADES 6–12

A Close Look at

CLOSE READING

TEACHING STUDENTS TO ANALYZE COMPLEX TEXTS | **GRADES 6-12**

BARBARA MOSS

DIANE LAPP

MARIA GRANT

KELLY JOHNSON

Alexandria, Virginia USA

1703 N. Beauregard St. • Alexandria, VA 22311-1714 USA
Phone: 800-933-2723 or 703-578-9600 • Fax: 703-575-5400
Website: www.ascd.org • E-mail: member@ascd.org
Author guidelines: www.ascd.org/write

Judy Seltz, *Executive Director;* Stefani Roth, *Publisher;* Genny Ostertag, *Director, Content Acquisitions;* Julie Houtz, *Director, Book Editing & Production;* Katie Martin, *Editor;* Donald Ely, *Senior Graphic Designer;* Mike Kalyan, *Manager, Production Services;* Cynthia Stock, *Typesetter;* Andrea Wilson, *Senior Production Specialist*

All web links in this book are correct as of the publication date below but may have become inactive or otherwise modified since that time. If you notice a deactivated or changed link, please e-mail books@ ascd.org with the words "Link Update" in the subject line. In your message, please specify the link, the book title, and the page number on which the link appears.

PAPERBACK ISBN: 978-1-4166-2009-9   ASCD product #115002   n5/15
PDF E-BOOK ISBN: 978-1-4166-2035-8; see Books in Print for other formats.

Quantity discounts: 10–49, 10%; 50+, 15%; 1,000+, special discounts (e-mail programteam@ascd.org or call 800-933-2723, ext. 5773, or 703-575-5773). For desk copies, go to www.ascd.org/deskcopy.

Library of Congress Cataloging-in-Publication Data

Moss, Barbara, 1950–
   A close look at close reading : teaching students to analyze complex texts, grades 6–12 / Barbara Moss, Diane Lapp, Maria Grant, Kelly Johnson.
      pages cm
   Includes bibliographical references and index.
   ISBN 978-1-4166-2009-9 (pbk. : alk. paper) 1. Reading (Secondary) 2. Reading comprehension.
I. Title.
   LB1632.M67 2015
   428.4071'2—dc23
                                                         2015000506

24 23 22 21 20 19 18 17 16 15   1 2 3 4 5 6 7 8 9 10 11 12

A Close Look at
CLOSE READING
GRADES 6-12

INTRODUCTION

Think about yourself as a reader. How well do you read? What do you read? Why do you read? Are you equally good at reading all types of materials?

Reading proficiency is developed over time. It involves having a purpose for reading and being able to adjust reading behaviors to accomplish that purpose. Inside or outside school, people read for different reasons. Often we read for sheer entertainment. At other times, we read to deeply analyze a position statement, to identify specific information, or to compare how different authors address the same topic. We might also read a text for a combination of reasons or approach it for different purposes at different times.

As Snow (2001), reminds us, reading comprehension is complicated and multifaceted:

> "Getting the gist" or "acquiring new knowledge" is too limited a definition of successful comprehension. In some cases, successful comprehension involves scanning quickly to find the bit of information one wants (as in using the Internet) or reading in order to apply the information immediately but then forget it (as in programming an electronic device). Surely we want to include in our thinking about comprehension the capacity to get absorbed and involved in the text (as when reading a page-turner), as well as reacting critically (as when disagreeing with an editorial). Good readers can do all of these, and can choose when each of these approaches to reading is appropriate. (para. 26)

Learning to become a skilled, purposeful reader requires the support of teachers who know how to create focused, personalized, varied, scaffolded, and motivating learning experiences (Guthrie & Wigfield, 2000; Lapp & Fisher, 2009; Marinak & Gambrell, 2008). Such teachers know when to provide direct instruction, how to guide students' developing understandings, and when to move to the side to support each student's growing independence. Their instructional approach allows students to take ownership for deciding their purpose(s) for reading and for determining if a selected text is helping them accomplish their intention.

To support the development of reading proficiency, it behooves teachers at each grade level and in every discipline to engage students in wide reading experiences that invite the exploration of ideas, issues, and players, discussing a myriad of positions on world topics. Texts introduced for different instructional purposes should be both hard copy and digital, including books, documents, magazines, newspapers, tweets, websites, and blogs. Introducing students to a broadened perspective supports the 21st century goal of developing civic, political, financial, scientific, and literary "movers and shakers" who are equipped to make well-informed decisions about their personal and professional lives and who are also aware of how their decisions affect the broader world community. Instruction that opens students' eyes to the roles they might play in creating global collaboration involves delicately balancing attention to students' personal interests and motivators with exposure to the great literary, scientific, and historical texts we want them to know, love, and return to often for both pleasure and deepened understanding. In this text, we assert, and reassert through classroom scenarios, that this goal can be accomplished only through focused, systematic instruction from expert grade-level teachers who realize that the way to extend a student's knowledge is to first focus on what that student already knows and then motivate and challenge him or her to go further.

Although the designers of the Common Core State Standards for English Language Arts & Literacy in History/Social Studies, Science, and Technical Subjects were very clear about the delineation of each college and career readiness anchor standard across the grade levels, they did not prescribe how these standards should be taught. We can, however, infer from the early Common Core documents (National Governors Association Center for Best Practices [NGA Center] & Council of Chief State School Officers [CCSSO], 2010a) that each teacher is expected to design and implement engaging, relevant, meaningful, continuously assessed, and standards-aligned instruction. The intent of the Common Core is that all students be prepared to fully participate as learners, innovators, collaborators, and communicators in their daily lives. Later in this Introduction and throughout this text we share more explicit discussion of the Common Core's intentions, both stated and inferred from later NGA Center & CCSSO documents (Coleman & Pimentel, 2012), and some of the concerns educators have about Common Core–influenced literacy instruction.

Reading to Learn Is a Lifelong Process

One means by which the Common Core addresses each student's preparation for lifelong learning success is through exposure to and close reading and analysis of a wide and increasingly complex array of informational texts. We believe this approach will be effective if it remains in the hands of skilled teachers who understand how to scaffold the instruction of complex texts in ways that support both learner engagement and comprehension. Researchers (Duke & Bennett-Armistead, 2003; Mohr, 2006; Pappas, 1993) note that, from the earliest years, many children prefer reading informational texts and that doing so prepares them to read for many purposes: to note key details, understand the nuances of carefully selected language, follow the development of ideas, infer author's perspective and implied information—all with the primary purpose of scrutinizing layers of information to arrive at a careful interpretation and evaluation of an author's message.

Students do, however, need more than just exposure to texts in order to become proficient readers; they also need the right kind of instruction from excellent teachers. Due to the outstanding work of researcher Jeanne Chall, you might be familiar with the adage that "in K–3 children are learning to read, and in 4–12 children are reading to learn" (Chall & Jacobs, 2003; Chall, Jacobs, & Baldwin, 1990); however, educators can hardly stop teaching reading after grade 3. The progression of reading skill development delineated in the Common Core standards underscores that, as students advance through the grade levels, they need systematic, focused, and purposeful instruction in order to develop and refine their analytic skills and comprehend increasingly complex texts in each content area. Richard Vacca (Moss, 2002) cautions that the "learning to read" and "reading to learn" dichotomy is a false one, and Laura Robb (2002) points out that "what many researchers have now shown is that for all children, learning to read and reading to learn should be happening simultaneously and continuously, from preschool through middle school—and perhaps beyond" (p. 23).

Just how this delicate teaching-and-learning dance occurs as students learn to closely read a text is our focus in the pages to come.

What's Your Latest Experience with Close Reading?

What formal reading instruction did you receive after 3rd grade? For most of us, the answer is "Little." Yet we have all had the experience of sitting in a classroom and struggling to make sense of the assigned text because we didn't have the right context for learning the content, or we didn't understand the language.

Teachers can and should challenge students to read increasingly complex texts, but we must remember that as students engage with texts and topics, they do so with variations in language, background knowledge, and reading skills. We must teach and support each student in both learning to read and reading to learn widely and deeply across grade levels.

Supporting students' close reading endeavors involves making a text's language, content, and structure increasingly accessible through purposeful repeated readings that are accompanied by text-focused conversations and questions that respond to the students' emerging thinking. These questions should push students back into the text, call their attention to additional aspects of the text's meaning and workings, and invite additional insights. Teachers who engage students in close reading instruction do so with the goal of making text analysis a habit of practice. Eventually, the students will be able to deploy the process independently whenever they need to find a way to support their comprehension.

What kind of close reading do you engage in outside of a school classroom? Maybe you're thinking about the other day, when you had to scrutinize the warning label on your new prescription medication. Or about how you pored over the assembly directions for a new piece of furniture or the Google Maps directions to that new restaurant. Maybe it was your close reading of the fine print on an insurance, health, or employment document or the details of a contract you had to sign. Or when you reviewed certain character descriptions in a novel to prepare for a book club discussion, took a close look at the district's new testing policy for points to raise at the faculty meeting, or read between the lines of your sister's e-mail message to try to figure out what she really hopes to get for her birthday. Diane recently had a close reading experience when she gathered with a group of friends to play Mexican Train, a game played with dominoes. As it happened, different players came in with different interpretations of the game's rules, and eventually, a copy of the official rules was downloaded and printed. For the rest of the evening, whenever a point of contention arose about proper procedure, these rules were closely read multiple times by multiple players and then collaboratively discussed before play resumed.

As Diane watched and listened, it was obvious to her that the way that the players kept returning to the game's directions (text) to scrutinize the language and the diagrams (structure) was very much like what students do as they return to a text for closer and closer analysis to find author clues and cues that help them understand what is being stated, what is being implied, and what is being left unsaid. Diane realized that she and the other players were not only closely reading the text but also closely reading the situation and one another's tone of voice, word choices, and body language in order to agree on how to proceed.

As we hope this example and your own have clarified, close reading is far from just a "school skill" to be taught and tested as part of Common Core implementation; it's a regular part of daily life. Every day, we and our students are called on to use cues and clues to arrive at reasoned interpretations of both spoken and written language, both inside the classroom and out in the world.

A Preview of the Text Ahead

The Common Core State Standards place close text reading in the spotlight as never before and give special attention to the close reading of informational text. While willing to teach students to engage in close reading of a wide array of texts, both literary (e.g., stories, poetry, drama) and informational, many educators are wondering what, exactly, this involves. Through our own teaching and conversations with our colleagues, we have arrived at one understanding of how to teach students to closely read texts, which we share with you in this publication. In the pages ahead, we use classroom scenarios to address a number of questions:

- What is the process for closely reading a text?
- Is the process of close reading similar across the grades and content areas?
- Why should students learn the process of closely reading a text?
- How does close reading align with the other classroom literacy practices—writing, speaking, and listening?
- Can close reading occur within a variety of grouping arrangements?
- How can the background knowledge and language readers need to engage with a text be "backfilled" rather than "frontloaded"?

- How can the complexity of a text be determined?
- What are text-dependent questions, and how do they support close reading?
- How often should students engage in close reading, and within what contexts?
- How does formative assessment during close reading support differentiated instruction?
- What do the Common Core assessments that focus on close text reading really measure?

In **Chapter 1,** we tackle the topic of complex texts from multiple vantage points. First we discuss the factors that make a text complex. Then we offer rubrics for evaluating the complexity of a text. Finally, we model how to use these rubrics to evaluate the complexity of both literature and informational texts. We highlight the fact that what a teacher identifies as the factors of text complexity must be addressed as explicit points of instruction. Identification of these factors depends on the characteristics of each of the students who will be reading the text as well as the features of the text. Using examples, we illustrate how both middle and high school teachers use the text complexity rubrics to identify the teaching points they will need to address if their students are to have successful close text reading experiences with both literary and informational texts. Many of the texts selected as examples are from Appendix B of the Common Core State Standards for English Language Arts (ELA) & Literacy, which provides exemplars of grade-level texts.

In **Chapter 2,** we focus on the reader and how information is processed during close reading. We also look at the process of close reading and the comprehension benefits it brings. The differences between shared and close reading practice and instruction, along with ideas about how often to engage students in close reading, are also addressed.

In **Chapter 3,** we discuss the practical tasks of planning, implementing, and managing close reading instruction. Using illustrations from both middle and high school classrooms, we look at how to do the following:

- Identify initial teaching points for a close reading
- Create effective text-dependent questions
- Prepare a text for a close reading
- Model text annotation and close reading
- Support students as they engage in close text reading
- Revise teaching points during a close reading
- Design various grouping configurations to support close reading

- Support English language learners and striving readers
- Use sentence frames to support academic language use during close reading conversations
- Differentiate instruction and instructional supports

We have been mindful to make these composite classrooms in our scenarios diverse—reflective of today's typical school environments, where students are likely to present a variety of linguistic, cultural, and academic differences. We are also careful to show how the identified strategies can be scaffolded to support the learning of all of these students.

Chapter 4 describes disciplinary literacy and then shares why close reading should be a component of learning in each of the disciplines. Noting that texts are classified by the Common Core standards as narrative, informational, persuasive/argumentative, and additional forms, we discuss the characteristics of each and offer justifications to clarify why there has been so much emphasis of late on reading informational texts, in both digital and print forms. We compare the Common Core's text exemplars and other texts, and we include a chart to provide an easy reference of informational texts across grade levels and disciplines. We also discuss how the development of close reading skills might progress within each discipline under the guidance of an expert teacher.

Engaging in a close reading involves communication through speaking, listening, and also writing. **Chapter 5** identifies the language, speaking and listening, and writing standards within the Common Core that support close reading experiences. We share examples of instructional routines that develop these literacies, paying special attention to the skill development associated with Writing Standard 1 (CCRA.W.1), in which students who learned to state opinions and support those opinions with data in the elementary grades move on to taking a stance and posing arguments. All of the instructional scenarios in this chapter illustrate the need to continually strengthen the language abilities of all students so they are able to engage in collaborative, student-to-student conversations about the texts they are closely reading and use the information learned from a close reading to support the stances they will later share through their written and spoken positions. We also include self-assessment measures that enable students to evaluate their own performance as listeners and speakers.

Chapter 6 emphasizes the value of formative assessment for student learning and instructional planning, particularly when it comes to teaching students to analyze complex texts. We begin by defining and illustrating the cycle of formative assessment and sharing examples of how to collect and make instructional use of formative assessment data. Then we take a look at the Common Core assessments under development and the specific tasks that are being assessed, along with the related standards. The instructional scenarios provided illustrate how teachers can use formative assessment data gleaned during and after instruction to modify and support their close reading instruction.

Before we proceed, however, we want to take a few minutes to talk about the elephant in the room. We mean, of course, the Common Core State Standards for English Language Arts & Literacy in History/Social Studies, Science, and Technical Subjects. Their focus on literacy across the disciplines and the close reading of both literature and informational text is likely why many of you are reading this book.

Common Core State Standards: FAQs

Although the expressed intent of the Common Core is to provide a common set of state-endorsed standards and assessments that will prepare all students with the skills they will need for success in college and workplace situations, a significant number of educators are expressing skepticism about this goal and concerns about the standards, their implementation, their assessment, and the consequences of that assessment. Fresh in many of these educators' minds is No Child Left Behind, with its publicly shared data on students' year-to-year achievement on statewide assessments, mandated program improvement for schools labeled as failing, and blame assigned to teachers when students did not meet identified benchmarks.

Let's address some of these concerns by addressing a few specific and frequently asked questions about the Common Core.

1. What exactly is the intent of the Common Core State Standards?

The Common Core State Standards are a scaffolded set of skill expectations to be met by students in grades K–12. The crafters propose that acquiring the identified skills will prepare students to succeed in college and the workplace.

There is one set of standards for English language arts, which is subdivided into the four literacy areas ("strands") of reading, writing, speaking and listening, and language. A second set of standards has been developed for mathematics. The ELA standards, the focus of this text, also include a separate section addressing how the anchor standards in the reading and writing strands should be addressed as literacy standards in the disciplines of history/social studies, science, and technical subjects in grades 6–12. In short, the anchor standards for each literacy area describe the skills students should master by the time they graduate. The grade-level versions of each anchor standard chart the gradual development of these skills.

For example, Reading Anchor Standard 10 (ELA-LITERACY.CCRA.R.10) notes that students should be able to read grade-appropriate complex texts. The 1st grade version of this standard calls for students to read texts of appropriate complexity for grade 1 with prompting and support. By grades 11–12, students are expected to be able to read and comprehend both literary and informational texts at the grades 11–12 level of complexity. We can infer that as students move from grade 1 to grade 12, the instruction they receive should help them acquire the skills they need to read texts that are both increasingly difficult and grade-level appropriate. If students master this standard, the reasoning goes, fewer of them will need remedial college courses and more of them will be on track to graduate within a four-year time period.

The skills students need to read and understand increasingly complex literary and informational texts are addressed in Reading Anchor Standards 2–9, which cover the ability to identify key ideas and details in texts, an awareness of the craft and structures underlying texts, and the ability to compare ideas in texts and synthesize new understanding. Reading Anchor Standard 1 (ELA-LITERACY. CCRA.R.1) calls for students to closely read texts. The grade-by-grade variations identify the incremental development of the skill of close reading for both literature and informational text. We can infer that this process of close reading will support students' ability to gain the skills they need to read increasingly complex texts as they move toward graduation and future work situations. We must be aware that these assumptions regarding the skill development for each standard across each grade level are not based on a body of research but instead represent the shared opinions of the experts who developed the standards. This should not cause alarm, because expert opinion has long been used to develop scope and sequence charts for basal readers. This realization should allow you, also an instructional expert, to be less constrained by these progressions and instead use them as a guide for grade-level performance.

2. Who determines the instruction needed to achieve the Common Core standards?

Nowhere in the standards are teachers told how to accomplish the skill development trajectory illustrated in the Common Core. On the contrary, the standards document notes that

> By emphasizing required achievements, the Standards leave room for teachers, curriculum developers, and states to determine how those goals should be reached and what additional topics should be addressed. Thus, the Standards do not mandate such things as a particular writing process or the full range of metacognitive strategies that students may need to monitor and direct their thinking and learning. Teachers are thus free to provide students with whatever tools and knowledge their professional judgment and experience identify as most helpful for meeting the goals set out in the Standards. (NGA Center & CCSSO, 2010a, p. 4)

In our analysis, concerns about teachers having a mandated curriculum are unfounded at this time; however, we encourage keeping a watchful eye to be sure that the more recent publishers' criteria for the Common Core State Standards (Coleman & Pimentel, 2012) are not moving in favor of published programs and materials that skirt teacher decision making and prerogative of use, as was initially published in the standards. Comments such as "Given the focus of the Common Core Standards, publishers should be extremely sparing in offering activities that are not text based" (p. 10) cause us to be cautious about what may really occur in future instructional implementation. However, since we do believe that published materials are a must for busy teachers, we remain optimistic that the individual teacher will be the determiner of what, how, and with whom both published and teacher-created materials are used in the classroom.

3. What role did the federal government play in developing the Common Core?

A third concern is that the standards were federally designed and are now being foisted on states. This is a misconception. As early as 2007, governors and state school administrators meeting as the Council of Chief State School Officers (CCSSO) voiced concerns about how many students entering college needed to take remedial English and math classes and advocated that K–12 schools better prepare students in these areas. Soon the National Governors Association (NGA) and Achieve, a private consulting firm, entered the discussion, noting that a review of state standards indicated that states had different expectations regarding what should be learned in school. With better coordination, they theorized, students throughout the United States could acquire the same skills, regardless of their school location. Together, NGA and Achieve began seeking advice from education experts about what these skills should be, consulting business leaders regarding the literacy skills needed for workplace success as well as higher education experts about the real expectations for entrance to a four-year college. The Gates Foundation supplied funding to advance these conversations and the resulting standards development. The federal government was not involved in these conversations; federal law prohibits the creation of national standards and related tests.

Former teacher and *Education Week* blogger Anthony Cody (2013) has noted that the Common Core standards were drafted by a group of 27 individuals, all but two of whom were affiliated with the College Board, ACT, Achieve, Student Achievement Partners, and America's Choice. University professors were the responders to the initial drafts. The development of the standards has been criticized because of the absence of teachers and parents in the early stages. This was indeed an oversight, but the process has since become more inclusive in continuing to solicit the voices of teachers and parents.

4. What role has the federal government played since the Common Core's initial planning stages?

The U.S. Department of Education offered Race to the Top funding to states with education standards it judged sufficiently rigorous to prepare students for success in college and the workplace. Many states adopted the Common Core as a way to access these funds. Although the Department of Education did not name Common Core adoption as a prerequisite for Race to the Top funding—and, in fact, did not require adoption of any specific set of standards—to some, the Race to the Top incentive smacks of government manipulation.

5. Were states required to adopt the Common Core standards?

States were not required to adopt the standards. They adopted them voluntarily.

6. Do the Common Core standards nationalize state curricula?

The standards identify goals that, if met, will ensure that students have the skills they need for academic success in grades K–12 and success in college and the workplace. Because the standards do not mandate instruction, states and teachers can decide the curriculum, texts, and instructional methods that best support students in accomplishing the standards' goals.

7. Do the Common Core ELA/literacy standards call for students to read more informational text and less literature (novels, poems, short stories, and other fiction)?

The distribution of informational and literary texts noted by the Common Core is aligned with the distribution of texts appearing in the National Assessment of Educational Progress (NAEP), which has been used for many years to assess students across the country. In 4th grade, the recommendation is that students read 50 percent literary text and 50 percent informational text. By 8th grade, the suggested distribution changes to a 45 percent literary/55 percent informational text split. By 12th grade, the suggestion is that 30 percent of reading focus on literature and 70 percent focus on informational text across the school day. What on the surface looks like a reduction in the amount of literature students will be reading actually reflects the Common Core's expanded focus on reading across the disciplines—in history/social studies, in science, and in technical subjects. The new expectation is that attention to how successfully students read informational texts should no longer be the exclusive purview of language arts teachers.

8. Will teachers need to teach to the Common Core's official assessments?

The Smarter Balanced Assessment Consortium ("Smarter Balanced") and the Partnership for Assessment of Readiness for College and Careers (PARCC) are separate, state-led consortia working collaboratively to develop assessments aligned to the Common Core. Members of the consortia include educators, policymakers, researchers, and community groups. The Department of Education has provided a four-year, $175 million grant to fund the consortia. Other funding has been provided by charitable foundations.

Because the Common Core assessments will measure attainment of the skills identified by the standards, there should be a close alignment between what is taught and what is assessed. Following a spring 2013 piloting of the assessments, many educators, students, and parents responded that the draft assessments were too long and too difficult. Less than one-third of the students who were assessed scored "proficient," with only 4 percent of English language learners reaching that mark. Hopefully, Smarter Balanced and PARCC will address these concerns through revisions of the assessments as they continue to gather insights from the tryouts that occurred with more than five million students in grades 3–8 and 11, a small sample of students in grades 9 and 10, and their teachers during the spring of 2014. Many teachers and students were also surveyed regarding their impressions of the test content and testing process. Despite very few and minor glitches with technology, the testing seems to have gone quite well, and the vast majority of surveyed students liked taking the assessments on computers and iPads. As test and survey data are further analyzed, test administration manuals and items will be revised to ensure further clarity. Language supports, including interactive glossaries in multiple languages and dialects, will also be assessed for clarity. Additionally, test versions shared through Braille keyboards and sign language interpreters will be evaluated to ensure that all students have equal access to appropriate testing materials. It appears that all related assessment documents will remain responsive to information received from school personnel.

9. Will curriculum materials be aligned with the Common Core standards?

This decision is left to states and school districts. Publishing companies have always considered standards in the creation of their materials. Pearson

Foundation, a major publisher of K–12 education materials, and the Gates Foundation have generated Common Core–related professional development for teachers. While many publishing companies are creating materials aligned to the Common Core, Secretary of Education Arne Duncan, speaking at a January 2014 meeting with ASCD, made it clear that the federal government would not be endorsing any set of materials. "In fact, not a word, not a single semicolon of curriculum will be created, encouraged, or prescribed by the federal government," Duncan said. "We haven't done so—and we won't be doing so, and that is how it should be" (Duncan, 2014, para. 24).

10. Will English language learners and students who struggle academically suffer because of the Common Core standards?

We believe that the Common Core will afford all students, including those who speak English as an additional language, those who have special needs, and those who are gifted, increased opportunities to acquire the language and skills needed to succeed. Like many successful intervention programs, the Common Core standards reflect high expectations for all students and identify the skill progression students need to meet these high expectations. Students grow when they are engaged in very purposeful instruction and interventions that are identified through formative assessment. Because of the Common Core standards' grade-by-grade focus on skill acquisition and development, teachers will be able to assess students' strengths and needs and target instruction accordingly. Remember, because the standards do not identify any prescriptive instruction, teachers will be able to use assessment data to design instruction that accommodates student differences.

11. Were the Common Core standards field-tested?

They were not. Education historian Diane Ravitch (2013) has argued that the Common Core standards should have been field-tested before implementation. While we agree, we see the early implementation of the standards as a "try on/ try out" period. Once teachers have an opportunity to develop instruction that is supportive of implementation, there will be real data to consider. We hope these data will be analyzed and the standards will be revised as needed to support better learning outcomes. As noted earlier in this discussion, during the spring of 2014, students across the country were engaged in PARCC and Smarter Balanced field testing to establish the validity and reliability of assessment items and to determine that they were fair for administration to all students. Schools and teachers also had a chance to determine their level of readiness for implementation of aligned instruction that is scheduled to begin in the spring of 2015. As teachers consider the resulting data, they will have an opportunity to assess the standards through day-to-day implementation and continuous formative assessment. For additional information regarding the spring 2014 tryouts, visit Smarter Balanced's report at www.smarterbalanced.org/field-test.

12. What is to be gained from continuing with the implementation of the Common Core standards?

As you read the standards, ask yourself if any of these skills are ones you would not want every child to possess. We believe you will agree that if every student gains proficiency with all of the skills the Common Core identifies, we will indeed have a nation of very powerful thinkers. There is nothing in the Common Core that, if accomplished, will harm students' potential for success.

In our opinion, the Common Core standards are worth a try. A nation with thinkers who exhibit the skills identified in the standards will be a nation of citizens who are able to interpret, critique, and evaluate what they hear and read, and able to compare perspectives and take a data-supported stance while creating and presenting a focused spoken or written argument. This text is designed to support you in using your skills as a teacher to give every student this opportunity.

We encourage you to continue to reflect on what you believe are the strengths and weaknesses of the Common Core standards. Your perspective will be informed by data you gather as you work with your students, and these data will guide your decisions about how best to support each student's literacy learning.

All of the instructional ideas we share in *A Close Look at Close Reading* are ones we and our colleagues in our professional learning communities use to support middle and high school students' close reading of both informational and narrative text across the disciplines and grades. They reflect the solutions we have crafted in response to legitimate concerns and actual instructional challenges. The rubrics, templates, checklists, guides, and forms we provide in this book are classroom tested, and we encourage you to download copies for your own use from the ASCD website (www.ascd.org/ASCD/pdf/books/CloseReading Tools612). Finally, each scenario and teacher mentioned in this book is real. We may not have used their real names, but every instructional composite is based on real classroom instruction implemented by our colleagues or ourselves.

As you think about the ideas and examples we share, remember that the success of every child depends on well-prepared teachers who understand how to design literacy instruction that includes close reading, talking, and writing about texts. Remember, also, that you are one of those teachers. We hope to convince you to give close reading instruction a try.

Barb Dione Maria Kelly

CHAPTER 1

UNDERSTANDING AND EVALUATING TEXT COMPLEXITY

In the United States today, teachers and administrators are buzzing about the Common Core State Standards, especially the English language arts (ELA) requirements for disciplinary literacy. The Common Core's ELA standards for grades 6–12 extend far beyond English class to disciplines including science, social science, and technical subjects, such as physical education. It's been said that this requirement for "cross-content or schoolwide literacy—reading, writing, speaking, and listening—is perhaps the most significant change faced by middle schools and high schools" (Achieve et al., 2013, p. 4).

What does this mean for your students? It means that they will read more than ever; they will be reading more challenging, complex texts than in the past; and you will be responsible for teaching them to analyze, understand, and learn from those texts. It will require big shifts in terms of the classroom experiences you provide, the texts you use with students, the reading tasks you assign, and the way you think about your instructional practice. According to the Partnership for Assessment of Readiness for College and Careers (2011), one of the assessment consortia for the Common Core State Standards,

> A significant body of research links the close reading of complex text—
> whether the student is a struggling reader or advanced—to significant gains
> in reading proficiency and finds close reading to be a key component of
> college and career readiness. (p. 7)

To create the instruction that will help each of your students achieve the goals of the Common Core standards and, in doing so, become more proficient readers and writers in your discipline and in all others, you need both a thorough understanding of the standards and a solid grasp of the concepts and practices related to text complexity and close reading. In this chapter, we will use a question-and-answer format to explore the questions about text complexity and close reading that we are most often asked by the teachers with whom we work.

A High-Level View of Text Complexity

Take a moment to review the following list of secondary texts and put them in order from least complex (1) to most complex (6):

_____ *The Sound and the Fury*
_____ *The Hunger Games*
_____ "The Meaning of the Fourth of July for the Negro"
_____ "How Aerodynamics Works"
_____ "California Launches 'Toilet-to-Tap' Water Purification Program"
_____ The King James Bible

What criteria did you use in your rankings? Did you think about the content and how accessible it might be to readers? Did you consider the kind of vocabulary likely to be used in these texts and their general language style? Maybe you considered the length of the text overall, how many syllables were in the longest words, the length of the sentences, and how many concepts might be bound within each sentence. And perhaps you factored in the authors' thematic purposes.

When ranking the complexity of these texts, you were thinking about **quantitative features**—ones that can be counted, like the number of syllables—and also about **qualitative features**—aspects such as the language used, the complexity of the shared ideas, and other attributes of the text, such as its structure, style, and levels of meaning. In your ranking, if you thought about how challenging the text would be for a specific reader or group of readers, you were considering a third dimension of text complexity, referred to as **reader/text factors.** All three dimensions factor in when it's time to select a text that is sufficiently complex for students to read closely.

Answers to 12 Frequently Asked Questions About Text Complexity

1. Reading Anchor Standard 10 of the Common Core standards states that students should read and comprehend complex literary and informational texts independently and proficiently. What does this mean?

The Common Core's ELA/literacy standards for grades 6–12 are arranged in three grade-level bands: grades 6–8, grades 9–10, and grades 11–12. Reading Anchor Standard 10 calls for students to read subject-appropriate narrative and informational texts that are within their specified grade-level bands. So, for example, at grades 6–8 level, the standard for informational text (RI.6.10) asserts that students will "read and comprehend literary nonfiction in the grades 6–8 text complexity band proficiently, with scaffolding as needed at the high end of the range" (NGA Center & CCSSO, 2010a, p. 39). When students reach the high end of a band (i.e., by the end of grade 8, grade 10, or grade 12), they are expected to be able to read texts in that band "independently and proficiently"—that is, without scaffolding.

2. Why is it so important that every teacher be aware of Reading Anchor Standard 10's call for students to read increasingly complex texts?

All teachers need to focus on Reading Standard 10 for the following reasons:

1. The standard applies to all students in all the content areas that are covered by the ELA/literacy standards, including history/social studies, science, and technical subjects.
2. It requires that teachers in grades 2–12 assign students texts that may be more challenging than those teachers have assigned in the past.
3. It means that teachers in all content areas in grades 2–12 will need to ensure that their students get a regular diet of complex texts.

In other words, students at all grade levels will benefit from instruction that helps build their understanding of the process of close reading and further develops the skills and stamina they will need to closely read complex texts. All teachers will need to create lessons that scaffold student understanding in ways that will allow them to read appropriately complex texts independently by the end of the school year.

3. Why do the Common Core standards call for students to read texts that are more complex?

The emphasis on increased text complexity in the Common Core can be traced to an intriguing study published by ACT (2006), the company that creates the widely used college readiness exam of the same name. This study examined 568,000 8th, 10th, and 12th graders' results on the three reading tests of the ACT and compared these scores against a benchmark level of "college readiness"— which predicted college acceptance, retention, and attainment of a 3.0 grade point average. Only 51 percent of the 12th grade students in the study met this benchmark.

The ACT researchers then took a closer look at student responses to determine what factors distinguished students who met the benchmark from those who did not. They divided the texts found on the tests into three levels (uncomplicated, more challenging, and complex) and analyzed student responses to each text type. Based on these data, ACT concluded that "students who can read complex texts are more likely to be ready for college. Those who cannot read complex texts are less likely to be ready for college" (2006, p. 11).

The texts students presently read at all grade levels are far less complex than they should be if students are to attain the literacy levels they will need for college and career success. For example, Williamson (2006) reports that the complexity level of "college and career texts," meaning the texts students typically read as part of college coursework or that are required for career success, is around a Lexile measure of 1350L (see pp. 22–24 for more about Lexile measures). This is 130 points *higher* than the complexity level of materials presently used with high school students in grades 11 and 12, which are typically around a Lexile measure of 1220L. While student reading materials in grades 4 and up have become easier over time (Adams, 2010–11), college texts have become more difficult (Stenner, Koons, & Swartz, 2010).

In order to close this "text complexity gap," the Common Core standards recommend students begin reading texts with higher Lexile measures in grades 2 and 3. It falls to teachers to provide the direct skill instruction and scaffolding that students need to do so. A wise teacher knows when and where to add scaffolds that support learning within each discipline and enable students to make sense of unfamiliar language, concepts, and stylistic devices used by the author; gain an understanding of text structures, purpose, and intent; and build surface or nonexistent topical knowledge. Put concisely, good instruction supports students' reading of increasingly complex texts, first by showing them how to tackle these texts and then by giving them many close reading opportunities.

4. What exactly does the term "text complexity" mean?

Text complexity refers to the *level of challenge* a text provides based on a trio of considerations: its quantitative features, its qualitative features, and reader/text factors. (These considerations are detailed in the answers to Questions 5–9.)

The concept of text complexity is based on the premise that students become stronger readers by reading increasingly challenging texts. Here is a simple analogy. Barb, one of the authors of this book, is a runner. She can continue to run at the same pace as she always has, which is very comfortable for her, but if she wants to run faster, she has to work at improving her speed—move out of her comfort zone and stretch herself. It will be a gradual process, requiring deliberate effort and lots of practice over a period of months (or, in her case, maybe years). In the same way, the writers of the Common Core want students to reach reading levels necessary for college and workplace success by high school graduation. To build the literacy skills identified in the Common Core State Standards, students in grades 2–12 need plenty of practice reading increasingly complex texts as they move from one grade level to the next. The writers of the Common Core reject the idea of putting students in "comfort level" instructional materials and keeping them there; instead, they challenge teachers to "ramp up" text difficulty as students move through each grade level in order to create increased challenge over time and support the continual development of literacy skill.

5. What's the difference between text complexity and "text difficulty"?

Be careful not to confuse text complexity with text difficulty. Some texts may be just too advanced for a student to read at a particular time—meaning that the student does not have the background knowledge, language, or reading skills necessary to unravel the complex ideas an author is sharing or understand the features the author is using to share these ideas. If it becomes clear during the close reading experience that a text you've selected for close reading is too difficult for your students—beyond their understanding of the topic, beyond their reading skill, or both—the proper response is to provide scaffolds during the experience.

These scaffolds might be additional questions you ask or an invitation for students to reread a section to focus on a perplexing word, phrase, idea, or structure. You might provide a cue or a prompt that leads students to recall previously learned information. You may need to look beyond scaffolds you originally planned and come up with new ones after observing students' annotations or listening to their conversations.

Scaffolds offered during the close reading are generally sufficient to support most students' comprehension of the text. However, if at the conclusion of the experience some students are still struggling, you will need to design additional contingency instruction that uses either the same text or a less complex text that is topically related in order to build students' background knowledge, language, and reading skills. If you do incorporate a new text, remember that it is not a substitute for the complex original but a scaffold back to it.

6. What are the quantitative features of text complexity?

Quantitative features of text complexity are the features that can be counted or quantified—sentence length, number of syllables, word length, word frequency, and other features that can be calculated on the computer. Typically, these calculations generate a grade-level designation, such as "6.5" (6th grade, fifth month).

7. What are Lexile text measures, and how do they correspond to grade-level designations?

Lexile text measures are a numeric representation of a text's readability. They have become the readability formula of choice for measuring the quantitative features of the texts recommended for use with the Common Core standards. Like other readability formulas (e.g., Accelerated Reader™ ATOS levels, the Fry

Readability Formula), Lexile text measures are based on factors such as word frequency and sentence length. However, rather than rate text in terms of grade levels, Lexiles generate a number that can range from 0L (the "L" is for "Lexile") to above 2000L. MetaMetrics, the company that created Lexile measures, also provides additional codes to clarify a text's appropriate audience. For example, texts that measure at 0L or below on the Lexile score receive a "BR" code for "beginning reader." Texts designated as "AD" ("adult directed") are those that are more appropriately read *to* a child than *by* a child. Texts coded "NC" ("nonconforming") may have higher Lexile measures than is typical for the publisher's intended audience, and those coded "HL" ("high low") have lower Lexile measures than expected for the intended audience. For information on additional Lexile codes, please see www.lexile.com.

There is no set correspondence between Lexile levels and grade levels; it's expected that students within a particular grade band will be able to comfortably read texts that fall within a range of Lexile levels. In Figure 1.1, you can see data on the typical Lexile levels of the middle 50 percent of secondary school readers midway through each school year juxtaposed with Lexile ranges of the texts recommended by the Common Core as challenging "stretch texts" necessary to keep students on track for mastering Reading Anchor Standard 10.

Figure 1.1 | **Typical Range of Lexile Levels in Secondary Readers and Common Core Stretch-Level Texts**

Grade	Mid-Year Lexile Levels of Middle 50% of Students	Text Demand of the Common Core Recommended "Stretch Level" Texts
6	665L–1000L	925L–1185L
7	735L–1065L	
8	805L–1100L	
9	855L–1165L	1050L–1335L
10	905L–1195L	
11–12	940L–1210L	1185L–1385L

Source: MetaMetrics (2014a, 2014b).

The guidelines for suggested Lexile bands in the Common Core are clearly higher than those indicating Lexile-to-grade correspondence. To experience these higher-Lexile texts in 8th grade social studies, for example, students may read *Narrative of the Life of Frederick Douglass* (1040L), one of the Common

Core's text exemplars listed in Appendix B of the standards document as part of a literature circle reading experience and then do a close reading from a stretch text like Raymond Bial's *The Strength of These Arms: Life in the Slave Quarters* (1140L). By giving our students experiences with texts at these "stretch" levels, we help to prepare them for the text complexity of career and college reading materials. However, just knowing that a text is at a "stretch" Lexile is not enough; we must also consider qualitative dimensions of these texts as well as our students' own skills and the nature of the tasks we give them.

8. What are the limitations of evaluating a text by quantitative features alone?

As you are probably aware, Lexile measures can sometimes be suspect. For example, Elie Wiesel's *Night* has a Lexile measure of 590L, placing it within the reading range of 2nd or 3rd graders. However, this book also contains mature content and weighty themes, addressing Nazi death camps, the death of family members, the loss of innocence, and life during the Holocaust. This text may not have complex language, but it certainly has complex themes that are beyond the grasp of most 8-year-old children. Rightfully, *Night* is a staple of high school classrooms, not elementary ones.

This discrepancy illustrates an important limitation of Lexile measures: They do not assess the *content* of a text. Quantitative measures of text complexity are the least reliable of the triad for just this reason. "Readability" measured in this way accounts for only about 50 percent of text difficulty (Shanahan, 2009). In order to get a more realistic perspective about text complexity we also need to consider a text's qualitative features and the knowledge, language, and sophistication of the students who will be reading that text.

9. What are the qualitative features of text complexity?

The qualitative features of a text are the aspects and nuances of it that can't be measured by a simple formula. They require careful content analysis by thoughtful teachers who scrutinize texts before sharing them with their students.

To further illustrate why it's impossible to determine the complexity of a text by simply counting its readability factors, imagine a 9th grader who is studying the life cycle of stars in Earth Science coming across this sentence: *The sun will burn out over a life span of about 10 billion years.* It's a simple sentence with easily decodable words, and a high school reader would be likely to know what each individual word means and be able to read the sentence with fluency and expression. Technically, most 9th graders would "understand" it. But they would have a deeper understanding if they also understood something about geologic time and the process of nuclear fusion, in which hydrogen atoms join together to form helium and energy. These understandings connect directly to the *life span* of a star and to the concept of a star *burning out.* To determine the true complexity of a sentence, then, we must also identify the related conceptual knowledge a reader needs for full comprehension.

When authors write, they make assumptions about the knowledge of the reader. When authors add features like examples, illustrations, and descriptions, they are helping to support the reader; without these supports, the reader must have more knowledge, related language, and motivation in order to stay with the text and comprehend its meaning. The conceptually required background knowledge, motivation, and proficiency with language needed on the part of the reader to comprehend a specific text are sometimes referred to as *knowledge demands.* Other qualitative dimensions of a text for a teacher to evaluate are *text structure, language features, meaning,* and *author's purpose.* To carefully analyze a text, teachers must consider the challenges of a text in view of each of these areas. Such a detailed analysis helps to flag dimensions of a text that may be challenging to students and will need to become specific teaching points during close reading lessons (see Chapter 3 for examples).

10. How do I go about analyzing the qualitative features of a text?

To determine the complexity of a text based on its qualitative features, you need to consider the students who will be reading the text and use criteria keyed to each dimension (text structure, language features, meaning, author's purpose, and knowledge demands) to analyze those areas that may interfere with students' comprehension. Both narrative and informational text can be evaluated by looking at these dimensions (see Figures 1.2 and 1.3), but the differences in these text types' content and purposes mean you'll need to use different criteria, which we'll look at now.

Figure 1.2 | **Qualitative Scoring Rubric for Narrative Text/Literature**

 Download

Dimension & Consideration	Questions	Scoring = 1 Easy or Comfortable Text	Scoring = 2 Moderate or Grade-Level Text	Scoring = 3 Challenging or Stretch Text
Text Structure: Organization	• Does the text follow a typical chronological plot pattern, or is it more elaborate and unconventional, incorporating multiple storylines, shifts in time (flashbacks, flash forwards), shifts in point of view, and other devices?	☐ The text follows a simple conventional chronological plot pattern, with few or no shifts in point of view or time; plot is highly predictable.	☐ The text organization is somewhat unconventional; may have two or more storylines and some shifts in time and point of view; plot is sometimes hard to predict.	☐ The text organization is intricate and unconventional, with multiple subplots and shifts in time and point of view; plot is unpredictable.
Notes on Organization				
Text Structure: Visual Support and Layout	• Is text placement consistent, or is there variability in placement, with multiple columns? • Are visuals compatible/consistent with the storyline?	☐ Text placement is consistent throughout the text and uses a large readable font. ☐ Illustrations directly support text content.	☐ Text placement may include columns, text interrupted by illustrations, or other variations; uses a smaller font size. ☐ Illustrations support the text directly but may include images that require synthesis of text.	☐ Text placement includes columns and many inconsistencies as well as very small font size. ☐ Few illustrations that support the text directly; most require deep analysis and synthesis.
Notes on Visual Support and Layout				

Text Structure: Relationships Among Ideas	• Are relationships among ideas or characters obvious or fairly subtle?	☐ Relationships among ideas or characters are clear and obvious.	☐ Relationships among ideas or characters are subtle and complex.	☐ Relationships among ideas or characters are complex, are embedded, and must be inferred.
Notes on Relationships Among Ideas			
Language Features: Author's Style	• Is it easy or difficult for the reader to identify the author's style? • Is the language used simple or more intricate, with complex sentence structures and subtle figurative language?	☐ The style of the text is explicit and easy to comprehend. ☐ The language of the text is conversational and straightforward, with simple sentence structures.	☐ The style of the text combines explicit with complex meanings. ☐ The language of the text is complex, may be somewhat unfamiliar, and includes some subtle figurative or literary language and complex sentence structures.	☐ The style of the text is abstract, and the language is ambiguous and generally unfamiliar. ☐ The text includes a great deal of sophisticated figurative language (e.g., metaphors, similes, literary allusions) and complex sentences combining multiple concepts.
Notes on Author's Style			
Language Features: Vocabulary	• Are the author's word choices simple or complex? • How demanding is the vocabulary load? • Can word meanings be determined through context clues or not?	☐ Vocabulary is accessible, familiar, and can be determined through context clues.	☐ Vocabulary combines familiar terms with academic vocabulary appropriate to the grade level.	☐ Vocabulary includes extensive academic vocabulary, including many unfamiliar terms.
Notes on Vocabulary			

Continued ↑

Figure 1.2 | Qualitative Scoring Rubric for Narrative Text/Literature (cont'd.)

Dimension & Consideration	Questions	Scoring = 1 Easy or Comfortable Text	Scoring = 2 Moderate or Grade-Level Text	Scoring = 3 Challenging or Stretch Text
Meaning	• Is the text meaning simple or rich with complex ideas that must be inferred?	☐ The text contains simple ideas with one level of meaning conveyed through obvious literary devices.	☐ The text contains some complex ideas with more than one level of meaning conveyed through subtle literary devices.	☐ The text includes substantial ideas with several levels of inferred meaning conveyed through highly sophisticated literary devices.
Notes on Meaning				
Author's Purpose	• Is the author's purpose evident or implied/ambiguous?	☐ The purpose of the text is simple, clear, concrete, and easy to identify.	☐ The purpose of the text is somewhat subtle, requires interpretation, or is abstract.	☐ The purpose of the text is abstract, implicit, or ambiguous, and is revealed through the totality of the text.
Notes on Author's Purpose				
Knowledge Demands	• How much and what kinds of background knowledge are needed to comprehend this text? • Do my students have the background knowledge to comprehend this text?	☐ Experiences portrayed are common life experiences; everyday cultural or literary knowledge is required.	☐ Experiences portrayed include both common and less common experiences; some cultural, historical, or literary background knowledge is required.	☐ Experiences portrayed are unfamiliar to most readers. The text requires extensive depth of cultural, historical, or literary background knowledge.
Notes on Knowledge Demands				

Figure 1.3 | **Qualitative Scoring Rubric for Informational Text**

 Download

Dimension & Consideration	Questions	Scoring = 1 Easy or Comfortable Text	Scoring = 2 Moderate or Grade-Level Text	Scoring = 3 Challenging or Stretch Text
Text Structure: Organization	• Is the pattern of the text clearly identifiable as descriptive, sequential, problem/solution, compare/contrast, or cause/effect? • Are signal words used to alert readers to these structures? • Are multiple structures used in combination?	☐ The text adheres primarily to a single expository text structure and focuses on facts.	☐ The text employs multiple expository text structures, includes facts and/or a thesis, and demonstrates characteristics common to a particular discipline.	☐ The text organization is intricate, may combine multiple structures or genres, is highly abstract, includes multiple theses, and demonstrates sophisticated organization appropriate to a particular discipline.
Notes on Organization				
Text Structure: Visual Support and Layout	• Is the text placement consistent, or is there variability in placement with multiple columns? • Are visuals essential to understanding the text without explanation? • Are visuals accompanying the text simple or complex? Do they require literal understanding or synthesis and analysis?	☐ The text placement is consistent throughout the text and uses a large readable font. ☐ Simple charts, graphs, photos, tables, and diagrams directly support the text and are easy to understand.	☐ The text placement may include columns, text interrupted by illustrations or other variations, and a smaller font size. ☐ Complex charts, graphs, photos, tables and diagrams support the text but require interpretation.	☐ The text placement includes columns and many inconsistencies, as well as very small font size. ☐ Intricate charts, graphs, photos, tables, and diagrams are not supported by the text and require inference and synthesis of information.
Notes on Visual Support and Layout				

Continued →

Figure 1.3 | **Qualitative Scoring Rubric for Informational Text (cont'd.)**

Dimension & Consideration	Questions	Scoring = 1 Easy or Comfortable Text	Scoring = 2 Moderate or Grade-Level Text	Scoring = 3 Challenging or Stretch Text
Text Structure: Relationships Among Ideas	• Are relationships among ideas simple or challenging?	☐ Relationships among concepts, processes, or events are clear and explicitly stated.	☐ Relationships among some concepts, processes, or events may be implicit and subtle.	☐ Relationships among concepts, processes, and events are intricate, deep, and subtle.
Notes on Relationships Among Ideas				
Language Features: Author's Style	• What point of view does the author take toward the material? • Is the author's style conversational or academic and formal?	☐ The style is simple and conversational, and it may incorporate narrative elements, with simple sentences containing a few concepts.	☐ Style is objective, contains passive constructions with highly factual content, and features some nominalization and some compound or complex sentences.	☐ Style is specialized to a discipline, contains dense concepts and high nominalization, and features compound and complex sentences.
Notes on Author's Style				
Language Features: Vocabulary	• How extensive is the author's use of technical vocabulary? • Can students determine word meanings through context clues?	☐ Some vocabulary is subject-specific, but the text includes many terms familiar to students that are supported by context clues.	☐ The vocabulary is subject-specific, includes many unfamiliar terms, and provides limited support through context clues.	☐ The vocabulary is highly academic, subject-specific, demanding, nuanced, and very context dependent.
Notes on Vocabulary				

Meaning • Is the amount and complexity of information conveyed through data sophisticated or not?	☐ The information is clear, and concepts are concretely explained.	☐ The information includes complex, abstract ideas and extensive details.	☐ The information is abstract, intricate, and may be highly theoretical.
Notes on Meaning			
Author's Purpose • Is the author's purpose evident or implied/ambiguous?	☐ The purpose of the text is simple, clear, concrete, and easy to identify.	☐ The purpose of the text is somewhat subtle or abstract and requires interpretation.	☐ The purpose of the text is abstract, implicit, or ambiguous, and is revealed through the totality of the text.
Notes on Author's Purpose			
Knowledge Demands • How much and what kinds of background knowledge are required to comprehend this text?	☐ The content addresses common information familiar to students.	☐ The content addresses somewhat technical information that requires some background knowledge to understand fully.	☐ The content is highly technical and contains specific information that requires deep background knowledge to understand fully.
Notes on Knowledge Demands			

Text Structure

How a text is structured or organized is the first key consideration for qualitative evaluation. Books with straightforward linear narrative plotlines, such as Jack London's *The Call of the Wild*, are generally easier for readers to comprehend than books with more elliptical structures, like Khaled Hosseini's *The Kite Runner*, which begins with a flashback that details a memory important to the main character and continues to use this device at critical junctures in the story. Well-organized informational texts often have one or more expository structures, which include description, sequence, compare/contrast, cause/effect, and problem/solution. The combination of these structures increases the level of challenge.

Visual supports and layout are another aspect of text structure that factors into text complexity. Illustrations and visual features such as maps, graphs, charts, and diagrams can support the reader's understanding, but sophisticated visual components may also increase the text's complexity. Layout features can also affect complexity, as can the text's font and the size of the type. Straightforward text layouts are generally the easiest for students to navigate, whereas layouts where multiple columns are interrupted by visuals can be very confusing.

When analyzing a text's structure and organization, also look at the relationships among ideas. These relationships can be simple or complex, but greater complexity means greater reading challenges. In a narrative text, you might consider the relationships among characters or among plots and subplots. In an informational text, you might look instead at the complexity of relationships among main ideas, facts and details, and the concepts discussed. For example, one of the challenges associated with reading *Romeo and Juliet* is keeping track of various characters like Benvolio, Mercutio, Tybalt, Paris, and Balthasar and connecting them to the main characters and the events of the plot.

Language Features

Language features, such as *writing style* and *vocabulary*, are the second important dimension of qualitative text complexity to consider. In a narrative text, the author's use of descriptive language and metaphors, similes, onomatopoeia, and other devices can make it difficult for students to understand the text's meaning. With informational text, the more conversational the author's style, the easier the text is for students to comprehend. This conversational style is one of the many strengths of Joy Hakim's *A History of US* series and a characteristic that distinguishes it from most textbooks. Here is how the author introduces a discussion of schools in the 19th century: "Remember, when you read history you need to put yourself in a time capsule and zoom back and try to think as people did then. If you do, you will find that America's citizens thought the United States was the most exciting, progressive place in the whole world" (Hakim, 2007, p. 120). One caution is in order here: While conversational informational texts like this are notable for their accessibility, students also need experiences with the more formal style of textbooks.

Consider the role of vocabulary in these two sentences:

> The man walked down the street, catching the eye of every girl he passed.

> The rakish young man sauntered down the boulevard, catching the eye of every young belle he encountered.

Clearly, the second sentence creates a different mood than the first sentence, but it also poses the challenge of more unfamiliar, somewhat archaic vocabulary. It is precisely these interesting word choices that make the text more complex, yet, at the same time, they create the rich mental pictures we experience when we read. Vocabulary is an important determiner of text complexity in both narrative and informational texts, and unfamiliar vocabulary poses even more challenge when context clues are lacking.

Vocabulary often poses particular challenges for students who are learning English as an additional language and students with identified reading or learning disabilities. Like every other child in your classroom, they will need their reading experience scaffolded in ways that support their learning.

Meaning

The meaning of a text—the sophistication of its ideas—is a third dimension of qualitative text complexity to factor into your evaluation. Is the book simple and one-dimensional, or are multiple layers of meaning present? For example, on one level, George Orwell's *Animal Farm* is a book about talking animals, but the author's allegorical message about a society gone wrong goes much deeper than that. It is important to have identified various levels of meaning before sharing a text with students so that your text-dependent questions can prompt students to look more deeply at the text meaning with each rereading.

Author's Purpose

The author's purpose is the fourth qualitative dimension to consider. Dee Brown's book *Bury My Heart at Wounded Knee*, a Common Core text exemplar for grades 9–10, is an extraordinary account of the genocide perpetrated by the dominant U.S. culture on Native Americans. In the Introduction, the author states his intention to fashion a narrative of the conquest of the Native American tribes as the victims experienced it. This author's purpose is evident and clearly stated. By contrast, in Martin W. Sandler's *Imprisoned: The Betrayal of Japanese Americans During World War II*, the author does not directly state his purpose, but over the course of the book, a reader can readily infer that his goal is to document the prejudice experienced by Japanese Americans during the war and to establish their innocence regarding the charges leveled against them.

Knowledge Demands

The fifth and final consideration for qualitative evaluation is the required background knowledge needed to navigate a text, which we mentioned earlier in the example about the sun burning out over its life span. Some books require students to know a lot about science, history, culture, or particular regions, while others are less background dependent. For example, students who know something about life during the U.S. civil rights movement will certainly appreciate Russell Freedman's *Freedom Walkers: The Story of the Montgomery Bus Boycott* more than students who know little about this time period. Conversely, a text like Gary Soto's poem "Oranges" can be easily understood without specific background knowledge about the time or place where it is set.

11. How do I evaluate the qualitative dimensions of text?

The rubrics presented in Figures 1.2 and 1.3 provide questions you can ask yourself about each of the qualitative dimensions we've covered. The criteria for each dimension for narrative texts (Figure 1.2) and informational texts (Figure 1.3) will help you determine whether to rate reading material as easy, moderately difficult, or challenging for students at a particular grade level. Remember, this evaluative process is important because it allows you to identify potential teaching points in relationship to each text and your particular group of students.

In Figure 1.4, we share how this rubric was used by 6th grade English teacher John Drake to identify teaching points when introducing his students to Sandra Cisneros's story "Eleven" (1991), a Common Core text exemplar for grades 6–8. Keeping his students in mind, he identified areas that might cause them difficulty and then used this information to plan instruction that would most effectively support their learning. The circled areas identify the possible points of struggle for Mr. Drake's students, and you can see his notes about how he plans to address these areas in his instruction.

Mr. Drake's annotated rubric shows that the text structure, vocabulary, and visual supports and layout of "Eleven" are within his 6th graders' comfort zone. The students do not need much support in building background knowledge about birthdays or the classroom setting, and most will relate to the experience of being embarrassed in front of peers. So Mr. Drake will tailor his close reading lessons to support students' understanding of characters' relationships, examine the text's style and language, explore its rich levels of meaning, and uncover the author's purpose. The text-dependent questions he plans to ask in these four areas redirect students back to the text to develop a deeper understanding of the story.

The next example, in Figure 1.5, illustrates how 10th grade history teacher Sora Pham assessed the qualitative aspects of Abraham Lincoln's "Gettysburg Address" (1863), a Common Core text exemplar for grades 9–10. To do so, she focused first on what areas of this informational text might be difficult for her students to grasp. Based on what you see in Ms. Pham's annotated template, what do you think her teaching points should be?

Ms. Pham's annotated rubric shows that she did not believe her students would struggle with the text organization, visual supports and layout, style, vocabulary, or purpose in Lincoln's great speech. But she suspected they would need more support with the required knowledge and the relationships among ideas. After all, this text is dense with reference to the U.S. Civil War and the events of the Battle of Gettysburg that she would need to help students uncover through text-dependent questions and multiple readings of the speech's three paragraphs.

By considering each of the qualitative criteria, teachers become more sensitive to the challenges of a text in terms of each dimension and are therefore better prepared to effectively instruct students as they encounter these challenging

Figure 1.4 | **Qualitative Scoring Rubric for Narrative Text/Literature Applied to Cisneros's "Eleven"**

↳ Download

Dimension & Consideration	Questions	Scoring = 1 Easy or Comfortable Text	Scoring = 2 Moderate or Grade-Level Text	Scoring = 3 Challenging or Stretch Text
Text Structure: Organization	• Does the text follow a typical chronological plot pattern, or is it more elaborate and unconventional, incorporating multiple storylines, shifts in time (flashbacks, flash forwards), shifts in point of view, and other devices?	☑ The text follows a simple conventional chronological plot pattern, with few or no shifts in point of view or time; plot is highly predictable.	☐ The text organization is somewhat unconventional; may have two or more storylines and some shifts in time and point of view; plot is sometimes hard to predict.	☐ The text organization is intricate and unconventional, with multiple subplots and shifts in time and point of view; plot is unpredictable.
Notes on Organization		*The structure is conventional and predictable and poses no challenges for students.*		
Text Structure: Visual Support and Layout	• Is text placement consistent, or is there variability in placement, with multiple columns? • Are visuals compatible/consistent with the storyline?	☑ Text placement is consistent throughout the text and uses a large readable font. ☐ Illustrations directly support text content.	☐ Text placement may include columns, text interrupted by illustrations, or other variations; uses a smaller font size. ☐ Illustrations support the text directly but may include images that require synthesis of text.	☐ Text placement includes columns and many inconsistencies as well as very small font size. ☐ Few illustrations that support the text directly; most require deep analysis and synthesis.
Notes on Visual Support and Layout		*Narrative text is consistent and easy for students to understand.*		

Text Structure: Relationships Among Ideas	• Are relationships among ideas or characters obvious or fairly subtle?	☑ Relationships among ideas or characters are clear and obvious.	☑ Relationships among ideas or characters are subtle and complex.	☐ Relationships among ideas or characters are complex, are embedded, and must be inferred.
Notes on Relationships Among Ideas		*Students are familiar with peer relationships like the one Rachel has with "stupid Sylvia Saldivar."*	*Students may not understand who the author is referring to when writing "they" or why mama is sad and needs to cry.*	
Language Features: Author's Style	• Is it easy or difficult for the reader to identify the author's style? • Is the language used simple or more intricate, with complex sentence structures and subtle figurative language?	☐ The style of the text is explicit and easy to comprehend. ☐ The language of the text is conversational and straightforward, with simple sentence structures.	☑ The style of the text combines explicit with complex meanings. ☑ The language of the text is complex, may be somewhat unfamiliar, and includes some subtle figurative or literary language and complex sentence structures.	☐ The style of the text is abstract, and the language is ambiguous and generally unfamiliar. ☐ The text includes a great deal of sophisticated figurative language (e.g., metaphors, similes, literary allusions) and complex sentences combining multiple concepts.
Notes on Author's Style			*Style of text includes inferences and similes (comparing growing older to an onion and tree trunk) and complex meanings (age of transition, internal struggle).*	
Language Features: Vocabulary	• Are the author's word choices simple or complex? • How demanding is the vocabulary load? • Can word meanings be determined through context clues or not?	☑ Vocabulary is accessible, familiar, and can be determined through context clues.	☐ Vocabulary combines familiar terms with academic vocabulary appropriate to the grade level.	☐ Vocabulary includes extensive academic vocabulary, including many unfamiliar terms.
Notes on Vocabulary		*Vocabulary is familiar, and words/phrases can be determined through context clues (underneath the year, wooden dolls).*		

Continued →

Figure 1.4 | **Qualitative Scoring Rubric for Narrative Text/Literature Applied to Cisneros's "Eleven" (cont'd.)**

Dimension & Consideration	Questions	Scoring = 1 Easy or Comfortable Text	Scoring = 2 Moderate or Grade-Level Text	Scoring = 3 Challenging or Stretch Text
Meaning	• Is the text meaning simple or rich with complex ideas that must be inferred?	☐ The text contains simple ideas with one level of meaning conveyed through obvious literary devices.	☑ The text contains some complex ideas with more than one level of meaning conveyed through subtle literary devices.	☐ The text includes substantial ideas with several levels of inferred meaning conveyed through highly sophisticated literary devices.
Notes on Meaning			*Students may not understand how this text is more than a story about a birthday but about a teacher-student relationship and feelings of powerlessness.*	
Author's Purpose	• Is the author's purpose evident or implied/ambiguous?	☐ The purpose of the text is simple, clear, concrete, and easy to identify.	☑ The purpose of the text is somewhat subtle, requires interpretation, or is abstract.	☐ The purpose of the text is abstract, implicit, or ambiguous, and is revealed through the totality of the text.
Notes on Author's Purpose			*Focus students' attention here, emphasizing how author gets us to feel what Rachel is feeling.*	
Knowledge Demands	• How much and what kinds of background knowledge are needed to comprehend this text? • Do my students have the background knowledge to comprehend this text?	☑ Experiences portrayed are common life experiences; everyday cultural or literary knowledge is required.	☐ Experiences portrayed include both common and less common experiences; some cultural, historical, or literary background knowledge is required.	☐ Experiences portrayed are unfamiliar to most readers. The text requires extensive depth of cultural, historical, or literary background knowledge.
Notes on Knowledge Demands		*Classroom setting will be familiar. Not all will relate to Rachel's reserve, but will understand feeling powerless or embarrassed.*		

Figure 1.5 | **Qualitative Scoring Rubric for Informational Text Applied to Lincoln's "Gettysburg Address"**

Dimension & Consideration	Questions	Scoring = 1 Easy or Comfortable Text	Scoring = 2 Moderate or Grade-Level Text	Scoring = 3 Challenging or Stretch Text
Text Structure: Organization	• Is the pattern of the text clearly identifiable as descriptive, sequential, problem/solution, compare/contrast, or cause/effect? • Are signal words used to alert readers to these structures? • Are multiple structures used in combination?	☑ The text adheres primarily to a single expository text structure and focuses on facts.	☐ The text employs multiple expository text structures, includes facts and/or a thesis, and demonstrates characteristics common to a particular discipline.	☐ The text organization is intricate, may combine multiple structures or genres, is highly abstract, includes multiple theses, and demonstrates sophisticated organization appropriate to a particular discipline.
Notes on Organization		*Single expository text structure with facts and information.*		
Text Structure: Visual Support and Layout	• Is the text placement consistent, or is there variability in placement with multiple columns? • Are visuals essential to understanding the text without explanation? • Are visuals accompanying the text simple or complex? Do they require literal understanding or synthesis and analysis?	☑ The text placement is consistent throughout the text and uses a large readable font. ☐ Simple charts, graphs, photos, tables, and diagrams directly support the text and are easy to understand.	☐ The text placement may include columns, text interrupted by illustrations or other variations, and a smaller font size. ☐ Complex charts, graphs, photos, tables, and diagrams support the text but require interpretation.	☐ The text placement includes columns and many inconsistencies, as well as very small font size. ☐ Intricate charts, graphs, photos, tables, and diagrams are not supported by the text and require inference and synthesis of information.
Notes on Visual Support and Layout		*Simple, comfortable visual layout for students. Easy to understand.*		

Continued →

Figure 1.5 | Qualitative Scoring Rubric for Informational Text Applied to Lincoln's "Gettysburg Address" (cont'd.)

Dimension & Consideration	Questions	Scoring = 1 Easy or Comfortable Text	Scoring = 2 Moderate or Grade-Level Text	Scoring = 3 Challenging or Stretch Text
Text Structure: Relationships Among Ideas	• Are relationships among ideas simple or challenging?	☐ Relationships among concepts, processes, or events are clear and explicitly stated.	☑ Relationships among some concepts, processes, or events may be implicit and subtle.	☐ Relationships among concepts, processes, and events are intricate, deep, and subtle.
Notes on Relationships Among Ideas			*Combines information about the U.S. Civil War, the Battle of Gettysburg, and President Lincoln's ideals.*	
Language Features: Author's Style	• What point of view does the author take toward the material? • Is the author's style conversational or academic and formal?	☑ The style is simple and conversational, and it may incorporate narrative elements, with simple sentences containing a few concepts.	☐ Style is objective, contains passive constructions with highly factual content, and features some nominalization and some compound or complex sentences.	☐ Style is specialized to a discipline, contains dense concepts and high nominalization, and features compound and complex sentences.
Notes on Author's Style		*Told from Lincoln's point of view, style is simple and contains a few concepts about freedom and liberty*		
Language Features: Vocabulary	• How extensive is the author's use of technical vocabulary? • Can students determine word meanings through context clues?	☑ Some vocabulary is subject-specific, but the text includes many terms familiar to students that are supported by context clues.	☐ The vocabulary is subject-specific, includes many unfamiliar terms, and provides limited support through context clues.	☐ The vocabulary is highly academic, subject-specific, demanding, nuanced, and very context dependent.
Notes on Vocabulary		*Students will be able to use context clues to determine meanings of such words/ phrases (final resting place, consecrate, died in vain).*		

Meaning	• Is the amount and complexity of information conveyed through data sophisticated or not?	☑ The information is clear, and concepts are concretely explained.	☐ The information includes complex, abstract ideas and extensive details.	☐ The information is abstract, intricate, and may be highly theoretical.
Notes on Meaning		Information is straightforward and concrete.		
Author's Purpose	• Is the author's purpose evident or implied/ambiguous?	☑ The purpose of the text is simple, clear, concrete, and easy to identify.	☐ The purpose of the text is somewhat subtle or abstract and requires interpretation.	☐ The purpose of the text is abstract, implicit, or ambiguous, and is revealed through the totality of the text.
Notes on Author's Purpose		The purpose is plain: to honor Civil War soldiers, liberty, and freedom.		
Knowledge Demands	• How much and what kinds of background knowledge are required to comprehend this text?	☐ The content addresses common information familiar to students.	☑ The content addresses somewhat technical information that requires some background knowledge to understand fully.	☐ The content is highly technical and contains specific information that requires deep background knowledge to understand fully.
Notes on Knowledge Demands			Students will need support in understanding references to the Civil War and events of the Battle of Gettysburg	

texts. No text evaluation is complete, [...]
and the task, which is the topic of the [...]

12. What are the reader/task factors of t[...]

The third leg of the text complexity tria[...] [...]
to reflections about students and their [...] levels of preparation [...]
the target text and the assigned learning [...]. Students are at the center of the
instructional enterprise, and this is as tr[...] with close reading of complex text[...]
as with any other learning experience. A[...]ording to Wessling, Lillge, and Van-
Kooten (2011), "Foregrounding student learning needs, abilities and interests provides a useful lens and necessary lens through which to interpret and implement
the [Common Core standards]" (p. 92). In other words, we cannot consider text
complexity without careful and deliberate consideration of our students and their
strengths and needs along with the demands of the tasks we plan to give them.

Complex texts and the demands of close reading require students to read in
ways that may be somewhat unfamiliar to them. Many are accustomed to reading
quickly and skimming and scanning texts in ways that may cause them to miss
important information. As Bauerline (2011) observes, "Complex texts require a
slower labor. Readers can't proceed to the next paragraph without getting the
previous one, they can't glide over unfamiliar words and phrases, and they can't
forget what they read four pages earlier. They must double back, discern ambi-
guities, follow tricky transitions . . . and acquire the knack of slow linear reading"
(p. 28). Developing these habits of practice requires time, experience, and effective teacher scaffolding.

Every day, as teachers plan lessons, they consider their readers in relationship
to the challenges of a text and consider if and how they will scaffold their instruction to create the optimum match between reader, text, and task. There are four
general areas of consideration that are essential to student success with close
reading of complex texts: (1) reading and cognitive skills, (2) prior knowledge
and experience, (3) motivation and engagement, and (4) specific task concerns.
A checklist like the one in Figure 1.6 can help you evaluate your students' readiness for a particular text.

Let's walk through this process, referring to our earlier example of "Eleven" as
it is read in a 6th grade classroom.

Figure 1.6 | **Comprehension Checklist**   Download

Reading and Cognitive Skills

☐ Do my students have the literal and critical comprehension skills to understand this text? If not, how will I scaffold the information?

☐ Will my students have the ability to infer the deeper meanings of the text rather than just achieve literal understanding? If not, what experiences will ready them for this?

☐ Will this text promote the development of critical thinking skills in my students?

What are my next instructional steps to support my students having a context for successfully reading the selected text?

Prior Knowledge and Experience

☐ Will my students grasp the purpose for reading the text?

☐ Do my students have the prior knowledge and academic vocabulary required for navigating this text?

☐ Are my students familiar with this particular genre and its characteristics?

☐ Do my students have the maturity level required to address the text content?

What are my next instructional steps to support my students having a context for successfully reading the selected text?

Motivation and Engagement

☐ Will my students be motivated to read this text based on its content and writing style?

☐ Do my students have the reading stamina to stick with this text with my support?

What are my next instructional steps to support my students having a context for successfully reading the selected text?

Task Concerns

☐ What is the level of difficulty of the task associated with this text?

☐ How much experience do my students have with this type of task?

☐ Have I created a moderately difficult task if the text is very challenging and/or created a more challenging task for an easier text?

What are my next instructional steps to support my students having a context for successfully reading the selected text?

Reading and cognitive skills. Students may have the literal comprehension skills to understand what it feels like to grow older. ("You don't feel eleven. Not right away. It takes a few days, weeks even, sometimes even months before you say Eleven.") However, a teacher may need to scaffold some of the deeper-level thinking skills that students may not have fully developed by comparing birthdays and growing older to an onion, a tree trunk, and wooden dolls. In all probability, many students will not automatically infer how the character feels about birthdays and how this age of transition creates an internal struggle within her. A teacher would probably need to make this a focal point for the lesson.

Prior knowledge and experience. "Eleven" is a story—a genre students are likely to be familiar with—and it has a clear story structure. Most 6th grade students will also have sufficient prior knowledge about having birthdays. But a teacher should carefully consider his or her specific group of students and how well they will be able to pick up the theme of inner conflict as the author's purpose.

Motivation and engagement. It is likely that students will have the motivation and engagement to read this text—if only to find out why the main character is struggling with having a birthday. In a close reading of this text, a teacher will probably want to focus attention on supporting students in other ways.

Task concerns. Obviously, this depends on the planned task. It's unlikely that all students will gain a rich understanding of "Eleven" if they are given 20 minutes to read the story independently and then explain its meaning. However, if the teacher provides a graphic organizer that the students can use for recording details and ideas about the story while they read, the task becomes infinitely more supportive.

For an example of how a teacher might examine the reader/task considerations with an informational text, we'll turn our attention back to the "Gettysburg Address."

Reading and cognitive skills. There are not too many words that students would have a hard time decoding in this text. As mentioned earlier, the vocabulary might give some students problems, but most 10th grade students would not struggle with the text's cognitive demands.

Prior knowledge and experience. The biggest concern might be students' lack of familiarity with why Lincoln is in Gettysburg dedicating "a portion of [this battle]field as a final resting place of those who here gave their lives that that nation might live" (para. 2). They may well need a bit more context about this time period to get a deeper understanding of the "great war" and the unfinished work that lay before the nation.

Motivation and engagement. Similarly, students without a great deal of prior knowledge about the Civil War era might not approach the text with much curiosity or eagerness. A teacher who understands the connection between prior knowledge and motivation might give students a bit of context to pique their interest and help them engage with the text.

Task concerns. Without careful consideration of the students themselves, assigning the "Gettysburg Address" could result in disengaged readers who check out in class and miss out on understanding the purpose, artistry, and historical impact of this famous speech.

13. How do I evaluate a text on all three dimensions of complexity?

For quantitative factors, we recommend using Lexile measures; for qualitative measures, the scoring rubrics in Figures 1.2 and 1.3; and for reader/task considerations, the checklist in Figure 1.6. Remember, all three dimensions of text complexity work in concert with the others. Considering only Lexile measures or only qualitative criteria, for example, will give you an incomplete picture of the text; you must also think about issues related to student needs and the tasks you might assign. The information you gain from analyzing these three dimensions will help you identify and prioritize the features you will address in class so that your students will be able to comprehend their reading.

⇒◆⇐

We hope that this chapter has answered many of your questions about text complexity, text evaluation, text selection, and how to identify related teaching points for close reading. In Chapters 2 and 3, we will discuss, through examples, how to make close reading a part of classroom practice. Understanding text complexity and close reading are major steps on the journey to achieving the major goal of the Common Core State Standards: for every student to become an expert, purposeful reader of increasingly complex texts.

CHAPTER 2

UNDERSTANDING THE ROLE OF THE CLOSE READER

There's been so much conversation about the importance of close reading that teachers may wonder if this practice involves just stepping aside and inviting students to read texts independently. While this is the eventual goal, close reading is a process, and it is highly unlikely that most students would know how to read and think deeply about a complex text if they had never been taught the process of doing so. To share expectations for close reading and to build a common language for discussing a close text reading with students, teachers will first need to model and discuss this process several times, using a wide array of texts selected for many purposes. The ultimate goal is for students to become independent readers who know when and how to engage in reading for entertainment as well as when and how to engage in close, rigorous reading.

The amount of instruction and modeling provided by the teacher for close reading will be dependent on the knowledge students have about the process. If they arrive in your classroom with a grasp of how to read closely, obviously you will have to do less. Once students know how to read a text and think deeply about it, they will be better able to do so independently. However, they will still need careful monitoring to determine how well they are comprehending the information they are reading and how successfully they are applying the skills associated with careful, close, rigorous, analytic reading.

In this chapter we address several questions regarding close reading and explore what it means for a reader to "read closely."

Making Sense of Close Reading: Six Key Questions

1. What is close reading?

Being a successful reader means being able to uncover the deeper meaning of a complex text through continued analysis, or, to borrow the language of Common Core Reading Anchor Standard 1 (CCRA.R.1), to be able *to determine what the text says explicitly, make logical inferences from it,* and *cite specific textual evidence when writing or speaking to support conclusions drawn from the text.* Close reading is a particular way of approaching a text in order to uncover, engage with, and understand the information and ideas it contains. It focuses students on

- *Detecting* the overall gist or meaning of the passage by thinking about major ideas; real or implied conflicts; the general sequence of events or information; the story arc; and stated or implied philosophies, claims, and evidence.
- *Authenticating* assumptions and interpretations by identifying and evaluating the credibility the author has to write the text; analyzing the author's language (words, tone, expressions, metaphors, etc.), style, structures used to share the information, and implications; and understanding how the author used language to promote the topics being addressed.
- *Determining* how the selected passage, whether a chapter from a textbook, a description of a character in a novel or story, a hypothesis of an experiment, or the presuppositions in a primary source document, fits into the whole text.
- *Evaluating* the relevancy and veracity of the passage by comparing it to ideas throughout the whole text and to other topically related information.
- *Arguing* a position or stance from a base of documentable insight gleaned from the text and related texts and experiences.

For students who are used to reading assignments that begin with the teacher frontloading most of the information they will need to comprehend a text, such as vocabulary words, elements to look for, or guiding questions, and conclude with teacher-led summaries that point out key ideas and explain what the text means and why it matters, a first encounter with close reading can be a shock. In close reading, it is the students who analyze a text's content and return to it as many times as they need in order to grasp how the language and ideas fit together to support comprehension. However, they must be taught to do so by a very insightful and supportive teacher.

Here are the most important points to remember about close reading:

- Close reading is just one type of classroom reading. Not all the reading students do can or should be close reading, and incorporating close reading into your classroom does not mean that you will no longer provide guided reading instruction with leveled texts, conduct shared readings, lead interactive read-alouds that include modeling and thinking aloud, or divide the class into book clubs for discussion, collaboration, and argument.
- Close reading requires students to become investigators of a short complex text and its meaning and deep structures (Adler & Van Doren, 1972). They work to identify the "bones" of the passage. Because many selected passages may be sections of larger texts, especially when reading a section of a textbook chapter, it is important to be sure that the selected segment contains all the information you are asking students to comprehend. This is often difficult because in a chapter, story, essay, and most text excerpts, meaning is developed through reading the entire text. Also, every reader's interpretation will always be influenced by that reader's prior knowledge and experiences; reading is an interactive process occurring between the reader and the text. For this reason, you must choose selections carefully to maximize every reader's potential to make a connection with the text during the close reading experience.
- Close reading requires students to read and reread, returning to the text at the word, phrase, sentence, and paragraph levels so that they will learn how the text works. The inferences they draw from the text will be supported by their initial and developing knowledge of the topic and by the language and the structure of the text.
- Close reading involves students answering text-dependent questions that keep them focused on what is within the four corners of the text rather than on their personal connections or reactions to the text. While a reader's response to questions asked during close reading should definitely draw from and relate to the information in the text, we must say again that reading is an interaction between the reader and the text, and no one can totally

disengage or be encouraged to disengage from prior experiences with a topic, language, and reading process when making inferences during reading about what the text says and means. We believe the authors of the Common Core documents want to move us away from the instructional practice that has become so prevalent in the last few years of asking students to make "text-to-self" connections—to answer questions like "How does this text relate to me?" or "What event in my life does this remind me of?" While this practice was never intended to conclude without a return to the text, it too often does. In the classrooms we have visited, we have seen many readers spend more time sharing personal experiences than talking about the text. During close reading or any type of reading experience, we must be careful to avoid having readers respond to a question solely using previous experience that is not associated with the text they are reading; both emphasis and evidence should be derived from that text. Here, again, we caution you to choose text passages very carefully and, as you write text-dependent questions, to be sure that you consider if students will be able to draw the needed inferences from the selected passage.

Understanding how well each student is able to comprehend the text offers insights to teachers about the instructional scaffolds needed. These scaffolds may be provided through additional text-dependent questions asked during the close reading or in subsequent instruction after close reading. Students will not become proficient readers of complex texts merely by being left to struggle in texts that far exceed their independent reading levels. If we expect them to become proficient, analytical, and independent readers of increasingly complex texts, we must teach them how to apply the knowledge and language they have, how to grow new knowledge and language bases, and how to monitor their understanding of text.

2. How does a close reading experience differ from shared and guided reading instruction?

A close reading experience differs from other reading instruction in several key ways:

- It focuses on short, challenging, complex texts (or challenging and complex sections of larger texts that have self-contained information) within a grade-level Lexile band rather than on grade-level texts.
- It limits the teacher's before-reading activities to a brief text introduction. Teachers do not initially build extensive background or model skills and strategies, as they do during a typical guided, shared, or read-aloud reading lesson.
- It begins with students independently "having a go" at the text—reading it on their own to get the gist or grasp its general message. During this first reading, students may annotate the text (using words, images, or marks) to identify points of confusion, challenging vocabulary, and other noteworthy features. Often, however, students read to get a general understanding of the text information by identifying big ideas and the text's overall structure.
- It features multiple rereadings, guided by text-dependent questions from the teacher, that promote a deepening understanding of how the text works, what it means, and how the information matters or can propel new questions and insights. To answer the questions, students reread the text (or listen to it) multiple times, engaging with it more deeply each time. While questions may be prepared in advance, they are often altered as teachers listen to student responses and conversations, and observe the annotations being made.
- It concludes with written activities, projects, or other experiences designed to extend what students have learned from their examination of the text or to provide opportunities for students to create and share new information from what they have learned. These expressions serve as assessments, providing the teacher with insight into students' subsequent instructional needs.

Figure 2.1 provides a more detailed look at the differences between a shared reading lesson and a close reading session, broken out into the familiar "Before, During, and After Reading" structure.

3. What is the purpose of close reading?

When students engage in a close reading, their goal is to gain insight into what the text says, how the message was constructed, and the author's intent. With such insights, a reader can critically and ethically evaluate the text message and how it works. The process of carefully examining the text's language, structure,

Figure 2.1 | **A Comparison of a Shared Reading Lesson and a Close Reading Session**

When	Shared Reading Lesson	Close Reading Session
Before Reading	• The teacher selects a text at or near students' reading levels and sets a purpose for student reading.	• The teacher selects a short, complex "stretch text" at the upper limit of students' grade-level Lexile bands; analyzes it for text complexity; and evaluates it to determine possible teaching points that, when addressed through questions and conversations, will support students' analysis of the passage.
	• The teacher builds background knowledge and/or vocabulary before students read.	• The teacher crafts text-dependent questions that will engage students in analyzing the identified points of need and focus—the teaching points.
	• The teacher and students might preview the text together.	• The teacher introduces the context for reading the passage. Teacher limits frontloading of vocabulary and background knowledge.
During Reading	• Depending on grade level, students read or listen to an entire story or passage.	• Depending on grade level, students read or listen to a short text that ranges in length from one paragraph to one page.
	• Students read along and listen to the text being read by the teacher. The teacher determines how to chunk the text and how many times it should be reread. While reading, the teacher might model and think aloud to demonstrate specific reading skills for students before they read. Modeled strategies might illustrate how to make sense of a text; these strategies might include predicting, visualization, questioning, clarifying, and summarizing.	• Students reread the text multiple times for different purposes as related to the text-dependent questions. They annotate as needed.
	• Students practice the modeled skill while reading the text. The teacher or students read a text, stopping to discuss teacher-generated text-independent and text-dependent questions about the text. Students may make text-to-text, text-to-self, and text-to-world connections to the text.	• While reading, students respond to text-dependent questions that focus on what's contained within the text.
		• First Reading: Students "have a go" at the text without teacher background building. Their focus for the reading is based on the lesson purpose and the text-dependent question(s). Teacher may ask students to read without annotating to get the gist or general understanding of the text. They may annotate the text if it naturally supports their analysis.
		• Students share ideas with peers. The teacher listens in and uses student collaborative conversations as formative assessment data to identify areas that are interfering with comprehension; these will become teaching points addressed through subsequent text-dependent questions asked by the teacher.

Continued ➜

Figure 2.1 | **A Comparison of a Shared Reading Lesson and a Close Reading Session (cont'd.)**

When	Shared Reading Lesson	Close Reading Session
During Reading	• Students may complete graphic organizers focused on lesson objectives.	• Next Reading: Students reread the text to explore text-dependent questions and deepen their understanding of the passage, vocabulary, text structure, and any other areas the teacher has assessed needs to receive focus. Students annotate the text to address a text-dependent question that focuses them more deeply on how the text language and structure work. The teacher may model a reading skill designed to address the lesson purpose or a teaching point. • Students share their annotations and responses with peers. Again, the teacher listens in and assesses their deepening understandings of the textual information. Based on assessments of conversations among the students and their annotations, the teacher asks questions that send them back into the text for a deeper reading. • Additional Readings: Students reread the text again, digging more deeply to answer text-dependent questions related to the meaning of the text, the author's purpose, and/or arguments presented in the text. They may complete graphic organizers or Foldables® during this time.
After Reading	• Students submit a written response to their reading, complete projects, or engage in other activities that demonstrate their comprehension of the text and the modeled strategy.	• Students respond to the text through projects or writing prompts that illustrate their abilities to take a stance, craft an opinion, evaluate a text, develop and support their stance with documented evidence, or create new related information.

facts, and details allows students to make the evidence-based inferences about the text's content and structure that are "the heart of meaning construction for learners of all ages" (Anderson & Pearson, 1984). By returning to the text multiple times, they have opportunities to deepen this understanding by

- Eliminating ambiguity regarding the text's message
- Analyzing context clues to figure out unfamiliar language
- Noting connections among ideas and key details
- Visualizing the organizational patterns the author used to share information
- Using what they remember to predict what comes next and to stay connected with the passage

- Summarizing aspects of the text as a means to draw conclusions
- Formulating a logical, text-supported evaluation and opinion
- Monitoring their understanding by continually self-assessing if the text is making sense to them and, if it isn't, figuring out what is causing the confusion

Using these insights, readers can be taught how to make a complex text comprehensible, which is exactly what proficient readers do once they no longer have the support of a teacher. It is during these returns to the text that the reader gains deeper insights into the topic and an expanded understanding of the topic and himself or herself as a reader.

In a practical sense, close reading mimics the process readers naturally engage in when attempting to read a text beyond their instructional level without teacher support. First, they look at a text and assess what they know about the topic by activating whatever related knowledge they have about the topic. Then, if they have a purpose for reading the text, they give it a go. If the text is challenging, the reading is seldom if ever "completed" the first time through. Instead, it is read and reread, and during the process, readers may leave the complex text for a while and seek to understand language or content through a less difficult, topically related text or source that provides the needed background. Then, having scaffolded their knowledge and gained needed language and understandings, they return to the complex text, properly prepared and newly empowered to understand.

Therefore, as suggested in Chapter 1, close reading is appropriate whenever you determine that the information in a text won't be easily or immediately accessible to your students. They will have to stretch a bit beyond their independent reading level for comprehension to occur. It's also a good choice when your students have some background knowledge that's related to the topic of the text but not enough, in your estimation, to gain a complete understanding of the author's message through just a single reading. According to Sheridan Blau (2003), the only texts worth reading in academic classes are those that students don't understand; helping them grapple with confusion builds comprehension and ultimately facilitates learning. It's the experience of returning to the text for analytic study of the message and the author's way of sharing the message that builds the reader's stamina and persistence for wrestling with a challenging text until the meaning and nuances become clear.

Of course, readers must be cautioned that when they are reading closely, they "must remain faithful to the author's text and must be alert to the potential clues concerning character and motive" (Rosenblatt, 1995, p. 11). This caution also applies when reading informational texts in regard to the need for the reader's interpretation of the text to be based upon, but not necessarily identical to, the author's message.

4. Why should "disciplinary teachers"—those who teach science, social studies, and technical subjects—make close reading part of their instruction?

Consider these reasons:

- An important goal of disciplinary literacy instruction is to help students learn to read and write like experts in the discipline. For example, students need to develop the abilities to *think* like scientists, historians, software engineers, and so on, and develop competencies associated with communicating and reading and writing like these disciplinary experts. To do so, they must understand the discipline, the language of the discipline, its discourse forms, its structures, and much more. Close reading can help students develop this knowledge through regular and repeated analysis of typical text types found in the discipline.

- The Common Core State Standards are designed to ensure that students are career- and college-ready by the time they graduate high school. Employers and universities want workers and students who are prepared to conduct and apply research, solve problems, and apply their skills and knowledge in a discipline. Universities are eager to eliminate the high level of freshman remediation in literacy, which is currently around 50 percent, and employers are keen to have employees who are workplace-ready in terms of their disciplinary knowledge and literacy abilities. Close reading in the disciplines can help to ensure both college and career readiness.

- The Common Core ELA/literacy assessments developed by Smarter Balance and PARCC require students to read content text passages and provide extended written responses to those passages. Giving students practice in close reading can prepare them to complete these assessments with skill and confidence.

5. How often should students engage in close reading?

While there is no definitive answer to this question, we believe that students should engage in daily close reading of texts that represent all areas of the curriculum (language arts, science, social studies, and mathematics). We are not suggesting that you should have your students engage in close reading every day but, rather, that close reading in all content disciplines should be a habit of practice throughout your school's faculty. So, for example, a student might read closely in Monday's American Literature class, in Tuesday's American History, in Wednesday's AP Biology, and so on. Obviously, teamwork and grade-level planning are essential to this approach. Unless students have frequent opportunities to read closely across the disciplines, they will not develop the skills they need to go beyond a surface reading of texts.

6. How do I begin close reading with my students?

Our experiences in the field have shown us that many middle and high school teachers become a little anxious when the conversation turns to close reading. They wonder how they can begin this practice when they have students who are just learning the English language or are otherwise struggling with decoding and reading with fluency. When speaking with these teachers, we point out that even struggling secondary readers can engage in silent, close reading of a well-chosen challenging text when the teacher follows a sequence of instruction that promotes and supports a focused interplay with the text that will advance understanding of the content.

Questions posed by the teacher push the students to think deeply about elements of the text as they read the text for the first time. Then, in repeated rereadings, the teacher asks increasingly challenging questions that draw the students' attention to and support the analysis of a particular pattern of language, the author's message and intention, key details of content and structure, presentation of the main idea, character traits, how the text relates to another text on the same topic, or any other aspect of the text that is worthy of critical examination.

The important point is that the questions asked during the close reading should do more than just cause the reader to repond. Questions should promote deep analysis of all of the features of the text. In this way, teachers support their students in thinking more intensely and analytically about the author's message and manner of presenting the message.

The Roles of the Reader in the Close Reading Process

Luke and Freebody (1999) remind us that literacy education does not mean helping readers develop isolated skills but rather helping them develop social, cultural, and economic practices that support critical analysis of text across the disciplines. As they explain in their four resources model of reading proficiency, this involves the students taking on four powerful roles: *code breaker, meaning maker, text user, and text critic.*

The reader as code breaker. To be a code breaker, the reader must first understand the alphabetic principle and that the sounds of language are associated with the symbols in a text. Becoming a code breaker involves gaining proficiency with *print concepts, phonological awareness, phonics and word recognition*, and *fluency*, which are identified by the Common Core standards as foundational for learning to read:

> These foundational skills are not an end in themselves; rather, they are necessary and important components of an effective, comprehensive reading program designed to develop proficient readers with the capacity to comprehend a range of texts across a range of types and disciplines. Instruction should be differentiated: good secondary readers will need much less practice with these concepts than struggling readers will. The point is to teach students what they need to learn and not what they already know—to discern when particular children or activities warrant more or less attention." (NGA Center & CCSSO, 2010a, p. 15)

Being able to apply these code breaking skills means students have the potential to understand a text at a surface or basic level.

The reader as meaning maker. Acquiring automaticity allows the reader to free up working memory to focus on meaning, which is why fluency is an important dimension of comprehension. Samuels (2007) notes that simply teaching students to "bark at words" (or speed read) is not enough to significantly improve their understanding; they must be taught that the print they are reading is bringing them a message from the author. Developing and struggling readers can begin this process of meaning making as they listen to complex texts read by their teacher and engage in very text-focused conversations that support their deepening understanding of text language, information, and features. However, these students should *also* engage in silent close reading of appropriately challenging texts.

The reader as text user. Thinking beyond the literal or basic level of meaning of the text involves learning to analyze the factors that influenced the author to share the message through the selected text structure. Being a text user means taking control of the reading interaction by returning to the text to think more intensely about the author's message and the language, style, and structures used to convey the message. While doing so, the reader is able to self-assess comprehension and decide which skills to apply in order to accomplish the purpose of reading. Here's an example. Think about your engagement with the text as you read the science passage that follows. Ask yourself: *What is this text saying? What do I already know about this topic? What's new to me? What problems, if any, am I having understanding the author's message?*

> Earth's internal and surface features are the result of constructive forces as well as destructive mechanisms. Volcanism, tectonic uplift, and folding and faulting of the crust often result in the formation of new features on Earth. These features may include mountains, valleys, and plateaus. At the same time, weathering, mass wasting, and erosion act to wear away geographic features. Earth is dynamic—always changing. It is shaped by forces that build up and forces that break down.

For some readers, vocabulary may be a roadblock to comprehension. This is particularly true of English language learners. Consider some of the challenging vocabulary in the passage above: *constructive forces, destructive mechanisms, tectonic, formation,* and *shaped.* A text user might go back to reread and focus on these terms, trying to derive meaning through various means, including context and structural analysis. She might even decide that some unfamiliar terms can be mentally noted for future consideration, even if exact definitions cannot yet be determined. When reading *constructive forces,* for example, a reader might not know exactly what the term means, but she could determine that it has something to do with building, because "construction workers" build homes. Similarly, in analyzing the word *formation,* the reader might deduce that this term has something to do with making something, as when you "form" clay to make a bowl, for example. In this passage, the barrier to comprehension could be language, but other obstacles could also curtail reading comprehension.

If the passage had contained many interrelated ideas, developing a graphic organizer might have helped the reader untangle the structure of the message. Or, if the reader determined that the information seemed to be at a more sophisticated level than her current understanding of the topic, she might have sought out and read another, less difficult text on the same topic as a way to gain the knowledge and language needed to return to the more complex passage. Whatever the reader's decisions while reading, being able to make them in support of her own comprehension indicates that she is a metacognitively aware text user who can engage in a conversation with the author by also engaging in a self-directed conversation that considers not only what skills she has that will support her analysis of the author's message but also the skills she must develop and the knowledge she must acquire.

The reader as text critic. When a reader is able to evaluatively interact with a text, she is functioning as a text critic—someone who understands that the text is not neutral and that the author is attempting to position readers to consider an issue from a specific vantage point. For an example, consider the following headlines. What is each positioning a reader to believe?

- *Are electric cars the best choice for all drivers?* Positions the reader to reflect on the various types of drivers there are and consider the idea that electric cars might not be suitable for all of them. The reader must then investigate, perhaps through a review of credible, research-based texts and media resources, whether or not electric cars have drawbacks for different kinds of drivers (e.g., long-distance drivers, short-distance commuters, parents with small children).
- *The use of genetically modified foods is the answer to global hunger problems.* Positions the reader to think that genetically modified foods can be produced in quantities great enough to fill voids in food supplies around the world. The reader must consider, possibly through a critical analysis of data and informational texts, which "global hunger problems" are being referenced and what their causes are in order to determine if the proposed solution of using genetically modified foods is viable. Additionally, the reader would want to consider drawbacks or concerns with the use of genetically modified foods.

- *A gluten-free diet will help you lose weight.* Positions the reader to consider the idea that consumption of gluten-containing foods, rather than consumption of fatty foods or overconsumption in general, may contribute to weight gain.
- *Recycling is useless because it takes more energy to collect and reuse recyclables than it does to make products from new raw materials.* Positions the reader to dismiss recycling because it is an energy-consuming endeavor that requires gas for trucks to pick up recyclables, energy to sort the items, and so on. The reader must consider real data to determine whether or not the energy costs of recycling are truly higher or lower than the energy costs of manufacturing new goods from raw materials. Additionally, the reader might consider the problems associated with accumulating trash if recycling is not in common use.

The ability to critically evaluate a text is a sophisticated process that requires practice. Teaching students the process of close reading as a way to scrutinize a text and its relationship with other texts should begin early in a student's school career and should be developed over time and across content areas.

⇒◆⇐

Teaching the process of close reading involves coming to understand it ourselves, and then supporting students through very purposeful instruction that enables them to closely read increasingly complex texts across the disciplines. According to Seymour Papert (quoted in Wurman, 2001), "The role of the teacher is to create the conditions for invention rather than provide ready-made knowledge" (p. 240). Nowhere is this more true than in close reading. In the next chapter, we'll explore the details of planning, conducting, and managing a close reading session.

CHAPTER 3

PLANNING, TEACHING, AND MANAGING CLOSE READING

In this chapter, we move on to the practical work of planning and implementing close reading sessions and the related management and grouping practices. We'll walk through the close reading planning process and then explore two extended examples of close reading in action, one set in a 6th grade science lesson and the other in a 9th grade English class. Then we'll delve deeper into classroom management practices and tools to support you as you reflect on your expanding knowledge of close reading practices and implementation.

Please bear in mind that there is no "set in concrete" pattern for planning and conducting a close reading session. The approach we offer is just one of many possibilities, but it is the one we have found to be successful in classrooms throughout the country—appropriate at all grade levels and across the range of disciplines and student abilities.

Before the Close Reading: Planning and Preparation Practices for Teachers

A close reading session requires careful planning, but it also requires that the teacher be willing to modify the plan based on developing student needs and gains. As explained in Chapter 2's overview of the process and illustrated in the classroom scenarios we will look at in the pages to come, every close reading is shaped not only by the learning goals and the composition of the classroom but also by the students' developing understandings and insights, by the confusions that emerge while encountering a complex text, and by how the teacher accommodates these various factors. To begin, let's look at the planning and preparation work that a teacher should engage in prior to involving students in close reading: (1) determine lesson purpose, tasks, and related standards; (2) select the text; (3) identify the areas of complexity and teaching points; (4) create text-dependent questions; (5) prepare the text for close reading and discussion; (6) model annotation methods; and (7) model how to closely read a text.

7 Steps

Determine the Lesson Purpose, Tasks, and Standards

① Slide 10

To begin planning a lesson that involves students in close reading, you will need to first identify the lesson's purpose(s) and tasks, and the related standards. The **lesson purpose** identifies the goal or objective of the lesson, but from a perspective that clarifies for students the "why" of what they are learning. Sharing the purpose with students helps them to maintain focus on the content. The **lesson tasks** clarify how the purpose is to be accomplished. Careful observation of students' performance in relation to these tasks provides opportunities to assess their growing understandings and skill development. These assessment insights support your next instructional steps. Finally, determining the content and literacy **standards** related to the lesson will provide focus, for both you and your students. You may select a single standard or address several standards within a single lesson.

It's not uncommon to mix up lesson purpose and standards. The key distinguishing factor is scope. Lesson purpose is smaller scale and more focused; it's what your students will accomplish during the lesson. By contrast, it's very rare that students will master a standard within a single lesson. For example, a lesson purpose for a close reading in Earth Science might be to *understand various types of rocks.* A related task might be to *write a summary of the reading* or to *share an e-mail with a friend that describes the different rock formations.* This close reading lesson could be one of several lessons designed to accomplish the content standard related to understanding that Earth is composed of several lateral geologic layers.

Select the Text *(Slide 11)*

Selecting a text for a disciplinary close reading involves careful consideration to ensure that the text not only addresses your identified lesson purpose and standards but also is both engaging and complex enough to push the knowledge levels of students (see Chapter 4). As discussed in Chapters 1 and 4, the complexity level of a text is determined by **quantifiable factors,** such as the number of words in a passage; **qualitative factors,** such as the knowledge demands and language features; and **reader/task factors,** which take into consideration the characteristics of the students who will be reading the text. Texts selected for close reading should be "compact, short, self-contained texts that can be read and reread deliberately and slowly" (Coleman & Pimentel, 2012, p. 4) during a class session. Students might be asked to tackle longer texts at other times in order to gain reading stamina and explore their interests.

not lengthy articles or novels

Questions to ask when making a selection include the following:

- Does the text or passage contain information that relates to a topic being studied or about to be studied?
- Is the text challenging, interesting, and well written? As students wrestle with it, will they be seeing a model of writing and language use worth emulating?
- Is the complexity of the text similar to or beyond the students' ability? Will they be stretched by reading it?
- What knowledge will students need in order to read this text? Do they have this knowledge? Does the text offer features, such as context clues, that will support the understanding of readers who don't have much prior knowledge of this topic? If not, how can this information be backfilled?
- Can the entire class closely read this text as it is and on their own, or would some students benefit from reading it partnered with other texts on the same topic to build concepts and language they need for better understanding? Will some students need advance instruction related to the topic in order to build necessary background knowledge, perhaps in a small-group setting? What other supports may be needed?

The goal is that every student will read complex texts at the high end of the grade-level band. However, each student must be supported with very purposeful instructional scaffolds. Most often, these are offered as text-dependent questions that deliberately push students back to sections of the texts to scrutinize author language and related clues that support their deepening understanding.

Determine the Areas of Complexity and Teaching Points

Next, use the rubrics in Chapter 1 (see Figures 1.2 and 1.3, pp. 26–31) or similar rubrics to identify areas of text complexity that may represent potential problem areas for your students—unfamiliar concepts, a complicated text layout, advanced vocabulary, particular language styles, and so on. From there, you must decide if these problem areas require instruction a few days prior to the close reading, or if they will serve as teaching points for the close reading—addressed through the discussions that occur after the first reading, during student conversations, and after subsequent rereadings.

There may be times when it will be clear that your students lack essential information they will need in order to make sense of the text. For example, if your students are reading a complex text about the causes and consequences of the Cold War, they will need to understand what the Cold War was, the time period in which it occurred, and the nations that were involved. It may be necessary to preteach this information in a class session prior to your reading session. (It's important not to load students down with information just before their first encounter with the text.)

If you are unsure if students will be able to comprehend these areas of complexity without preteaching, err on the side of letting them try it. In our experience, when students grapple a bit with difficult material, they often generate insights we do not expect. If they stumble during their first reading, use collaborative discussion to clarify the information prior to their next reading.

Once you begin the close reading session, you will need to watch and listen carefully to your students and ask questions that help them to grasp the needed information and deepen their understanding of the passage. You can also note which students need additional supports, which can be provided in a small-group setting. This arrangement is often particularly appropriate for English language learners, who may need the support of both the teacher and their peers to master challenging concepts.

Create Text-Dependent Questions

In close reading, text-dependent questions related to the identified teaching points serve to focus students' interactions with the text. Text-dependent questions differ from the kinds of "text to self" and "text to world" questions students may be used to answering in response to a reading in that they do not focus on personal connections to the reading; instead, they require students to focus explicitly on what the text itself has to say. The answers to text-dependent questions may not be found easily, and answering may require students to read and reread. Questions and prompts that relate to identified teaching points (e.g.,

Identify the language that communicates the gist of the author's message) should be created in a way that returns readers to the text for rereading and deeper analysis (e.g., *What words and phrases tipped you off to what the author really wants the reader to understand?*). Although it's often recommended that these questions "be answered by careful scrutiny of the text" (Coleman & Pimentel, 2012, p. 5)—that is to say, readers must be true to the meaning suggested in the text—we believe student experience and knowledge also play a role in their ability to connect ideas across texts in order to evaluate the veracity of information in texts. This transaction between the reader and the text (Rosenblatt, 1978) enables readers to make text-supported judgments as they search, synthesize, infer, and evaluate the texts they are reading in an attempt to analyze an author's message and intention.

Asking students text-dependent questions does not mean asking only low-level, literal questions that involve regurgitation of easy-to-find information. On the contrary, text-dependent questions should invite students to interpret the theme or major points of information, analyze vocabulary, observe the effects of the author's word choices and use of dialect, and examine text structure and language features as a means to understand and evaluate the complexity of the message.

After generating a set of questions based on the key ideas, insights, or points from the text students should understand (e.g., theme, main idea, persuasive techniques), the teacher organizes these questions in a way that moves students from a very literal interpretation to higher levels of analysis, synthesis, and evaluation as they develop insights that enable them to argue a position. Remember, because you will write most of these questions prior to the first reading, you must be prepared to revise them or generate new ones after listening to students' responses.

A simple distinguishing feature of text-dependent questions is that they could not be answered by someone who has not read (or listened to) the particular text. Text-dependent questions differ further from non–text-dependent questions because they *push the students back into the text* rather than *take them away* from it. For illustration, consider Figure 3.1, which shows text-dependent and non–text-dependent questions generated for the passage "Space Probe," from Phillis Engelbert's *Astronomy and Space: From the Big Bang to the Big Crunch* (2009), a Common Core informational text exemplar for grades 6–8. As you review this figure, also notice that the purpose for each question is indicated. In

Figure 3.1 | **Text-Dependent and Non–Text-Dependent Questions for Engelbert's "Space Probe"**

Progression of Questions (Informational Text)	Text-Dependent Questions	Non–Text-Dependent Questions
General Understanding	What are the main points of this article?	Have you ever seen the moon at night?
Key Details	What kind of information did the Soviet Union's Luna probes provide?	What does the moon look like?
Vocabulary	What does it mean when the author notes, "Encounters were also made with Mars in 1976 by the U.S. probes *Viking 1* and *Viking 2*"?	What descriptive words could you use to describe the moon? Mars?
Text Structure	What academic terms are used to show sequences in time?	What sentence could you write using a problem/solution text structure?
Author's Purpose/Message	What is the author's purpose in writing this article?	Why is space exploration important to us?
Inferences	What kinds of knowledge have space probes provided us over the years?	Is space exploration worth its high cost?

many instances, these questions will reflect categories found on qualitative scoring rubrics like those we looked at in Chapter 1.

Consider what distinguishes the text-dependent questions from the non–text-dependent ones. The first of the text-dependent questions assesses students' general understanding of this text rather than their literal comprehension (their ability to respond "yes" or "no" to a point made in the text). Similarly, the second text-dependent question, related to key details, drives students back into the text to see what kind of information the Luna probes provided. Now look at both questions intended to assess vocabulary. The non–text-dependent question, which prompts a student to think about descriptive words that could describe the moon and Mars, is certainly related to the topic of space probes, but it could be answered without returning to the text. By contrast, the text-dependent vocabulary question requires students to go back and reread to get an understanding of the key word *encounters* from its context.

Now, look at the the non–text-dependent question about text structure. It asks for comparision words that are not derived from the text. The contrasting text-dependent question sends students back to the text to find the language used by the author. Similarly, the inference and argument text-dependent questions require that students look to the text for evidence and clarification, while the non–text-dependent questions can be answered without the text, by using other content knowledge. Clearly, the use of well-crafted text-dependent questions is what facilitates the students' closer look at the text and deepens their understanding of text-based content.

Here is one protocol for generating text-dependent questions:

1. Identify key ideas or concepts in the text.
2. Think about questions that might orient students to the general meanings of the text.
3. Focus on vocabulary and text structure. Determine what key terms and patterns of text structure (problem/solution, compare/contrast, etc.) are used in the text.
4. Determine the most difficult sections of the text, and develop questions that focus on these areas. Consider complex phrasing, dense material, and places where inference is required.
5. Consider the appropriate grade-level versions of Common Core Anchor Standards 1 and 8, both the versions for ELA and those for literacy in history/ social studies, science, and technical subjects, and create additional questions to focus students on particular elements of these standards.
6. Develop a series of text-dependent questions that require students to delve deeper with each subsequent reading. Depending on the text, students may need to read or listen to the text multiple times.

Our colleagues Doug Fisher and Nancy Frey (2013) have developed the model shown in Figure 3.2 to guide the creation of text-dependent questions. Their model illustrates a progression of questioning that moves from parts to the whole, focusing first on words before expanding to sentences, paragraphs, longer passages, and the overall text. At the same time, they call for these questions to direct students' attention to increasingly sophisticated aspects of the text, moving from key details to the author's purpose to inferences, opinions, and arguments. While this model identifies a hierarchy of complexity, it is not intended to suggest that teachers must ask a question that addresses each area or that there is only one place to begin. The types of questions that should be asked are dependent on the lesson purpose, the areas of complexity within the text, and the kinds of cognitive and language scaffolding the students need.

We have carried over the categories in Fisher and Frey's model to the template in Figure 3.3, which you might use to jot down a few questions that will support your lesson focus and the skill and knowledge development your students need.

Figure 3.2 | **A Model for the Progression of Text-Dependent Questions**

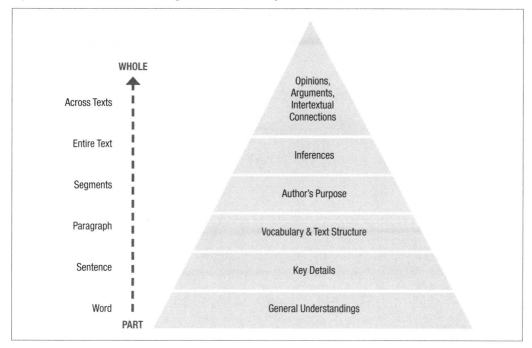

Remember that the responses your students generate during the close reading should largely guide the questions you ask. Depending on their initial comprehension and the lesson purpose, you may need to skip some questions or add additional ones. Every plan for close reading evolves because of the performance of the readers.

Here's an example of how the use of text-dependent questions can direct students' attention to details and concepts and encourage them to evaluate and critique text content. During a close reading of "Space Probe," Angel Washington, a 7th grade science teacher, checked in on a conversation between two students working together to determine the author's purpose for writing the piece:

> *Alexandra:* OK, I see where the author writes, *The purpose of such missions is to make scientific observations, such as taking pictures, measuring atmospheric conditions, and collecting soil samples, and to bring or report the data back to Earth,* but I don't know why the author wrote about this.

Figure 3.3 | **A Template for Preparing Text-Dependent Questions**   Download

Progression of Questions (check)	Text-Dependent Questions	Evidence-Based Answers	Page/Para. #
☐ General Understanding ☐ Key Details ☐ Vocabulary and Text Structure ☐ Author's Purpose ☐ Inferences ☐ Opinions, Arguments, Intertextual Connections			
☐ General Understanding ☐ Key Details ☐ Vocabulary and Text Structure ☐ Author's Purpose ☐ Inferences ☐ Opinions, Arguments, Intertextual Connections			
☐ General Understanding ☐ Key Details ☐ Vocabulary and Text Structure ☐ Author's Purpose ☐ Inferences ☐ Opinions, Arguments, Intertextual Connections			
☐ General Understanding ☐ Key Details ☐ Vocabulary and Text Structure ☐ Author's Purpose ☐ Inferences ☐ Opinions, Arguments, Intertextual Connections			

Paloma: Me neither. The author writes about lots of space probes: Luna probes, *Voyager 1* and *Voyager 2,* a Ranger probe. And it says NASA landed *Surveyor* on the Moon. It's a lot of information, but what's the point?

It was clear to Ms. Washington that these students needed additional questions to help them grasp the concept of author's purpose. To focus their thinking in that direction, she followed up with Alexandra and Paloma:

Ms. Washington: Here, in paragraph 6, it says that during its year in orbit, *Mariner 9*'s two television cameras transmitted footage. What did the cameras show? Are there other places in the text that show what else we learned about Mars or about the Moon from space probe data? Now think again about why the author might share all this information about space probes. Do you gain this knowledge when you read this?

Cued to notice how much we learn from space probes, and prompted to connect the idea of gaining knowledge to the author's purpose, Alexandra and Paloma recall that one possibility for author's purpose is to inform the reader. Alexandra notes, "I think the author wants to tell us about the great things that space probes have helped people understand about space. So the author's purpose is to inform."

We want to reiterate that although the kinds of questions we are suggesting are answerable with information from the text, as Shanahan (2013) explains, such questions are not always lower-level, *right-there* questions. To the contrary, text-dependent questions can require readers to draw on prior knowledge to intently focus on various aspects of the text. In "Space Probe," a question about *the meaning and function of space probes* might lead a reader to think about *probing* as the act of asking a series of questions. The reader might make associations with probes used in medicine. While drawing on this understanding of various aspects of the word *probe,* the reader might be able to better ascertain that the mechanical device called a *space probe* does investigate—as a person does when asking questions or when using a medical probe. Such connections could help forward an understanding of the role of a space probe. The bottom line is that when you are creating text-dependent questions, regardless of where those questions fall on Bloom's taxonomy, they must compel readers to go back into the text to examine information, data, research, illustrations, charts, and other aspects of the text. The points the readers consider may later connect to their evaluation or analysis of the text, as when Ms. Washington's question to Alexandra and Paloma returns them to "Space Probe" to note that television footage and photos have provided information about the surface of Mars and about the Moon.

Posting sentence frames on the document camera or the whiteboard or writing them on sentence strips held in a pocket chart are ways to scaffold student responses or focus students on particular aspects of content. Notice how the following sentence frames push responders to use academic vocabulary words and phrases:

> The author explains the meaning of space probes by describing the data from _____.
>
> The author explains the function of probes by stating that the Mariner probes _____ and the Viking probes _____.
>
> When probes go out into space, they _____. This explains the function of space probes.

Frames like these can be very useful in supporting a range of learners' abilities to talk about a text. You can alter sentence frames to be more or less complex, depending on the needs of the students.

After you have asked questions that continually push the readers back into the text in a way that helps them accomplish the learning targets, most will have a very good understanding of the text. But this doesn't complete the learning process; remember, a primary goal of good instruction is for students to gain the degree of mastery necessary to function on their own as empowered, independent learners. Therefore, it is important to emphasize that each reader must also become his or her own interrogator during and after a close reading, which means each reader must ask internal questions that are very similar to those that you generate and use to steer students back to the text for deeper understanding. Being able to ask and answer these questions involves a close observation and analysis of the text. Here are a few examples of the kinds of questions you want your students to ask themselves:

- What is the author's message at this point in the text?
- What words or phrases are confusing me? Can I find clues from the author to help me understand them?
- What interesting or different ways does the author use language to help me to better understand the message?

- What techniques is the author using to share the information?
- Is the message changing throughout the passage?

When the passage being closely read is literature rather than an informational text, readers can ask similar questions that address the features of a narrative (e.g., plot, character development, setting).

With both text types, and regardless of whether you're asking the questions or students are, it's a good idea to require students to provide the evidence that supports their responses. This sheds light on how the reader has come to a specific conclusion and also provides insights for assessment regarding the veracity of the reader's interpretation.

Prepare the Text for Close Reading and Discussion

 It's important not to overlook the simple but powerful practice of setting up the texts used for close reading sessions in a way that facilitates directed rereading, discussion, and reference for evidence. This means using a pen, pencil, or sticky notes to number the lines, paragraphs, or stanzas so that it will be easy for everyone to find and refer to the same portion of the text. You can do the numbering in advance for readings that you'll distribute to students, and with textbooks and other texts that can't be written in, you can ask the students to use sticky notes to number the paragraphs or lines on their own. When reading text aloud to emerging readers, be sure to use a finger to point to the line or section being read.

Provide Instruction and Modeling on Text Annotation

 Text annotation is an essential literacy learning skill and one that is very useful for students during the process of close reading. Annotation promotes active engagement during the act of reading, preventing students from simply skimming a text. When you direct closely reading students to look for and annotate aspects of a text that are important to lesson goals, you are facilitating their *attention to* and *understanding of* the text. You are providing them with a way to recall the text's details, which will support discussion and further exploration. In addition, text annotation gives students a way to identify where their comprehension is breaking down. According to Kelly Gallagher (2004), "Teaching students to identify the precise areas where they begin having trouble is the first step to helping [them] cope with their confusion" (p. 67). Text annotation can help students pinpoint those areas of confusion. In this way, annotation facilitates student attention to the text as well as their own comprehension monitoring.

Of course students (and adults!) can overuse annotation. Many of us have had the experience of returning to a text we annotated by highlighting every other sentence in a different color and wondering *What was I thinking?* There really is no end to what can be annotated: confusing or difficult vocabulary, literary devices (metaphor, simile, imagery, personification, etc.), rhetorical devices and author style (figurative language and dialect, tone, diction, syntax, etc.), text structure (description, sequence, cause/effect, compare/contrast, problem/solution), text features (captions, sequences, footnotes), main ideas, key details, supporting evidence, student questions or areas of confusion, and on and on. Because the possibilities are endless, it's essential to teach students to annotate for distinct purposes and to establish consistency with the markings used within a given class.

Annotations are generally classified into the following categories: language, questions, predictions, opinions, author's craft, author's message, connections, reflections, and arguments. For example, when reading to focus on language, students might circle confusing words (marking them with a *C*) and interesting words (marking them with an *I*). They might note key words and phrases by drawing boxes around them, underline major points, draw an arrow when making connections to information in another text, or write *EX* when the author provides an example. There is no standard set of markings, so the one you design should fit the instructional purposes of your lessons.

It's not a bad idea to kick off any close reading session with a few words of guidance on and modeling of text annotation, even if it's just to remind students of the classroom's standard markings and symbols. Figure 3.4 shows a variety of charts that work well for students in grades 6–12, including one designed for annotating in math class.

As you share a text with your students, model for them the features to consider while reading. For example, explain that annotations help us return to a text to clarify confusing words, questions we have, important features and points within the text, language we like, and so on. Also explain that it's important to use a consistent pattern of markings so it's easier to remember which features we were thinking about while reading. Provide students with time to practice and discuss the annotations, including how the annotations support conversations about text, rereadings of text, and writing about text.

Figure 3.4 | **Annotation Charts**

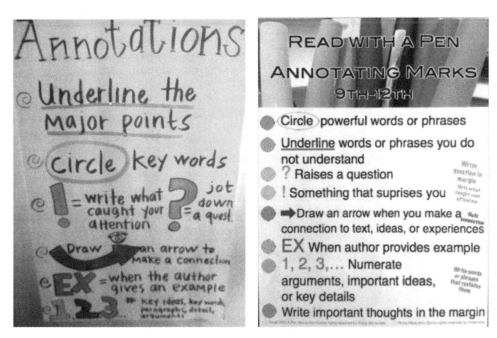

For Middle School Students   **For High School Students**

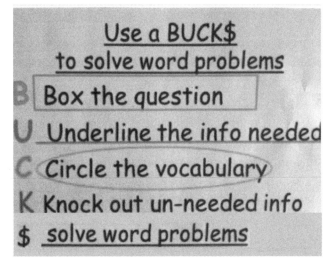

For Word Problems in Math Class

Once you have finished modeling how to annotate a text and students have practiced various text annotations, invite them to give it a try. Using a new passage, have them read and annotate. Remind them to refer to the annotation chart as needed. Have them discuss their annotations with a peer, and then spend a few minutes doing this as a class to be sure that everyone understands and is using the same system and symbols.

As students grow more comfortable with reading and annotating, you might experiment with allowing multiple annotations at the same time—not just circling unfamiliar words but also including questions next to ideas that are unclear. When students have become comfortable with the annotation system you use in your classroom, encourage them to personalize their interactions with text by adding new symbols and categories of their own. Once they have an understanding of the rationale for annotating and how to do it effectively, text annotation can become an expectation of close reading.

Another mode of annotation, referred to earlier, is highlighting different features in a text with different colors. For example, students might highlight unfamiliar words in yellow, and language that identifies the author's position on a topic in green. This method of color-coding must be consistent, of course, and it must appear on the annotation chart. Colored pencils can also be used to circle and underline key words or phrases that relate to the identified purpose. They're often a better choice than highlighters, because a student reading with a colored pencil in hand is much more likely to add related margin notes than a student reading with a highlighter. By the time students reach grade 6, they are generally old enough to capture their thoughts on the page, whether these are questions, predictions of confusing words, or connections made to other parts of the text. As they work to make sense of complex text, these notes may be more helpful than relying just on symbols and letters. Of course, students who are English language learners or striving readers and writers can benefit enormously from making simple annotations (even just a ? in the margin) or by sketching their notes and reactions.

If you are having students closely read and annotate passages within their textbooks, you may want to distribute photocopies of the pages in question for students to mark up and keep in their textbooks. This gives them a durable record of their reading thoughts in a form that preserves the surrounding supports of the textbook's pictures, charts, and graphs. It's especially beneficial when reading science or social studies texts, as the visuals help to support students' analysis.

Model How to Closely Read a Text

Teaching students to closely read a text begins by modeling the close reading practices in which students should engage and ends with students being able to independently apply these practices whenever they read closely. Because close reading skills are developed over time, modeling the process is not a "one and done" situation; you should expect to model close reading both when you first introduce the practice to students and as needed prior to and during subsequent close reading sessions.

Important to remember

Here's a look at how Lin Ryan, a high school physics teacher, modeled close reading to introduce the process to her class. First, she selected a passage on a topic that she found interesting and thought her students might as well:

Advancements in Electric Car Design

Electric cars are not for all drivers; however, engineers are working to make them more attractive to future buyers. Electric cars' capacity for speed has increased dramatically in recent years, and world speed records for these vehicles now top 300 miles per hour. Additionally, advancements in efficiency are making some potential buyers consider bypassing a gasoline-powered vehicle for a new, slick, electric-powered model. Internal combusion engines have efficiencies lower than 30 percent, far below the effiencies of 60 percent and higher available in some electric cars. Another attraction for drivers is that in many areas, electric cars are eligible for carpool lane access. If the traffic on the freeway is heavy during your rush hour commute, then an electric car may be just the solution you need to get you moving to work, school, home, or wherever you are traveling.

Ms. Ryan began the class session by explaining to her students that the topic of electric cars was one that she had been hearing lots about in the popular press and from her friends. She explained that when she realized that she didn't know enough about the topic of electric cars to be able to participate in conversations with friends or follow the more sophisticated discussion in print, she decided to teach herself more about electric cars. To do that, she explained, she had to read articles about them very closely to be sure that she really understood what she was reading. "Right now," she told her students, "I'm going to show you how I conduct a close reading."

Ms. Ryan posted the passage she'd selected and read it aloud, annotating the text and thinking aloud about it, analyzing the language and message. In particular, she noted the term *efficiency*, and wondered how efficiency was measured. Continuing to think aloud, she pointed out the use of the problem/solution text structure (through the use of if/then) and commented on the fact that engineering was connected to science. She asked herself questions to kick off targeted rereadings ("Which type of car has an internal combustion engine? I'm going to reread this section to see if I can figure it out. . . ."). She concluded by discussing with students how the close analysis of the text language and organization helped her gain initial insights about the author's message, and how she gained an even deeper understanding by returning to the passage for additional rereadings. Specifically, Ms. Ryan noted that engineers have designed electric cars that reach higher speeds and are more efficient. She speculated that, in this context, *efficiency* might have something to do with the amount of energy needed to run the car compared to the amount of work that you get out of the car. ("I remember this from studying machines," she added.) Once Ms. Ryan's students seemed comfortable with the practice of close text reading, she felt confident in releasing the responsibility for subsequent close text readings to them. However, she knew that modeling would continue to be a valuable tool for her whenever her students struggled to apply a new strategy or grasp new content.

During the Close Reading: An Illustration of Teacher and Student Practices

Figure 3.5 provides an overview of teacher and student practices throughout the whole close reading process: before, during, and after the session. Notice that the first five practices of the teacher—the planning work of identifying the lesson purpose and standards, selecting a text, determining potential problem areas, generating text-dependent questions, and any preparatory text annotation or close reading modeling required—should occur *before* students see the passage to be closely read. Teacher practices 6–15 support students *during* and *after* the close reading. We'll now explore both through some classroom scenarios. As you read these, be sure to pay attention to how the questions the teachers ask correspond to the identified teaching points.

Figure 3.5 | **Close Reading Practices of Teachers and Students**

When	Teacher Practices	Student Practices
Before the Session *(Pre-planning and preparation work)*	1. Select an appropriate text that relates to the identified lesson pupose. 2. Identify potential problem areas and teaching points. 3. Create text-dependent questions. 4. Prepare the text for close reading. 5. Model annotation methods and close reading, as necessary.	
During the Session	6. Ask text-dependent questions. 7. Promote rich and rigorous conversations that support the lesson purpose(s). 8. Observe students' oral and written responses to identify the next appropriate question to ask. 9. Invite rereadings as needed to support students' deep text analysis. 10. During each reading, collect observational data to determine the next questions and instructional paths to support students' analysis. 11. Backfill rather than frontload information through questions that draw students' attention to the text meaning and workings (i.e., language structure, purpose, and intent). 12. Ensure that conversations and experiences connect to the text and the lesson purposes. 13. Initiate a "best use" activity that invites students to share their understandings and create new information.	1. Read, analyze, and annotate the text for a specific purpose. 2. Engage in focused, collaborative conversations that address an identified purpose. 3. Reread to expand understanding about the text. 4. Converse with others to share interpretations and seek clarity. 5. Reread and continue collaborations as needed until a deep understanding of the text features and author's message is achieved.
Beyond the Session	14. Encourage students to employ close reading practices independently. 15. Meet with small groups as needed to ensure that everyone has deeply comprehended the text.	6. Complete a "best use" activity to illustrate a deep understanding and use of the text information. 7. Understand the value of the practice of close reading well enough to apply it without the involvement of others.

A Look at Close Reading and Thinking in Grade 6

Before the reading. Jan Greenfield teaches science, and her 6th graders are just learning to negotiate complex texts. To help them move forward in their reading, she conducted a personal close reading of an informational text that explains how waves are reflected, absorbed, or transmitted through various materials (see Figure 3.6).

To ensure that she properly identified potential problem areas for readers, Mrs. Greenfield used the Qualitative Scoring Rubric for Informational Text (see Figure 1.3, p. 29) to analyze the text. Her assessment of the text yielded this information:

- *Text Structure—Organization:* Challenging/stretch text; organization includes multiple text structures that convey chronology or conditions or time sequence (*when the molecules vibrate, when light passes through the glass windows*), cause/effect, problem/solution, description, directions, and compare/contrast.

Figure 3.6 | **A Middle School Science Text Prepared for Close Reading**

1   Light waves behave in many different ways. The behavior of an electro-magnetic wave depends on the material it hits. An incoming wave that strikes a material is called an incident wave. When an incident wave hits a material, or medium, and is returned by bouncing off, it is reflected. When you see your image in a mirror, you are viewing light waves that come from you, strike the mirror, and bounce off.

2   Consider an incident wave that moves straight through a medium. This wave is transmitted. When light passes through the glass windows of a car, it is being transmitted. Light can also pass through media like water and plastic. Sunlight can travel through raindrops.

3   Absorption happens when particles of the wave hit atoms and molecules in the medium, causing them to vibrate. When the molecules vibrate, the material becomes hotter. Light waves that strike a black shirt you are wearing are absorbed. On a sunny day, you might feel the increasing heat produced by absorption.

- *Text Structure—Visual Supports and Layout:* Moderate/at grade level; text is partnered with a diagram of reflection, transmission, and absorption.
- *Text Structure—Relationships Among Ideas:* Moderate/at grade level; relationships are sometimes implied—for example, the author states, *When you see your image in a mirror, you are viewing light waves that come from you, strike the mirror, and bounce off.* Students might infer that viewing your reflection involves the function of your eyes. Also, they might infer that the light waves that come from you and bounce to the mirror are produced by a light source like the sun or a lamp.
- *Language Features—Author's Style:* Challenging/stretch text; the style is specialized to science (several complex sentences such as *Absorption happens when particles of the wave hit atoms and molecules in the medium, causing them to vibrate.*)
- *Language Features—Vocabulary:* Moderate/at grade level; discipline-specific with some unfamiliar science words and academic language—words like *incident, increasing,* and *produced.*
- *Meaning:* Moderate/at grade level; some information is complex (patterns of wave behavior that are dependent on the material the incident wave strikes).
- *Author's Purpose:* Moderate/at grade level; the purpose is subtle and requires interpretation. Students may be able to determine that this is about the effect of the medium on an incident electromagnetic wave.
- *Knowledge Demands:* Moderate/at grade level; students had some background knowledge because most knew that light could be described as a wave. They had talked about this in class.

Given this analysis, Mrs. Greenfield concluded that the text was at a moderate level of complexity overall, although it did have some elements that would require students to stretch their thinking. She prepared by crafting text-dependent questions that addressed the potential areas of need. For example, she planned to have students go back into the text with her for second and third readings so that they could respond to the following questions: *Where does the author use words to describe how the incident wave moves?* and *The author talks about how light behaves. What sentence tells you about this?*

First reading and discussion. Because Mrs. Greenfield knew that it was critical for her 6th graders to build the capacity to engage with complex texts, she made the first reading a "cold reading." She had modeled close reading and annotation in a previous class session, and students knew that, initially, they might "not get it all." She had stressed that they would need to persevere, to wade through some complex and unfamiliar language, and to reread the text more than one time. She had also reassured them that she was going to provide questions and time to talk with classmates as they engaged in subsequent readings. To provide just a bit of support, she had students create a Foldable (see Figure 3.7) where they could capture notes about three key questions after their first reading and annotation: *What happens to the incident wave when it is reflected? What happens to the incident wave when it is transmitted? What happens to the incident wave when it is absorbed?*

Mrs. Greenfield observed students as they engaged in the first close reading. She monitored their initial phase of annotations, mentally noting which words and phrases were circled and which concepts were distinguished with question marks, indicating the need for further clarification. After students read and annotated, they analyzed content independently by recording ideas in their Foldables. Then they partner-shared their Foldables with one another, sharing details they remembered.

Next reading and discussion. Mrs. Greenfield noticed that some students struggled with sequencing information (she had predicted as much in her preparation for this close reading). She asked this text-dependent question: *Where does the author use words that tell you the order of events when light is reflected?* Students read closely, making annotations that would help them answer

Figure 3.7 | **A 6th Grade Foldable® Graphic Organizer**

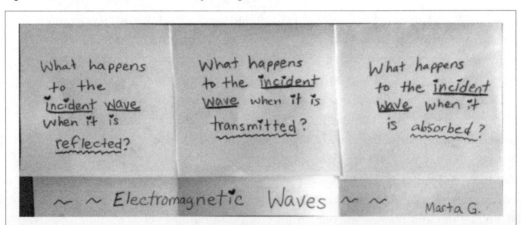

this question. When everyone had finished reading, they once again shared responses, and Mrs. Greenfield once again listened in, seeking evidence that the students understood the movement of a wave from an object, to the mirror, and back to the viewer's eyes.

Subsequent readings and discussions. Once she was confident students understood the content, Mrs. Greenfield was ready to focus them on the craft evident in the text. Specifically, she wanted students to notice the author's use of descriptive language—words like *incoming* and *increasing.* Addressing the 6th grade version of Common Core Reading Informational Text Standard 4 ("Determine the meaning of words and phrases as they are used in a text, including figurative, connotative, and technical meanings" [RI.6.4]), she prompted with a question she had generated when planning the lesson: *What words does the author use to describe how the incident wave moves?* She asked questions about the author's choice of words: *What words does the author use to help you understand the effects of absorption?* After asking the questions, Mrs. Greenfield invited her students to do a third close reading, again making annotations to address the questions.

At this point, students had read and thought about the text multiple times. Mrs. Greenfield introduced an additional and challenging text-dependent question intended to help them think more deeply about the text: *How do various media affect the behavior of an incident wave?* By asking this question she was also addressing Reading Informational Text Standard 3 ("Analyze in detail how a key individual, event, or idea is introduced, illustrated, and elaborated in a text [e.g., through examples or anecdotes]" [RI.6.3]). The challenge for students was to use their knowledge of mediums, a topic they had discussed previously, to connect the movement of light to the material it strikes. Mrs. Greenfield asked them to do one last close reading, requesting that they seek out text-based evidence for their forthcoming conversations about these questions. After this rereading, they discussed clues in the text, such as the real-world examples of media (e.g., mirrored surfaces, glass, raindrops, and black shirts).

Although everyone can learn and benefit from revisiting a complex text multiple times and engaging in peer and whole-class partner talk about it, it's understandable that not all students will understand every text equally well or come to that understanding within the same time frame. Then again, these students must have access to the critical content information every text presents. In these circumstances, a good option is to work with the subset of struggling students to revisit the concepts by introducing a partner text at a comparable level of language complexity that covers the same content but places fewer knowledge demands on readers and requires them to bring less background knowledge. Once the students grasp the critical concepts, they can be directed back to the initial, more complex text.

This is just what Mrs. Greenfield did with five students whose comprehension seemed to be stalled. She invited them to join her in taking a closer look at images she had found on a NASA website (http://missionscience.nasa.gov/ems/03_behaviors.html) that clarified the concepts of *reflection, transmission,* and *absorption.* She then sketched a picture to illustrate transmission, and encouraged the five students to closely read her sketch and the online images, just as they would closely read a text.

> *Mrs. Greenfield:* Let's start with the reflection picture. How would you describe the movement of light?
>
> *Jaleesa:* Look there, in the reflection picture, the arrow is hitting something and bouncing off.
>
> *Mrs. Greenfield:* OK, yes. We can see it right there. Now, what does this image represent?
>
> *Charles:* The arrow is a beam of light, hitting an object, like a mirror. It bounces off.

Mrs. Greenfield guided Jaleesa, Charles, and the others in their small group to "read" the other images in a similar manner. In this way, she scaffolded the learning, and then she sent these students back to the original complex text to address questions like *What evidence does the author provide to let you know that light can move in different ways?* and *How does the medium affect the movement of a light wave?* After noting the five students' responses to these last questions, she felt comfortable that they had achieved the necessary deep understanding of the initial text.

Writing activity. Satisfied that her students all understood the information in the text, Mrs. Greenfield asked them to complete the following language frame, referring to the information they'd found in the text and captured in their Foldables:

> Light waves behave _____. When light strikes
> _____, it _____. In other cases,
> light might hit a _____ and _____. Finally, if light
> _____, then _____. The evidence for
> these ideas can be found _____ in the text.

When the students finished their writing, they shared it with others at their table. In this lesson, Mrs. Greenfield provided her 6th graders with opportunities to use academic language during their close reading and thinking, their peer collaborations, and their writing. She did this while addressing multiple Common Core reading and writing standards tailored for middle school history/social studies, science, and technical subjects:

RST.6–8.1. Cite specific textual evidence to support analysis of science and technical texts.

RST.6–8.2. Determine the central ideas or conclusions of a text; provide an accurate summary of the text distinct from prior knowledge or opinions.

RST.6–8.5. Analyze the structure an author uses to organize a text, including how the major sections contribute to the whole and to an understanding of the topic.

RST.6–8.6. Analyze the author's purpose in providing an explanation, describing a procedure, or discussing an experiment in a text.

WHST.6–8.2. Write informative/explanatory texts, including the narration of historical events, scientific procedures/experiments, or technical processes.

WHST.6–8.9. Draw evidence from informational texts to support analysis, reflection, and research.

A Look at Close Reading in Grade 9

Before the reading. Ninth grade English teacher Jacob Mestman planned his next close reading session with two goals in mind. First, he wanted to give his students an opportunity to struggle a bit with how word choice and usage help readers visualize characters. Second, he wanted to expose them to an example of descriptive writing that could serve as a model for their own writing efforts. The complex text he chose for these purposes was an excerpt from Chinua Achebe's 1958 novel *Things Fall Apart* (see Figure 3.8), a Common Core text exemplar for grades 9–10.

Like Mrs. Greenfield, Mr. Mestman identified potential problem areas prior to the close reading session. Using the Qualitative Scoring Rubric for Narrative Text/Literature (see Figure 1.2, p. 26), he planned his lesson based on the following general assessment of the text and his students:

Figure 3.8 | **A High School Literary Text Prepared for Close Reading**

1   Okonkwo was well known throughout the nine villages and even beyond. His fame rested on solid personal achievements. As a young man of eighteen he had brought honor to his village by throwing Amalinze the Cat. Amalinze was the great wrestler who for seven years was unbeaten, from Umuofia to Mbaino. He was called the Cat because his back would never touch the earth. It was this man that Okonkwo threw in a fight which the old men agreed was one of the fiercest since the founder of their town engaged a spirit of the wild for seven days and seven nights.

2   The drums beat and the flutes sang and the spectators held their breath. Amalinze was a wily craftsman, but Okonkwo was as slippery as a fish in water. Every nerve and every muscle stood out on their arms, on their backs and their thighs, and one almost heard them stretching to breaking point. In the end Okonkwo threw the Cat.

3   That was many years ago, twenty years or more, and during this time Okonkwo's fame had grown like a bush-fire in the harmattan. He was tall and huge, and his bushy eyebrows and wide nose gave him a very severe look. He breathed heavily, and it was said that, when he slept, his wives and children in their houses could hear him breathe. When he walked, his heels hardly touched the ground and he seemed to walk on springs, as if he was going to pounce on somebody. And he did pounce on people quite often. He had a slight stammer and whenever he was angry and could not get his words out quickly enough, he would use his fists. He had no patience with unsuccessful men. He had had no patience with his father.

4   Unoka, for that was his father's name, had died ten years ago. In his day he was lazy and improvident and was quite incapable of thinking about tomorrow. If any money came his way, and it seldom did, he immediately bought gourds of palm-wine, called round his neighbors and made merry. He always said that whenever he saw a dead man's mouth he saw the folly of not eating what one had in one's lifetime. Unoka was, of course, a debtor, and he owed every neighbor some money, from a few cowries to quite substantial amounts.

5   He was tall but very thin and had a slight stoop. He wore a haggard and mournful look except when he was drinking or playing on his flute. He was very good on his flute, and his happiest moments were the two or three moons after the harvest when the village musicians brought down their instruments, hung above the fireplace. Unoka would play with them, his face beaming with blessedness and peace. Sometimes another village would ask Unoka's band and their dancing egwugwu to come and stay with them and teach them their tunes. They would go to such hosts for as long as three or four markets, making music and feasting. Unoka loved the good fare and the good fellowship, and he loved this season of the year, when the rains had stopped and the sun rose every morning with dazzling beauty. And it was not too hot either, because the cold and dry harmattan wind was blowing down from the north. Some years the harmattan was very severe and a dense haze hung on the atmosphere. Old men and children would then sit round log fires, warming their bodies. Unoka loved it all, and he loved the first kites that returned with the dry season, and the children who sang songs of welcome to them. He would remember his own childhood, how he had often wandered around looking for a kite sailing leisurely against the blue sky. As soon as he found one he would sing with his whole being, welcoming it back from its long, long journey, and asking it if it had brought home any lengths of cloth.

Source: Things Fall Apart by Chinua Achebe, 1994, pp. 3–5.

- *Text Structure—Organization:* Moderate/at grade level; organization includes narrative text structures that describe, such as *He was tall but very thin and had a slight stoop.*

- *Text Structure—Visual Supports and Layout:* Not applicable. No visual supports are included in this text to either confuse students or support their understanding.

- *Text Structure—Relationships Among Ideas:* Moderate/at grade level; relationships were sometimes implied in this text. For instance, the author writes that *He* [Okonkwo] *had a slight stammer and whenever he was angry and could not get his words out quickly enough, he would use his fists. He had no patience with unsuccessful men. He had had no patience with his father.* This implies that Okonkwo believed his father to be unsuccessful.

- *Language Features—Author's Style:* Moderate/at grade level; although commas are used in some complex sentences, the style is written at grade level for these 9th graders.

- *Language Features—Vocabulary:* Challenging/stretch text; many words and phrases (e.g., *threw in a fight, improvident,* and *folly*) might challenge students.

- *Meaning:* Moderate/at grade level; some information is complex (*He always said that whenever he saw a dead man's mouth he saw the folly of not eating what one had in one's lifetime*).

- *Author's Purpose:* Challenging/stretch text; the purpose requires some interpretation. Students may not be able to determine that this passage shows contrasts between characters.

- *Knowledge Demands*: Moderate/at grade level; students have some background knowledge about texts that explore cultural traditions and themes.

Given this analysis, Mr. Mestman chose to focus his lesson on how the author used language to help readers visualize and contrast characters. As shown in Figure 3.9, he prepared a set of text-dependent questions and evidence-based answers designed to steer readers to a deeper understanding of this lesson purpose. He knew that these questions and answers were just a place to start; during the lesson, he might need to add or skip questions, based on his students' responses.

Mr. Mestman also prepared for sharing the lesson by copying the short passage on legal-size paper so students would have space to add margin notes, such as questions they had about the text, in addition to highlighting, underlining, and circling words and phrases. He made copies of the passage for all students

Figure 3.9 | **Text-Dependent Questions and Evidence-Based Answers for Achebe's *Things Fall Apart***

Progression of Questions (check)	Text-Dependent Questions	Evidence-Based Answers	Page/Para. #
☑ General Understanding ☐ Key Details ☐ Vocabulary and Text Structure ☐ Author's Purpose ☐ Inferences ☐ Opinions, Arguments, Intertextual Connections	What is happening in this passage?	Characters who live in a village are introduced and described.	Paragraphs 1–5
☐ General Understanding ☑ Key Details ☐ Vocabulary and Text Structure ☐ Author's Purpose ☐ Inferences ☐ Opinions, Arguments, Intertextual Connections	Who is mentioned in the passage?	Amalinze the Cat, a wrestler Okonkwo, a fierce fighter Unoka, Okonkwo's lazy father	Paragraph 1 Paragraphs 2–3 Paragraphs 4–5
☐ General Understanding ☐ Key Details ☑ Vocabulary and Text Structure ☐ Author's Purpose ☐ Inferences ☐ Opinions, Arguments, Intertextual Connections	What words does the author use to describe the characters?	Amalinze—great wrestler, undefeated for 7 years, wily craftsman Okonwko—well-known, tall, huge, severe look, could pounce on someone Unoka—happiest when playing flute, face beaming, loved the season, "loved it all"	Paragraphs 1–2 Paragraphs 1 & 3
	What is the purpose for using these words to describe the characters?	These words provide a lot of contrast.	Paragraph 5

so they could annotate major ideas, confusing words, surprises, and questions to deepen their understanding of the setting and the characters.

First reading and discussion. Mr. Mestman began the lesson by stating the purpose: "As we read today, I want you to pay close attention to how the author's language helps us visualize and understand the characters. Let's number our paragraphs and then do a first reading to get a feeling for what the text is saying." When everyone had finished, Mr. Mestman checked for a general understanding of the passage. Students talked in pairs and at their tables about what they had read, while Mr. Mestman moved among the small groups, listening in to decide which of the text-dependent questions he'd prepared would move the group to a deeper understanding. As he observed the students' conversations and annotations, he used a prepared form (see Figure 3.10) to capture formative assessment data. We will take a closer look at the process of formative assessment during close reading in Chapter 6.

Second reading and discussion. Mr. Mestman asked his students to return to the text a second time to pay close attention to any words, phrases, or details that helped them create vivid mental pictures of characters. "What words describe the characters so well that you can picture them or so that you would know them if they walked through our classroom door right now?" he asked. "What words make you 'see' Okonkwo and Unoka?" Because he wanted the students to notice the key language details the author used, he asked that they annotate by circling words that described the characters. After everyone had read and annotated the passage the second time, Mr. Mestman invited them to work with a partner to complete the simple graphic organizer shown in Figure 3.11.

Students in this 9th grade class were used to transferring annotations and margin notes to a graphic organizer. As they charted and chatted, Mr. Mestman took the opportunity to check in on his students' progress toward achieving the lesson purpose. Observing that they were now attending to the precision of the author's language choices, he said, "Now that you have added some words that help you to visualize the characters, please add to your graphic organizer, recording a *P* next to the words and phrases that created positive visual images and characteristics in your mind and an *N* next to those that are negative."

Students were able to identify some of the more obvious words and phrases and label them correctly with a *P* or *N*. Students correctly identified words that created negative images (e.g., *bushy eyebrows, pounce on someone*) as well as more positive images (e.g., *his face beaming with blessedness and peace*) as part of their text evidence. Mr. Mestman knew at this time that another reading was necessary in order for the students to understand the author's juxtaposition of the two main characters: the heavily breathing, severe Okonkwo and the beaming Unoka, who "loved it all."

Additional readings and discussion. Students had read this text twice on their own, and Mr. Mestman felt that by reading part of the text aloud to them, he might help them uncover some of the less obvious positive and negative visual images key to understanding the juxtaposition of the two characters. Rather than read the whole text, he read paragraphs 3 and 5, pausing to show students which words he was adding to his graphic organizer and why. Mr. Mestman pointed

Figure 3.10 | **An Observation Form for Formative Assessment of Close Reading**   **Download**

Text: _____

Date: _____

Preplanned Text-Dependent Questions	Observations of Students *Who is confused?* *What are the misconceptions?*	New Text-Dependent Questions to Further Student Understanding

Figure 3.11 | **A Graphic Organizer for Capturing Text Evidence**

Text evidence describing Okonkwo	Text evidence describing Unoka

out and added *slight stammer, use fists to get words out,* and *no patience with unsuccessful men* as phrases that give negative images and *blessedness, peace, and loved good fellowship and children* as words and phrases that create positive ones. Because his students were nodding and had expressions of understanding on their faces, Mr. Mestman decided that they were ready to tackle the other paragraphs on their own. He watched as they reread the rest of the text silently, adding to their graphic organizers.

At this point, Mr. Mestman knew that his students were ready to be pushed back into the text to consider the author's use of foreshadowing. His next instructional purpose was to prompt his students with questions about how the author used language to help foreshadow future events in the text. "Think about how the author describes these characters," he said. "Were you surprised by this? Why, or why not? What would be the purpose of using contrasting language when describing the main characters? What might you expect to happen in this text?"

Writing activity. As an exit slip for this lesson that would also be used for formative assessment, Mr. Mestman asked students to respond to the following prompt: *What language does the author use to describe Okonkwo and Unoka, and how might this language help foreshadow what we will read about tomorrow?* He also posted a set of sentence frames students could use to shape their written response, encouraging anyone who needed them to use them:

The author uses _____ to help me understand that _____.

Okonkwo is described as _____. This creates a _____ visual image.

Unoka is described as _____. This creates a _____ visual image.

By using the words _____ and phrases _____, the author is foreshadowing that _____.

Both of the classroom examples offered in this chapter are intended to provide insight into the process of close reading and one way it might be planned and implemented. We encourage you to create a close reading structure that works for your students and is adaptable enough to address the teaching points of the text you are using. For example, your students might need to read some passages twice and other texts more than twice. The focus and details of a close reading always depend on the text, the lesson purpose, and the reader's familiarity with the topic of the passage. Some texts might contain language that requires in-depth attention, while others might require more attention to key details. Ultimately, rereading helps students gain a better understanding of the key ideas and details of the author's message and become aware of how the author used writing to convey that message.

The **Planning Guide for Close Reading,** shared in Figure 3.12, can serve as a resource for planning and conducting your next close reading.

Managing Close Reading

Now that we've examined the process of close reading in action, let's address just how close reading fits into a daily classroom schedule and how to employ it in a way that will accommodate different student strengths and grouping arrangements.

Scheduling: Making Close Reading an Integral Part of the School Day

It's impractical to make close reading a daily practice, but it should be a regular part of the weekly schedule. Although many upper-grade teachers give students reading assignments, typically they're to be completed outside of class. Furthermore, when some teachers identify texts as difficult, they tend to read those texts aloud, deliver a lecture on the content, or provide hands-on activities in lieu of a

Figure 3.12 | **A Planning Guide for Close Reading**   Download

CLOSE READING PRE-PLANNING

Lesson Purpose: _____

Common Core State Standard(s): _____

Date: _____   Grade: _____   Discipline: _____

Step 1: Select the Text

Text should be short, complex, and worthy of a close read. Remember to include a wide range of genres over time.

Title: _____

Author: _____

Page(s) or chunk(s) of text: _____

Step 2: Determine the Areas of Complexity/Potential Problem Areas and Teaching Points

Think about your students and aspects of the text that may interfere with their comprehension. Those chosen should become the focus of your teaching points. Refer to your qualitative rubric.

Literary Texts
- ○ Text Structure
- ○ Language Features
- ○ Meaning
- ○ Author's Purpose
- ○ Knowledge Demands

Informational Texts
- ○ Text Structure
- ○ Language Features
- ○ Meaning
- ○ Author's Purpose
- ○ Knowledge Demands

Step 3: Generate Text-Dependent Questions

Develop several high cognitive level questions that you may ask, depending on students' conversations with you and each other. Questions should require students to use the author's words. Prompt students to use text evidence. Use the progression of text-dependent questions as a scaffold. Focus on those that will best support your students in acquiring the knowledge needed to expand their comprehension.

1. _____

2. _____

3. _____

4. _____

5. _____

6. _____

Continued →

Figure 3.12 | **A Planning Guide for Close Reading (cont'd.)**   Download

CLOSE READING SESSION

Remember to number the paragraphs or chunks of text. Limit frontloading when introducing the text.

First Reading

The first reading of a text should allow the reader to gain a general understanding of what the text says. Encourage students to annotate while reading to identify big ideas, if that is your initial focus. You may also want to use the first reading to have students identify (circle) words that are difficult for them. This provides insight into comprehension interference. Base your direction during the first reading on your prior assessment of the text complexity as it relates to your students.

Purpose Setting: Let's read to find out . . .

○ Teacher Read   ○ Student Read

First Discussion: Partner talk and check meaning
Students dialogue about their understanding of the text or about the difficult text language, if that was your direction to them. Listen, and assess what students have understood. The next questions asked should build from these insights.

Next Reading

Based on the responses of the students, ask a question or two that pushes them back to the text to expand their thinking. This reading of the text should focus the reader's attention on how the text works by prompting consideration of author's use of language and the structure of the text. Encourage students to annotate while attending to text-dependent questions.

Text-Dependent Question:
Evidence-Based Answer (include p. # or para. #):

Text-Dependent Question:
Evidence-Based Answer (include p. # or para. #):

Next Discussion: Partner talk and check meaning
Students dialogue about their understanding and language of the text at a deeper level. Listen and assesses what students have understood and determine what next questions to ask.

Additional Readings

Additional readings of the text should allow the reader to draw inferences and make intertextual connections through a deepening understanding of the text's language, structure, and meaning. Encourage students to annotate while attending to text dependent questions.

Text-Dependent Question:
Evidence-Based Answer (include p. # or para. #):

Text-Dependent Question:
Evidence-Based Answer (include p. # or para. #):

Additional Discussions: Partner talk and check meaning
Students dialogue about their understanding of the text at this deepened level. Listen and assess what students have understood and determine whether more text-dependent questions and additional readings are needed.

Writing as an Assessment and/or to Extend Meaning

A writing activity allows students to demonstrate their understanding of the text and serves as a performance assessment.

reading assignment. According to Snow and O'Conner (2013), "These practices may be effective in ensuring students are exposed to required content, but they do not support students in learning to read the complex texts required in the content areas" (p. 2). They deny students the opportunity to struggle with texts and, by doing so, to develop the disciplinary literacy skills so critical for career success. The incorporation of close reading in each content area classroom provides ways to make disciplinary reading part of regular classroom practice, and it gives students rich opportunities to engage in literacy experiences that will help them to better master the content in your discipline.

What if you already incorporate plenty of reading experiences in your classroom? In that case, try regularly substituting close reading for a portion of the reading you typically assign. Remember, though, that close reading is more time-consuming, so you may wind up devoting a whole class period to a single close reading instead of planning for 20 minutes of independent reading on Tuesday and 40 minutes of shared reading on Wednesday. You might also conduct a close reading once or twice a week during the time usually used for small-group instruction. In this set up, students can begin the close reading experience in a large-group setting and follow up with small-group experiences for the second or third readings.

Here's an example from Mr. Mestman. When he finished reviewing the exit slips his students had submitted, he counted six students who did not identify the vocabulary the author used to describe the main characters and could not articulate in writing the purpose of such language. He decided to bring those students together in a small group and work with them closely while the rest of the class first used Voki, an educational tool (www.voki.com), to create speaking avatars that illustrated their understanding of the characters and then shared these avatars with one another.

Mr. Mestman's work with the group of six students was structured and deliberate. He distributed prepared copies of the same passage of *Things Fall Apart* and read the first paragraph, modeling how he thought about some of the vocabulary and how the adjectives gave him a clearer understanding of the character Amalinze, and encouraging students to add words and phrase to their graphic organizers. Moving on to paragraph 2, he and the students worked together to identify, define, and understand the characteristics of Amalinze and Okonkwo. Mr. Mestman contined to release more and more responsibility for understanding by allowing the students to work in pairs to identify key vocabulary and make connections while reading. Finally, Mr. Mestman was comfortable with the students' developing understanding and asked them to read paragraphs 4 and 5 on their own. At each stage—with the teacher, with their peers, and individually—students added to their original graphic organizers. Mr. Mestman finally checked the group's understanding through a more formal response: having them create Vokis (speaking avatars) to assume the perspective of either Okonkwo or Unoka and explain how he was different from his father or son.

As students gain skill in close reading, they can read closely across the disciplines, which provides additional opportunities to work the process into the school day. Knowledge of content and text structures will grow as students analyze textbooks, primary source documents, maps, charts and graphs, and math problems. With proper support, students' close reading proficiency will grow, and their confidence and independence will increase. In Chapter 4, we will provide suggestions for teaching close reading across the disciplines.

Differentiating Close Reading

All students can learn to read closely, provided their teacher is able to differentiate instruction for those who need additional supports to effectively read complex text, such as English language learners and striving readers.

One approach is to use the Gradual Release of Responsibility (GRR) instructional framework (Fisher & Frey, 2014; Pearson & Gallagher, 1983). After the first independent close reading, you might model a strategy (*I do it*) as you read the text aloud, have students try out the strategy in a group rereading (*we do it together*), have students try out that strategy with a partner in another pass (*you do it together*), and then have students employ the strategy independently (*you do it alone*).

Consider the approach taken by 9th grade teacher Kaila Tricaso, who had her students closely read a scientific journal article about burn injuries (Corry, Pruzinsky, & Rumsey, 2009) as a complement to their study of Chris Crutcher's *Staying Fat for Sarah Byrnes*, a novel about a girl whose burn scars make her an outcast. Ms. Tricaso chose this particular informational text because of the stretch it provided her 9th graders in terms of vocabulary and meaning (see the Qualitative Scoring Rubric for Informational Text, Figure 1.3, p. 29). For this lesson, she distributed copies of the article, projected one copy for all to see, introduced its title ("Social Functioning and Adjustment to Burn Injuries"), and set the lesson purpose: "We're going to read this article to learn more about burn injuries and explore how Sarah Byrnes might relate to the information it contains." As she read the three-paragraph article aloud, students followed along, thought about the lesson purpose, and made annotations on their personal copies (*you do it alone*), some by circling or highlighting words like *psychosocial rehabilitation, unsolicited, social ramifications,* and *prominent* and making notes in the margins and some by drawing quick sketches. When this first reading was complete, students shared their annotations, first with a partner and then with the whole group (*you do it together*). Ms. Tricaso reminded them to cite evidence from the text when explaining how Sarah, the character from their novel, might relate to the information in the article.

Before the next reading, Ms. Tricaso said to the students, "Now I will read the first paragraph again, modeling for you what it can teach me about burn injuries. Notice how I think aloud and how I use annotations to make the text mine. You might want to add more notes to your copy as you watch me." This *I do it* stage is important, as it allows students to see the language and the thinking processes that are involved with comprehending difficult text. Ms. Tricaso went on to read the title of the article again, thinking aloud about what social functioning might have to do with burn injuries. Then, as she read, she highlighted the phrase *prominent challenges inherent in long-term psychosocial rehabilitation following a major trauma such as a burn injury,* thinking aloud about how Sarah Byrnes did seem to be facing challenges in terms of her body image and interactions with people and wondering what psychosocial rehabilitation might entail. Then she asked her students if this second reading had helped them learn anything new about how people who had been burned function in society and adjust to their scars. They shared these responses as a whole group. During a third reading (*we do it together*), Ms. Tricaso read the next paragraph, asking students to take a closer look at the words and phrases the author used. "What more did you learn about burn injuries? After I read, please work with your partner to annotate on your paper other descriptions of your new learning." When the students later shared their ideas with the whole group, Ms. Tricaso asked text-dependent questions such as *What evidence from the text tells us that there are social ramifications of having a burn injury? How do we know what some of the proactive social strategies are to overcome social challenges? How does the information here relate to Sarah Byrnes? What do you think Sarah would say after reading this article?* Ms. Tricaso concluded this GRR/close reading lesson by asking groups of students to put all their notes and knowledge together to come up with a complete summary of the article (*you do it together*). She explained that they could share their descriptions in writing, through an oral presentation, or as an illustration.

Another way to scaffold instruction for struggling middle or high school readers is to involve them in using fluency strategies. For example, if your students are reading a complex stretch text excerpt from a text exemplar, you might ask your English language learners or striving readers to engage with the text after the first reading by using a fluency routine like paired repeated readings. With this scaffold, they will be better prepared to focus on text comprehension during a second reading and a whole-group discussion afterward. Or, if a text contains lots of challenging academic terms, it can be effective to have students work with a partner to create 4-Square Word Cards that contain a definition, a picture of the term, a synonym for the word, and a sentence containing the word (see Figure 3.13). If the text has an unfamiliar structure, you can call student attention to that structure through text-dependent questions of increasing difficulty.

Differentiating instruction for English language learners should involve the use of oral language as part of every close reading experience. Partner talk can be invaluable for English language learners as they grapple with challenging texts. They might share with a partner their initial impressions of the text, retell the text to a partner, or summarize key points from the text. The use of sentence frames can also facilitate this process.

Figure 3.13 | **A 4-Square Word Card to Scaffold Academic Vocabulary**

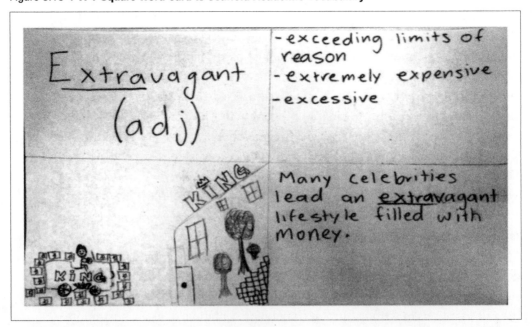

Grouping Arrangements That Support Close Reading Instruction and Learning

Effective grouping patterns can help to ensure student success with the complex texts required for close reading. Over the course of the close reading experience, students should have large-group, small-group, paired, and individual learning arrangements.

Here's an illustration that shows an approach taken by 8th grade social studies teacher James Farrell. He and his students, who were predominantly English language learners, decided to do a close reading of Walt Whitman's poem "O Captain! My Captain!" (a Common Core text exemplar) as part of a unit on the U.S. Civil War. Mr. Farrell began the lesson by sharing with his students that the purpose for reading this text was to explore the author's feelings about the death of the captain. During the first reading, students worked *independently* to read and annotate the text, focusing on main ideas, unknown vocabulary, and areas of confusion. While guiding the *large group* in a follow-up discussion of the text, Mr. Farrell noted that several students had difficulty identifying the poem's various shifts in tone, from joyous and jubilant to deeply melancholic.

Before the second text reading, he began by modeling how to analyze the shifts in tone in the first stanza by examining the author's word choices, and then students worked *in pairs* to analyze the shifts in tone in the next two stanzas. Following this, students shared their understandings of these shifts, and Mr. Farrell recorded those responses on the board. After students read the text a third time, Mr. Farrell put the students into small writing groups. He directed them to consider what they knew about what happened in 1865 (the year the poem was written) and to consider who the captain in the poem might be, what the ship might represent, and the narrator's emotions about the captain. He asked them to use Storybird.com, a digital story-building tool, to write a short paragraph explaining their answers to these questions and to provide three pieces of evidence from the poem in support of their opinions. In this way, he used a variety of grouping patterns during key phases of the lesson: students worked individually during the first reading, discussed the text in a large group, worked in pairs during the second reading, and created small writing groups in response to the close reading.

Consider using the checklist shown in Figure 3.14 to reflect on your current familiarity with text complexity and close reading as well as your current implementation practices. This form might also be the centerpiece of the discussion of these topics in a professional learning community (PLC).

Figure 3.14 | **Close Reading Expertise and Implementation Self-Assessment**   Download

TEACHER EXPERTISE	Beginning	Progressing	Accomplished
1. Am I aware of the kinds of texts that are appropriate for close reading?			
2. Do I understand the quantitative factors of text complexity?			
3. Do I understand the qualitative dimensions of text complexity?			
4. Can I identify reader/task features that influence text complexity?			
5. Can I evaluate a text for complexity based on quantitative, qualitative, and reader/task factors?			
6. Can I identify potential close reading teaching points based on my text and reader assessments?			
7. Do I understand the steps in close reading and how it differs from traditional reading instruction?			
8. Do I understand how to create effective text-dependent questions?			
CLOSE READING IMPLEMENTATION	**Beginning**	**Progressing**	**Accomplished**
1. Have I made close reading a part of my regular classroom schedule?			
2. Do I implement close reading in my classroom on a daily basis?			
3. Does close reading occur in content area subjects as well as language arts time?			
4. Do student close reading experiences incorporate the Gradual Release of Responsibility model?			
5. Do I use formative assessment to determine students needs and next steps for instruction during close reading?			
6. Do I differentiate instruction based on formative assessments as part of close reading experiences?			
7. Do I use a variety of grouping arrangements to support close reading instruction and learning?			

Based on a reflection on my knowledge of close reading practice, what are my next steps for professional development?

How do I plan to begin?

On your own or with the members of your PLC, use the checklist to reflect on what you understand about close reading and how you use text complexity and close reading strategies. Identify the aspects of close reading implementation you are doing effectively and those that are more problematic. Over time, the information you gather with this form can be helpful as an informal record of progress and may be useful in planning individual or schoolwide professional development experiences.

Finally, in this book's Appendix A, **A Guide for Administrators,** we provide suggestions for how administrators can support whole-school implementation of close reading instruction, a Close Reading Observation Guide designed to parallel the Planning Guide for Close Reading shared in Figure 3.12, and resources administrators can consult to learn more and find information to share with teachers. By creating common understandings around the practice of close reading, administrators can better support teachers as they work to become proficient in this practice.

◆

As we have seen, in close reading, the teacher uses a combination of planning, structured implementation, and thoughtful management to set conditions under which students create their own deep knowledge and understanding of a text and an author's message. As both teachers and students increase their familiarity with close reading practices, they will find that close reading promotes the kind of critical thinking essential to success in school and in the workplace. In the next chapter, we explore how teachers can move close reading beyond the boundaries of the language arts classroom and into disciplinary instruction.

CHAPTER 4

READING CLOSELY ACROSS THE DISCIPLINES

As a middle or high school English language arts, social studies, science, or mathematics teacher, odds are you don't think of yourself as a literacy teacher. You are correct. You are a teacher of English, social studies, science, or mathematics. However, your job also involves engaging students in thinking, talking, writing, and reading within your discipline, because this is what learning a discipline entails, and this is what will be expected of your students if they eventually choose a career in your discipline. In this chapter, we will support you in thinking about how close reading relates to your discipline; why, how, and when to engage students in close reading of complex texts; and what materials to use to do this.

Let's begin by taking a step back. One of the most radical changes of the Common Core State Standards is that they make literacy a critical part of instruction in all disciplines and at all grade levels. This is a departure from the No Child Left Behind era, when social studies and science instruction took a back seat to reading and mathematics. In grades 6–12, the Common Core State Standards for English Language Arts & Literacy are divided into two sections: the English language arts standards cover reading, writing, speaking and listening, and language; and the literacy standards focus specifically on the connection of the ELA anchor standards to the disciplines of history/social studies, science, and technical subjects. (If you're reviewing the standards document, the literacy standards begin on page 59.) According to the Common Core's creators, this division reflects the ELA teacher's essential role in developing students' literacy skills, and simultaneously recognizes that teachers in the other subject areas have a critical responsibility to address and support students' literacy development within their disciplines. The introduction of literacy standards to history/social studies, science, and technical subjects is in no way intended to supplant content area standards from the various states; the Common Core standards are a supplement aimed at increasing students' literacy in the content they will encounter in all disciplines.

In short, then, the literacy that the Common Core calls for is *disciplinary literacy*—that is, using reading, reasoning, investigating, speaking, and writing to develop content knowledge related to a particular discipline (McConachie & Petrosky, 2010). This embrace of disciplinary literacy acknowledges how central reading and writing are to the real-world work of historians, mathematicians, scientists, software engineers, and those in other technical disciplines (Zygouris-Coe, 2012). While science teachers, for example, may think of science as a hands-on pursuit, fully 50 percent of the work that scientists actually do involves reading (Hunt Institute, 2011).

Note that disciplinary literacy is not just another name for *content area literacy* (Shanahan & Shanahan, 2012). The latter focuses on generic strategies, such as questioning and summarizing, that students can use to boost general comprehension while reading textbooks in social studies, mathematics, science, and other classes. Disciplinary literacy, by contrast, includes specific literacy practices that disciplinary experts have identified as ones they use to make sense of information within their disciplines. These practices are not generic; they are unique to each area of study. For example, Shanahan and Shanahan (2008), studying the literacy practices engaged in by experts in the various disciplines, found that chemists read texts with the intent to study them more deeply through replication of the identified processes and tasks, while historians perceive texts as interpretations that often hold bias. The goal of disciplinary literacy instruction is to teach students to use those specific strategies, different for each discipline, as they read all kinds of texts within that area of study.

This chapter looks at reading and writing strategies that pertain to close reading across all of the content areas. While we use the terms *content areas* and *disciplines* interchangeably, the close reading and other literacy practices we discuss can be applied to all of the content areas rather than to the work done exclusively by scientists, historians, mathematicians, and rhetoricians. We view close reading as a literacy practice that supports an analytic investigation of a text in any discipline and that, through the text-dependent questions being asked, can help students investigate texts in ways similar to how a disciplinary expert might interact with a text. In our discussion of close reading, we will share

- Ways to use multiple text types for close reading across the disciplines.
- The rationale for focusing on informational texts during close reading.
- How students build discipline-specific knowledge through experience with increasingly challenging texts.
- Resources for text exemplars and text sets for close reading in the disciplines.
- Examples of what close reading looks like in science, social studies, and mathematics.

Let's get started.

Why Reading Closely Across the Disciplines Is Essential

To review some key points from Chapter 2, close reading represents an intimate, analytic encounter with a text. Shanahan (2012) argues that close reading is "an intensive analysis of a text in order to come to terms with what it says, how it says it, and what it means" (para. 5). When you read a challenging text—say, a primary source document, an insurance policy, or a complicated chart—you naturally find yourself reading and then rereading to grasp the text's meaning. This ability to read and reread with a laser-like focus on the information the author presents on the page (or "within the four corners of the text") is a highly valuable skill in *every* discipline and in various aspects of everyday life.

There are many reasons for close reading to be a component of all disciplinary learning and instruction. Here are three we find particularly compelling.

Embedded Disciplinary Literacy Instruction

The Common Core envisions literacy instruction as something that is embedded within the curriculum of all disciplines rather than something confined to the ELA classroom. The practice of close reading is an ideal means for achieving this kind of literacy integration. Through close reading, a teacher can increase the amount of reading students do in social studies, science, and other subjects and promote long-term retention of content-related information.

Close reading also gives students practice mastering the "ways of knowing" pertinent to each discipline. For example, one important way of knowing that is characteristic of social studies is understanding how a text's author shapes the information he or she delivers. When historians read, they interpret a text by asking themselves who the author of that text is, what the author knows about the topic, and what the author's biases might be. If necessary, they analyze information in historical maps and charts, and they make connections among economics, religion, government, and cultural topics (Wineburg, 1991, 1998). So, for example, when 10th graders do a close reading of Ronald Reagan's "Address to Students at Moscow State University," a Common Core exemplar for grades 9–10, the teacher can frame the experience in ways that require students to continually revisit the text and, in doing so, expand their understanding of both President Reagan's objectives and the broader geopolitical context as they consider and reconsider the meaning of his message.

Opportunity to Acquire and Develop Discipline-Based Knowledge

The Common Core standards expect students to use reading experiences to build a coherent body of knowledge in the various disciplines as they move through the grades. As their knowledge in the discipline grows, so will their ability to grasp and assimilate the new ideas they will encounter in their reading. As Lee and Spratley (2010) remind us, "If you don't know content you will have a difficult time understanding the texts, and if you don't understand the texts you are unlikely to learn content" (p. 3). Ideally, daily close reading sessions should be structured so that each experience builds on the one before it; in this way, students use text to build conceptual knowledge over time.

Teachers can collaborate with colleagues across grade levels to ensure an ever-expanding trajectory of challenge in the texts provided for close reading and an ever-expanding range of content understanding. For example, in 9th grade science, students might read Annie J. Cannon's "Classifying the Stars," a Common Core text exemplar for grades 9–10, as a way of exploring the way that visible light can be broken into component parts. Carefully crafted text-dependent questions would direct students to note these key elements of spectral analysis. Then, in 12th grade Physics, students might closely read Mark Fischetti's "Working Knowledge: Electronic Stability Control," another Common Core text exemplar, as a way to investigate the design and development of the hydraulic systems connected to the technology of electronic stability control. In such a case, students would explore how these advancements use actuators to correct trajectories of motion during braking. In a later semester, they might dig even deeper to understand how the yaw sensor works.

Although in this example, the specific content is different—one text is about spectral analysis and the other is about hydraulics—both deal with topics in physics that utilize technical and academic language that is specific to science writing. A teacher may provide students with the opportunity to wrestle with a complex science text at a challenging level in 9th grade and then progressively move them to higher Lexile levels and greater text complexity in 10th, 11th, and 12th grade, as they develop the skills that will enable them to negotiate the intricacies of this type of discipline-specific text. Similar instructional progressions can be implemented in other content areas, from English to social studies to mathematics.

Close reading experiences with disciplinary texts help students build content knowledge over time through mastery of academic vocabulary, sensitivity to text structure, increased understanding of linguistic and discourse forms, and a developing understanding of authors' purposes. They push students to monitor their comprehension as they reread to note key ideas; ask themselves questions about the content; visualize people, places, processes, and events; and make predictions and connections among related topics. Students develop facility with close reading at different rates, and some may need more support than others. Fortunately, the skill development progression in the Common Core standards can help teachers identify the instructional interventions that each student needs.

Modeling of Disciplinary Literacy Practices

Close reading of disciplinary texts gives teachers a way to model for students how to address the unique comprehension challenges associated with particular content within a particular subject area. For example, a common difficulty students face when reading scientific texts is understanding how to identify characteristic text structures like problem/solution and cause/effect. When a teacher models what to look for and how to note it, homing in on constructions like *if/then*, *when/then*, or *because*, students develop a better sense of how to notice these text structures themselves—and use them in their own scientific writing. Science readers also need to understand how data, diagrams, charts, graphs, or tables connect to text and be able to interpret trends in charts and graphs. An astute teacher will model how to notice the axes of a graph, including units, and then how to determine if a value is increasing or decreasing relative to another quantity. These are just two examples of disciplinary literacy skills that are rarely taught explicitly, yet are essential to comprehension of scientific texts.

A teacher who models disciplinary literacy strategies within the context of close reading demonstrates for students how scientists, historians, mathematicians, writers, and other professionals read and reread to unlock the deeper meanings found within complex texts. With these tools at their disposal, students are better prepared to engage with various disciplines' critical content, vocabulary, forms of discourse, and linguistic and text structures. Each new close reading experience positions them to strengthen these skills and increases their readiness to meet the demands of college and the workplace. At the end of this chapter, we provide examples of how teachers use close reading to model learning across the disciplines.

Using Multiple Text Types and Genres in Disciplinary Close Reading

The Common Core State Standards make *texts* central to classroom instruction as never before. Consider that the word *text* represents 19 percent of the total words in the Common Core ELA/literacy standards document, compared to less than 1 percent of typical state standards documents (Burkins & Yaris, 2012). It's notable, too, that all the key instructional shifts that the Common Core requires (Common Core State Standards Initiative, 2014) relate to texts.

Here is how the ELA/literacy standards document sums up the kind of reading students should do:

> Students must read widely and deeply from among a broad range of high-quality, increasingly challenging literary and informational texts. Through extensive reading of stories, dramas, poems, and myths from diverse cultures and different time periods, students gain literary and cultural knowledge as well as familiarity with various text structures and elements. By reading texts in history/social studies, science, and other disciplines, students build a foundation of knowledge in these fields that will also give them the background to be better readers in all disciplines. Students can only gain this foundation when the curriculum is intentionally and coherently structured to develop rich content knowledge within and across grades. (NGA Center & CCSSO, 2010a, p. 40)

Why is deep, wide, and broad text reading so important? Because it translates into big improvements in student learning. Increasing the range and variety of texts increases reading competencies (Kuhn & Stahl, 2000) and improves achievement—not only in reading but in other content areas as well (Guthrie, Schafer, Von Secker, & Alban, 2000). The truth is, most teachers present students with a pretty limited range of texts. Remembering that literacy knowledge comes from literacy experiences (Palincsar & Duke, 2004), if we want students to read and comprehend multiple text types, if we want them to reap the full benefits of close reading, they need exposure to lots of different complex texts and instruction on how to read those texts.

Certainly by the middle school years, texts from the different disciplines vary dramatically. As Buell (2009) puts it, they represent "different worlds . . . different purposes, different writing styles, different organizations, different language, different modes of communication, different visual layouts, different expectations of relevant background and experiences, and different uses of knowledge" (p. 230).

Each genre has unique features, and reading comprehension is genre dependent (Duke & Roberts, 2010). Genre-specific strategies help students understand the unique features of each text type. In other words, the reading processes needed to comprehend a historical fiction book about the bombing of Pearl Harbor, like Graham Salisbury's *Under the Blood-Red Sun,* are very different from those required to take information from a literary nonfiction text focused on the same historical event, like Walter Lord's *Day of Infamy: The Classic Account of the Bombing of Pearl Harbor.* These two texts are written for different purposes, using different language and structures. *Under the Blood-Red Sun* is the story of a fictional Japanese American boy in Hawaii whose life changes dramatically after the bombing. It is written with attention to character description and the depiction of Tomi's courage when he and his family are faced with prejudice. *Day of Infamy* painstakingly recounts the actual events of the attack on Pearl Harbor, providing descriptions of the hour-by-hour planning and its aftermath based on primary sources, including letters, diaries, and interviews. It shapes a voluminous amount of information about the event, using narrative devices that place the reader at Pearl Harbor on that fateful day. Students need explicit instruction in specific strategies unique to reading and writing in a particular genre if they are to successfully negotiate the many text types they should encounter as part of close reading.

One of the demands of the Common Core's writing standards is that students be capable of writing in three different genres: *narrative, informative/explanatory,* and *persuasive/argumentative.* Through close reading experiences with each genre, students will gain experience with all three of these text types, and that will make writing in each genre easier. As you will see in Chapter 5, language and writing experiences can be closely aligned with close reading practices.

The Common Core's ELA/literacy standards specifically mention and reference a wide range of genre examples across grades 6–12, and we'd like to take a closer look at them now. For discussion, we have divided the genres recommended and referenced in the standards into three categories: *literature, informational text,* and *additional forms.*

Literature

Literary study of stories, dramas, and poetry often occurs in the English language arts classroom, but literature need not be confined to that discipline. Teachers of social studies, science, and technical subjects can also use these literary forms for close reading experiences by incorporating carefully selected pieces of literature into their instruction or grouping selected stories, poems, dramas, and informational texts into text sets to be used when studying a particular concept, era, theory, or theme. (Later in this chapter we will provide more information on text sets.) According to the Common Core State Standards, students in grades 6 and 7 are expected to spend 50 percent of their in-school reading time reading literature; by grade 8, the percentage drops to 45 percent, and by grade 12, it is 30 percent. Despite what some have suggested, the Common Core standards do not advocate the abandonment of literature study, but it is true that most of the literature students read will be in English class, and most of that literature can be categorized as stories, dramas, and poetry. Within those three categories, however, there is an astonishing range of choice.

Stories are imaginative narratives that include characters, plots, and settings. Stories can be short or long, and they take many different forms, including the following text types:

- *Adventure stories*—fictional stories with fast-moving plots that usually relate unexpected and dangerous events. A classic example is Robert Louis Stevenson's *Treasure Island*, a story of buccaneers and buried gold.
- *Allegories*— stories in which characters, settings, and plots represent a deeper symbolic or spiritual meaning. For example, in Herman Melville's *Billy Budd, Sailor*, an exemplar for grades 11–College and Career Ready (CCR), Billy Budd represents goodness, and Claggart, the master-at-arms, represents evil.
- *Fables*—short tales containing a moral, like *Aesop's Fables.*

- *Fantasy*—highly imaginative fiction often containing magic and imaginary worlds. Susan Cooper's *The Dark Is Rising* is a Newbery Honor book and an excellent text exemplar for grades 6–8 that features an imaginary world where the struggle between Light and Dark prevails. The main character, Will Stanton, fights the forces of the Dark using the magic he has learned from the Old Ones, who are the keepers of the Light.
- *Folktales*—stories that have been passed down via oral tradition and retold over time. For example, Virginia Hamilton's haunting "The People Could Fly," a text exemplar for grades 6–8, is a retelling of an African American folktale in which slaves elude their masters by literally taking flight.
- *Historical fiction*—stories with settings and some actual people from the historical past but with fictional or fictionalized main characters. For example, the text exemplar *Roll of Thunder, Hear My Cry*, by Mildred D. Taylor, describes the injustices suffered by an African American family in Mississippi in 1933.
- *Legends*—traditional tales of a group, first told orally and later in written form, like the King Arthur stories.
- *Mysteries*—narratives that involve solving a crime or getting to the bottom of an unexplained event. The famous Sherlock Holmes stories by Arthur Conan Doyle focus on a fictional detective whose powers of logical reasoning allow him to solve even the most complicated mysteries.
- *Myths*—stories that explain the mysteries of life and the world. The books in Rick Riordan's popular *Percy Jackson & the Olympians* series combine aspects of Greek mythology with a contemporary setting. Percy, the main character, is the son of Poseidon, the Greek god of the sea.
- *Novels*—long prose narratives that describe human experiences through fictional characters, settings, and events. Amy Tan's *The Joy Luck Club*, for example, is a novel with a contemporary setting that explores the complicated relationship between four Chinese American women and their Chinese-born mothers. It is a text exemplar for grades 9–10.
- *Parodies*—narratives that imitate another work in an effort to mock or ridicule that work, its author, or its style. One of the earliest and best-known parodies is Miguel de Cervantes's *Don Quixote*, a text exemplar for grades 11–CCR, which sends up the style of the chivalric romances popular in the 1500s.
- *Satire*—a literary form in which humor is used to attack human foibles through wit, irony, and other devices. Nikolai Gogol's "The Nose," a text exemplar for grades 9–10, is a satirical short story that ridicules the social conventions of 19th century Russia.

Dramas—plays that contain one or more acts—are the second type of literature noted in the Common Core. They can be read or performed by actors, and they are often captured on video or film. Dramas on the Common Core exemplar list include contemporary works like *The Diary of Anne Frank: A Play* by Frances Goodrich and Albert Hackett, an adaptation of Anne Frank's diary (grades 6–8); classic modern works like Henrik Ibsen's *A Doll's House* (grades 9–10), a three-act play critical of 19th century marriage norms; and ancient classics like *Oedipus Rex*, a tragedy by Sophocles first performed in 429 BCE (grades 9–10).

Poetry, the third type of literary text called out in the Common Core, is a written form that uses sound, meaning, and rhythm to convey experience. The following forms of poetry are specified in the standards:

- *Narrative poems*—poems that tell a story and often include characters and a narrator. Henry Wadsworth Longfellow's "Paul Revere's Ride," a text exemplar for grades 6–8, tells the story of Revere's ride to warn the colonists of the British troops' advance during the American Revolution. This poem was familiar to generations of American school children but is less well known today.
- *Lyrical poems*—poems that express feelings or emotions and have a songlike quality. Many of the Common Core text exemplars represent classic literary works, and Percy Bysshe Shelley's lyrical poem, "Ozymandias," a text exemplar for grades 9–10, is one of these—a renowned work that explores the enduring theme of the transience of human glory and power.
- *Free verse poems*—poems without a particular meter, rhyme, or other poetic conventions. Free verse poems included on the text exemplar list for grades 11–CCR include Walt Whitman's "Song of Myself," illustrating the author's poetic vision, and former U.S. Poet Laureate Rita Dove's "Demeter's Prayer to Hades," a contemporary poem with references to classical mythology.
- *Sonnets*—a classical poetic form with 14 lines and a specific rhyme scheme. Shakespeare's "Sonnet 73," a text exemplar for grades 9–10, uses metaphor to address the theme of aging.
- *Odes*—a subset of lyrical poems that have a formal structure and address a serious or contemplative topic. John Keats's "Ode on a Grecian Urn," a text exemplar for grades 11–CCR, is considered one of the finest odes in the English language. In it, the narrator reflects upon an ancient urn and the nature of art as depicted in an image frozen in time.

- *Ballads*—a subset of narrative poems, often intended to be sung, composed of simple stanzas and a refrain. William Butler Yeats's "The Song of Wandering Aengus" is a ballad that retells a Celtic myth about Aengus Og, a god of youth and beauty. It is a text exemplar for grades 6–8.
- *Epics*—long narrative poems about serious topics detailing heroic deeds and events. Homer's *The Odyssey*, a grades 9–10 text exemplar, is a classic epic poem about Odysseus's exploits in ancient Greece.

Informational Text

"Informational text" is an umbrella classification for a wide range of nonfiction text types written to inform readers about all kinds of topics in science, social science, current events, the arts, and more.

Informational texts have a strong presence in the Common Core State Standards. A key recommendation of the Common Core is that middle graders spend 55 percent of their reading time focused on informational text, with that percentage increasing to 70 percent by the end of high school (NGA Center & CCSSO, 2010a). The English language arts standards also recommend emphasis on one type of informational text—literary nonfiction. In fact, the standards state that because the ELA classroom must focus on literature (stories, drama, and poetry) and literary nonfiction, "a great deal of informational reading in grades 6–12 must take place in other classes" (p. 5).

There are at least three justifications for the Common Core's emphasis on informational text types. First, research indicates that students are not spending enough time reading complex informational texts. Within the disciplines in secondary school, it's generally assumed that the textbook serves as a common information source, but how much textbook reading are students actually doing? Studies suggest very little, whether in school or for homework (Wade & Moje, 2000). We would estimate that in many schools, students are spending only 10–15 minutes a day actually reading the content-based information they need to master social studies, English, or science. In some cases, teachers choose to read textbooks aloud to students or deliver content through lectures or Power-Point presentations that demand minimal reading on the part of students, rather than teach students how to read textbooks on their own. If students are to be prepared to read for information in college and in the workplace, they need far more access to and experience with informational texts than they are getting now—as well as strategies for reading informational texts across the disciplines.

The second justification for emphasizing informational text is that it is the favorite type of reading for many adolescents, particularly adolescent boys (Smith & Wilhelm, 2002). In a study focused on middle graders, when given access and opportunity to read books that interested them, both boys *and* girls showed motivation to read informational texts (Moss & Hendershot, 2002). It simply makes sense to capitalize on this interest by providing relevant informational texts in every content area—texts that engage adolescents in learning about the real world. Through this engagement, they increase their content knowledge, academic vocabulary, and understanding of informational discourse. At the same time, they develop the habit and love of reading so critical to creating lifelong readers.

A third and final justification for emphasizing informational text is that school and workplace success depends on the ability to read it. According to Kamil (2004), "Nothing is more important to a student's success in school than the ability to read and write expository text." Furthermore, the literacy demands of today's technological society require that students be able to read and write the largely expository text that appears on Internet websites (Kamil & Lane, 1997). As Pearson (2004) notes, "It is competence with expository reading, not narrative reading, that most concerns educators and future employers" (p. 222).

Think about the reading you do every day. You may read a newspaper, the various e-mail messages in your inbox, your students' social studies text, notes from parents, online news stories and interviews, part of a novel, or a few articles in a favorite magazine. We read online and offline, and we encounter a multiplicity of text types—some narrative, but a lot more informational. If we are to adequately prepare students for college and the workplace, we need to give them the tools they need to succeed when reading informational texts.

Informational texts are the second major category represented in the Common Core State Standards. As noted, they encompass a broad range of texts. Just as stories include realistic fiction, historical fiction, adventure stories, mystery stories, fantasies, and other forms, informational texts range from biographies, which are often written more like stories, to functional texts, like bus schedules and directions for downloading apps. Many teachers involve students in the study of biography, but this is just one type of the many kinds of informational text that students need to encounter. The Common Core identifies four specific categories of informational texts: *literary nonfiction, expository text, argument, and procedural texts.* Students should experience each of these types of texts in close reading experiences.

Literary nonfiction refers to texts that present factual information but use a narrative format, including narrative devices like metaphors, similes, and dialogue. A piece of literary nonfiction usually has a clear beginning, middle, and end, and it combines narrative elements, like protagonists, plots, and themes, with informational ones (Duke & Bennett-Armistead, 2003). Literary nonfiction is designed so that readers will gain both enjoyment and information and will learn to appreciate the author's craft in terms of word choice, phrases, and structural elements. The narrative aspects of the text act as a bridge to the information it provides.

Literary nonfiction includes the following text types:

- *Biography*—an account of a person's life written by another. High school text exemplars like *America's Constitution: A Biography*, by Akhil Reed Amar, explore more sophisticated forms of biography in which the focus extends beyond people to "living" documents like the U.S. Constitution.
- *Autobiography*—a full account of a person's life so far, written by the person himself or herself. *Narrative of the Life of Frederick Douglass, an American Slave, Written by Himself* combines Frederick Douglass's first-person look at his own life story with a powerful anti-slavery argument.
- *Personal memoir*—an account of a specific period in a person's life written by the person himself or herself. A personal memoir is distinguished from an autobiography by its focus on a more limited time frame and the writer's experiences during that particular time.

Joy Hakim's (2005) *The Story of Science: Newton at the Center* is a grades 9–10 informational science text exemplar that represents the best in literary nonfiction. It traces the history of science through time, using catchy titles; clear, reader-friendly explanations; and copious visuals, including maps, graphs, charts, and more. Note her explanation of thermodynamics:

> The first law of thermodynamics is easy. Energy can't be created or destroyed:
> it just changes its form. That's it. The first law is kind of a bookkeeping affair.
> It says that it doesn't make any difference to nature what form energy takes, as
> long as it keeps its books in balance. (p. 400)

Note how Hakim's conversational style and her analogy to bookkeeping help make a very complex concept accessible to teen readers.

Expository texts include informational trade books, textbooks, news articles, feature articles, encyclopedia entries, and historical documents. They are generally structured using patterns like description, sequence, causation, problem/solution, and comparison/contrast. Written in a third-person, academic style, expository texts use rhetorical structures like examples and repetition along with text features like subheadings, captions, sidebars, photos, and charts and tables. They often include visual features like maps, graphs, and charts.

Expository text types include the following:

- *Informative/explanatory texts*—texts written to convey information through exposition.
- *Textbooks*—wide-ranging books providing information related to a discipline of study (e.g., chemistry, world history, mathematics).
- *Encyclopedia entries*—articles that provide information pertaining to the entry's name. "Geology," an entry in *U*X*L Encyclopedia of Science*, edited by Rob Nagel, is a typical example (and a Common Core text exemplar for grades 6–8). It is dense, contains much technical language, and provides specific information about geology and its forms.
- *Historical documents*—texts that preserve and describe the records of a government, nation, or society.
- *Visual texts*—maps, charts, graphs, political cartoons, or other documents that use images to convey information. One example would be *FedViews*, a text exemplar for grades 11–CCR. This online periodical published by the Federal Reserve of San Francisco presents brief commentary on current economic indicators accompanied by illustrative charts and graphs.

Expository texts are sometimes, but not always, less engaging for students than literary nonfiction because they focus mainly on straight factual information. Consider the following expository paragraph:

> Plant and animal cells have different structure. While both plant and animal cells contain cell membranes and nuclei, plant cells have some additional specialized structures. Many animals have skeletons to support their bodies. Plants do not have skeletons for support but they do have particular structures. For instance, plants have a *cell wall*. The cell wall is a rigid structure outside

of the cell membrane composed mainly of cellulose. The cell wall gives the plant cell a defined shape, which helps support plant parts. In addition to the cell wall, plant cells contain the *chloroplast*. The chloroplast allows plants to harvest energy from sunlight. Specialized pigments in the chloroplast (including the common green pigment *chlorophyll*) absorb sunlight and use this energy to change sunlight into sugar. Because of this *photosynthesis*, the plant can live and grow.

Note the repetition of key terms like *structure* and *specialized*, and the use of examples. This text contains almost no narrative features; the author's purpose is strictly to inform the reader. Without multiple close readings of this passage, many students would struggle to comprehend it.

Functional/procedural texts provide instructions on how to complete a task. They show steps in a process or combine words and graphic elements to communicate the process to readers. Close readings of procedural texts on topics like how to use a search engine, how to do an online library search, or how to complete a craft activity combine practice in reading procedural texts with practical student needs and interests.

Procedural text types include the following:

- *Technical texts*—information and directions about how to perform a particular task (e.g., hang a light fixture), frequently accompanied by forms and graphic information. The "What to Do" sections of the grades 6–8 text exemplar *Math Trek: Adventures in the Math Zone*, by Ivars Peterson and Nancy Henderson, are procedural texts that explain how to complete specific mathematical tasks.
- *Science experiments*—directions for how to carry out a specific investigation.
- *Technical manuals*—instructions about how to operate things, such as a computer, a cell phone, and so on.

Persuasive and argumentative texts employ appeals designed to persuade an audience to the author's point of view. These can include appeals to reason or evidence, to audience needs or desires, or to the writer's credibility (Duke, Caughlan, Juzwik, & Martin, 2011). Appendix A of the Common Core ELA/literacy standards document cites a variety of research identifying argumentation as an essential skill for college readiness, and the teaching of argument—identifying it, analyzing it, and using it in written and spoken language—is central to the standards in grades 6–12. Writing that falls into the genre of argumentative/persuasive text includes the following:

- *Opinion pieces*—texts in which the author takes a position on an issue and argues its merits.
- *Advertisements*—promotional communications used in marketing to alert and persuade consumers.
- *Editorials*—articles written by an editor that state and support an opinion about a particular topic of public interest.
- *Essays*—typically short prose pieces that advance an author's argument. They can include observations, author reflections, or even political manifestos. Thomas Paine's *Common Sense*, an essay in the form of a pamphlet, advanced the argument that the colonies should seek immediate independence from Britain. It is a Common Core text exemplar for grades 11–CCR.
- *Persuasive letters*—texts in letter format that take a position and support it with evidence. In Martin Luther King Jr.'s "Letter from Birmingham Jail," a grades 9–10 exemplar, the author is responding to a letter to a newspaper written by eight white clergymen critical of his civil rights efforts. In this letter, King uses ethos, pathos, and logos—Aristotle's three rhetorical tools of persuasion—to bring those who read it over to his position.
- *Letters to the editor*—letters to a newspaper or magazine editor expressing the author's beliefs regarding a particular topic of public interest.
- *Reviews*—critical pieces in which the author expresses and supports an opinion about the merit or content of a movie, book, play, piece of music, game, restaurant, product, or the like.
- *Brochures/flyers*—deliberately biased descriptions or advertisements in which the author works to persuade a reader to take action.
- *Comments sections*—comments in response to online articles, posts on social media sites, or blog entries in which the writer states an opinion about the material presented.
- *Persuasive speeches*—writing crafted to be heard that presents a specific argument designed to persuade readers of a position. For example, Learned Hand delivered his "I Am an American Day Address," a grades 9–10 text exemplar, to an audience of 1.5 million gathered in New York's Central Park on May 21, 1944, arguing that the spirit of liberty resides in the American people, not in the country's laws or government.

As noted, the skill of writing to craft an argument is first addressed in the Common Core standards at the 6th grade level, and it remains a focus through grade 12. Texts that expose students to well-crafted arguments can provide models for writing development. Carla Killough McClafferty's *Fourth Down and Inches: Concussions and Football's Make-or-Break Moment*, for example, is an excellent mentor text for helping students read closely to evaluate arguments for and against playing football in view of the dangers of concussions. This book provides an ideal opportunity to teach argument in physical education, a subject area included as a technical subject in the Common Core State Standards.

To further students' ability to produce argumentative writing, teachers in grades 6–12 might regularly ask students to closely read a collection of short persuasive texts and then synthesize the information those texts present into a new claim, backed with evidence. For example, students in a 7th grade social studies class exploring the question "Is social media really social?" might closely read and annotate articles from the *New York Times* with headlines like "Who Gives a Tweet? Evaluating Microblog Content Value," "Why Most Facebook Users Get More Than They Give," "Social Selection and Peer Influence in an Online Social Network," and "Social Networking Sites and Our Lives." There are several websites that provide articles, facts, and videos about topics to explore in an argumentative fashion. We particularly like the collections at ProCon.org and Debate.org.

Other Text Forms

There are many other kinds of texts that are not easily classified because they are distinguished more by form than by content:

- *Graphic texts/novels,* which run the genre gamut, including science fiction novels, contemporary fiction, biographies, memoirs, and beyond.
- *Audio texts,* including podcasts, audiobooks, and radio programs
- *Video texts,* including films, videos, and other visual formats.
- *Multimedia texts,* combining audio, images, video, animation, and other forms.
- *Digital texts,* which include blog posts or online discussions and electronic versions of written texts that students can access online or download onto tablets or other electronic devices.

Note that all of the content of the text types listed here can fall into any genre: fiction, nonfiction, fantasy, opinion pieces, reviews, and so on.

Digital texts merit a closer look, because when today's students are not in school, a lot of what they read is digital text. The Common Core acknowledges the need for students to read more of these digital texts in school—specifically online texts. The text exemplars even include some online texts. Furthermore, the Common Core assessments being developed by Smarter Balanced and PARCC will be administered online, necessitating that students have experience reading these text types in a classroom setting.

Although the research on online comprehension is relatively new, it does suggest that online reading and offline reading are not the same, and that children require different comprehension skills and strategies in order to read effectively online. Consider these findings:

- When children are reading online, the skills of locating and critically evaluating information are extremely important (Zawilinski & Leu, 2008).
- Students may need specific instruction in online reading comprehension skills before they can successfully comprehend online texts (Leu et al., 2005). For example, students must know how to use search engines effectively in order to locate websites appropriate to their area of investigation. Similarly, students need to be taught to evaluate the "truth value" of the information they find online in order to assess its value and integrity.
- A comparison of results on a standard statewide reading comprehension assessment and an online reading comprehension test showed that some students who performed poorly on the print assessment were among the highest performers on the digital version (Leu et al., 2005). This finding supports the claim that print reading comprehension and digital reading comprehension are different things.

Invasive Plant Inventory from the California Invasive Plant Council is an online text exemplar for grades 6–8 science. A teacher might assign a couple of key sections for close reading. For example, the section titled "Inventory Categories" discusses the categories used to rate plant species according to ecological impact, and a teacher might start a close reading with a general understanding question (*What's the main point of this section?*) and follow it with a vocabulary-related question like *How does the author clarify the term "dispersal rate"?* Finally, addressing a key concern that many have with classroom use of online resources, the teacher might ask a question to focus students on the article's credibility: *Do you think the contents of this section are valuable and credible?* To explore the credibility of the text, students need to review its authorship and determine whether or not its contents are supported by research. This is a skill that requires guided instruction, but close reading provides a workable situation for practice—one in which a teacher can conduct formative assessment as the students discuss their findings and opinions.

Texts are written for different purposes using different language. The fictional story is written with attention to character description, emotive language, and story structure. The online science content text is constructed using data, academic language, topical words, and quotes from science researchers. Students benefit from explicit instruction in specific strategies unique to reading and writing in particular genres if they are to successfully negotiate the many text types they should encounter through close reading.

Text Exemplars: A Powerful Resource for Close Reading

So where can teachers find examples of the various types of texts? We recommend the text exemplars provided in Appendix B of the ELA/literacy standards document (NGA Center & CCSSO, 2010b). We've referred to them already, but it's important to take a moment to review why the text exemplars are such a great resource for busy teachers. The exemplars, online at www.corestandards.org/assets/Appendix_B.pdf,* are a list of (and a collection of extracts from) narrative and informational texts arranged in grade-level bands: 6–8, 9–10, and 11–College and Career Ready (CCR). They are offered to give teachers representative examples of the kinds of complex texts appropriate for classroom use, and include stories, poetry, dramas, and informational texts arranged by content area at each grade-level band. In Appendix B of the standards document, the exemplars are explained as follows:

> The . . . text samples primarily serve to exemplify the level of complexity and quality that the Standards require all students in a given grade band to engage with. Additionally, they are suggestive of the breadth of texts that students should encounter in the text types required by the Standards. The choices should serve as useful guideposts in helping educators select texts of similar complexity, quality, and range for their own classrooms. They expressly do not represent a partial or complete reading list. (NGA Center & CCSSO, 2010b, p. 2)

---

* Our own Appendix B, beginning on page 207, will show you where within the standards document to find the text exemplars we mention in this book.

According to the ELA/literacy standards document, these texts were chosen by a work group who took recommendations from teachers, educational leaders, and researchers who had used the titles successfully with students at the specified grade levels.

You are probably wondering how the texts recommended for use with the Common Core are different from the texts you use now. First, the texts recommended may represent a broader range of genres than you may be using in your classroom, whether in a core reading program or in disciplinary textbooks. By specifying titles in seldom-taught genres like literary nonfiction and informational texts, the Common Core elevates these genres to a more prominent place with the hope that they will get more attention in classrooms. Consider, for example, Elizabeth Partridge's *This Land Was Made for You and Me: The Life and Songs of Woody Guthrie* (2002), a history/social studies text exemplar for grades 6–8. This award-winning title not only immerses students in the life of an iconic American musician but also provides them with a deepened understanding of both the effects of the Great Depression on ordinary Americans and Guthrie's efforts to tell stories of these ordinary Americans through his music. It takes a "posthole" approach to history, providing a depth of information on the Great Depression that a textbook simply can't deliver.

Second, the exemplar texts include more classic works than you may currently be teaching. For example, in the grades 11–CCR band, Alexis de Tocqueville's *Democracy in America* is a social studies text exemplar; Ralph Waldo Emerson's essay *Society and Solitude* is recommended for English language arts, and John Allen Paulos's *Innumeracy: Mathematical Illiteracy and Its Consequences* is recommended for science, mathematics, and technical subjects.

Finally, the text exemplars are probably more complex than the textbooks you are presently using. Keep in mind, however, that recommended complexity levels are to be mastered by the end of the grade-level band. Titles you teach now may appear at earlier grade levels on the text exemplar list. For example, Joy Hakim's *A History of US: Liberty for All? 1820–1860*, which is a common supplemental textbook for 8th grade American history, appears as a text exemplar at the grades 4–5 band. The poetry titles for grades 6–8, while not evaluated by Lexiles, include the aforementioned "Song of Wandering Aengus," a selection that has typically been reserved for study by high school students. The complexity of these texts suggests that students will need to grapple with them through close reading in order to understand them. As we illustrate in the scenarios in

Chapter 6, many students who at first do not succeed when reading a particular complex text may need to be engaged in subsequent small-group instruction that prepares them to return for a later, *successful* reading of the text.

Recommended Text Exemplars for Disciplinary Literacy

Teacher responses to the text exemplars are often, "But these are so hard! How can our students read these books?" Carol Jago makes an important point: "In our effort to provide students with readings that they can relate to, we sometimes end up teaching works that students can read on their own [instead] of teaching more worthwhile texts that they most certainly need assistance negotiating. . . . Classroom texts should pose intellectual challenges for readers and invite them to stretch and grow" (Common Core, 2012a, pp. viii–ix). She correctly notes that students will need teacher assistance in negotiating these complex texts, especially in terms of background knowledge and vocabulary expertise requisite for both text-explicit and text-implicit comprehension.

You don't need to look too far to find good complex texts for close reading. If you are an English teacher whose class is reading a short story or poem from a literature anthology, you might pick a couple of paragraphs or a page. If you are a science teacher whose students are studying issues related to global warming, you might have them closely read a current newspaper article on the topic or a functional/procedural text that involves completing an experiment related to quantitative chemical analysis through titrations. They could even closely read a chart or graph by noting axes, trends, and analyses. If you teach American history and your students are studying Civil War–era laws about slavery, you might assign a primary source document advertising a runaway slave. In all of these disciplines, students themselves may identify close reading passages of interest to them and their peers, as long as these passages meet the quality criteria. As noted and illustrated in Chapter 2, texts selected for close reading should be

- Short, ranging from a few sentences to a few pages. They may also be subsections of a larger text.
- "Worthy" texts—that is, texts with depth, layered meaning, and important messages.
- Texts that require students to dig deeply and reread to get at the author's message and language choices.

- Texts that are not too challenging for students to first attempt to read independently, yet sufficiently challenging to require teacher support through scaffolded questioning.
- Texts that you have systematically evaluated for complexity (see the qualitative and quantitative rubrics in Chapter 1) and related teaching points.

The titles listed in Figure 4.1 are texts that we recommend. All are Common Core exemplar texts. All are written by quality authors of different genres, and all are worth students' attention—either in their entirety or as excerpts. We hope that these titles may prompt those of you who generally stick to the textbook

Figure 4.1 | **Recommended Text Exemplars for Close Reading in Various Disciplines**

Grade Level	English Language Arts	History/Social Science	Science, Mathematics, and Technical Subjects
6–8	*Black Ships Before Troy: The Story of the Iliad* *The Diary of Anne Frank: A Play* *Dragonwings* "The Railway Train" *A Wrinkle in Time*	*Freedom Walkers: The Story of the Montgomery Bus Boycott* *The Great Fire* *This Land Was Made for You and Me: The Life and Songs of Woody Guthrie* *Vincent Van Gogh: Portrait of an Artist*	*Cathedral: The Story of Its Construction* "The Evolution of the Grocery Bag" *Geeks: How Two Lost Boys Rode the Internet out of Idaho* *The Number Devil: A Mathematical Adventure*
9–10	*The Book Thief* *The Glass Menagerie* "The Raven" *To Kill a Mockingbird*	*Black, Blue and Gray: African Americans in the Civil War* *Bury My Heart at Wounded Knee: An Indian History of the American West* *The Longitude Prize* *The Story of Art, 16th Edition*	"Classifying the Stars" *Life by the Numbers* *The Race to Save Lord God Bird* *The Story of Science: Newton at the Center*
11–CCR	*The Great Gatsby* "Mother Tongue" *Our Town: A Play in Three Acts* *Their Eyes Were Watching God*	*1776* *America's Constitution: A Biography* Selections from *The American Reader: Words That Moved a Nation* *Mirror of the World: A New History of Art* "What to the Slave Is the Fourth of July? An Address Delivered in Rochester, New York, on 5 July 1852"	*Google Hacks: Tips and Tools for Smarter Searching, 2nd Edition* *Innumeracy: Mathematical Illiteracy and Its Consequences* *The Tipping Point: How Little Things Can Make a Big Difference* "Untangling the Roots of Cancer"

during social studies, mathematics, and science instruction to explore other reading materials, including primary source documents and online articles.

Text Sets for Close Reading in the Disciplines

Text sets are multigenre sets of books related to a single theme or essential question. In the Common Core era, with standards stressing the importance of student experiences across texts rather than just within a single text, they are tremendously useful. Many teachers have already discovered the power of linking books together in ways that let students explore different aspects of a time period, topic, or experience. As Gay Ivey (2010) puts it, "[Students] can't learn much from just one book. . . . What we really want students to be able to do is read across texts critically and analytically. We have become overly concerned with whether students can comprehend a particular text and not concerned enough about whether students can use multiple texts or grapple with big ideas" (p. 22).

Closely reading excerpts of books in text sets can engage students with important concepts that span more than one text. By seeing the same topic through multiple lenses, students expand their viewpoints, gaining exposure to voices that are often silenced. Guided by text-dependent questions, they can examine, compare, and analyze aspects of these texts in a way that leads to in-depth reflection on big ideas. These texts are also an excellent source for student independent reading on a content-related topic (Moss, 2011).

During a study of the Great Depression, for example, 7th grade American history teachers might pair Jerry Stanley's literary nonfiction title *Children of the Dust Bowl: The True Story of the School at Weedpatch Camp* with Christopher Paul Curtis's historical fiction *Bud, Not Buddy* and Karen Hesse's *Out of the Dust,* a long narrative poem written in free verse. All three texts provide rich portrayals of Depression-era America but from different perspectives: the plight of the Okies in California, the story of an African American boy in Michigan who tries to find his jazz musician father, and the story of a young girl's suffering in Oklahoma at the height of the dust storms. By jigsawing these titles, students can share what they learn about social and economic issues of the time, music, government programs, protests, strikes, and so on. A unit featuring this text set would address the Common Core's Reading Literature Standard 9: "Compare and contrast a fictional portrayal of a time, place, or character with an historical account of the same period as a means of understanding how authors of fiction use or alter history" (CCRA.RL.9.7).

Or, in a science unit focused on applying engineering design principles to find real-world applications of content, students investigating the processes and practices of technological advancements might read John Katz's *Geeks: How Two Lost Boys Rode the Internet out of Idaho,* a Common Core text exemplar chronicling the life of two technologically savvy teens, strategically paired with articles about technological innovations, like *ScienceDaily*'s "Hi-Tech Innovation Gauges Science Learning in Preschooler."

Figure 4.2 shows a few sample text sets useful for teachers in several different content areas. We also encourage you to explore the following resources and create text sets of your own:

- The grades 6–8 and grades 9–12 versions of the *Common Core Curriculum Maps: English Language Arts* (Common Core, 2012a, 2012b) contain sample thematic units that incorporate lists of texts representing classic and contemporary literature, readings on science and social science topics, and texts related to the arts and music. Sample unit titles include "Authors and Artists," "Epic Poetry—Heroism," "A New Nation," and "Science or Fiction?"
- The Cooperative Children's Book Center (http://ccbc.education.wisc.edu/default.asp) compiles lists of text sets suitable for middle and high school on themes related to every content area. Here, you'll find topics like science and scientists, social justice, the environment, and much more.
- Room for Debate (www.nytimes.com/roomfordebate) is a *New York Times* blog in which different arguments about issues or news events are discussed by four to six contributors. Each response is only four or five paragraphs, making this a great resource for close reading of topical issues, including "Do we still need libraries?" "Is organic food worth the expense?" and "When should young people be considered adults?"
- The Teachers College Reading and Writing Project (http://readingand writingproject.org) contains many text set resources for teachers. Its collection of digital science text sets and digital nonfiction text sets related to popular culture, science, and social studies can be particularly helpful.

Close Reading in ELA/Social Studies, Science, and Mathematics

In this section, we share examples of what is involved when engaging students in a close reading in a variety of disciplines, focusing on how to address both content learning requirements and standards and incorporate the reading of informational

Figure 4.2 | **Examples of Text Sets**

Grade Level & Discipline	Unit Topic	Texts Included	Rationale
6th grade social studies	Ancient Civilizations	• *Black Ships Before Troy: The Story of the Iliad* by Rosemary Sutcliff (historical fiction)* • *A Short Walk Around the Pyramids and Through the World of Art* by Phillip Isaacson (literary nonfiction)* • *The Eagle of the Ninth* by Rosemary Sutcliff (historical fiction) • *Roman Shipwreck Raised After 2,000 Years* (documentary video) from *National Geographic* online	Together, these texts give students glimpses into the myths, daily lives, and art and architecture of ancient Greece, Egypt, and Rome.
8th grade social studies	The U.S. Civil War	• "O Captain! My Captain!" by Walt Whitman (poem)* • *Harriet Tubman: Conductor on the Underground Railroad* by Ann Petry (biography)* • *Narrative of the Life of Frederick Douglass, an American Slave, Written by Himself* (autobiography)* • Videos from the PBS television series *Africans in America*	These texts provide students the opportunity to analyze different and contrasting perspectives on the events of the period.
10th grade Biology	Viruses and Viral Infection	• *The Hot Zone: A Terrifying True Story* by Richard Preston (literary nonfiction)* • "The Hunt for Ebola" by Joshua Hammer (article in *Smithsonian Magazine*) • "Criminal Profiling Technique Targets Killer Diseases" from Queen Mary University of London (research summary on *Science Daily*) • *The Plague* by Albert Camus (philosophical/allegorical novel)	These texts provide students with an opportunity to investigate the local and global impacts of disease on societies and to consider the moves of the science and medical professions as they work to combat such epidemics.
10th grade American History	The Causes and Consequences of War	• "1941 State of the Union Address" by Franklin D. Roosevelt (speech)* • "Hope, Despair and Memory" by Elie Wiesel (speech)* • *The Book Thief* by Markus Zusak (historical fiction)* • "Second Inaugural Address" by Abraham Lincoln (speech) • *The Killer Angels* by Michael Shaara (historical fiction)	These selections give students the opportunity to compare and contrast the causes and consequences of two major American wars, the Civil War and World War II.
8th grade English language arts	The American Experience in Literature	• *Little Women* by Louisa May Alcott (historical fiction) • *The Adventures of Tom Sawyer* by Mark Twain (historical fiction)* • "Chicago" by Walt Whitman (poem) • "The People Could Fly" by Virginia Hamilton (folktale)* • "Eleven" by Sandra Cisneros (short story)*	These titles immerse students in diverse experiences of characters in literary works with American settings that are both historical and contemporary.
10th grade English language arts	The Human Quest	• *The Odyssey* by Homer (myth)* • *The Grapes of Wrath* by John Steinbeck (historical fiction)* • *The Joy Luck Club* by Amy Tan (contemporary novel)* • "Ozymandias" by Percy Bysshe Shelley (lyrical poem)* • *I Know Why the Caged Bird Sings* by Maya Angelou (memoir)* • "I Have a Dream" by Martin Luther King (speech)	These selections help students explore the human propensity for seeking—whether seeking a better life, a link with the past, or a future of freedom in the form of civil rights.

*Common Core text exemplars

text in compliance with the Common Core. Be sure to take note of the text type used in each example and the specific instruction that is customized to the discipline.

Close Reading in English/Humanities

The Common Core State Standards call for middle and high school students to closely read a wide array of texts, and to cite evidence to support their written and spoken analyses and arguments. Caitlin Allen teaches Humanities—a course combining aspects of a traditional ELA course (literature) with art and global studies. As part of her efforts to help her 6th grade students achieve these standards, she invites them to explore topics through the close reading of various types of texts. For example, when teaching her students how to analyze arguments to familiarize them with the tools of argument and how arguments are crafted, one of the "texts" she incorporated into her instruction was the movie *The Great Debaters*, a historical account of how the debating team at the all-black Wiley College gained entry into intercollegiate competition with white schools in the 1930s American South.

Because she wanted her students to begin with a close reading of the language used by the movie's debaters in a key scene, she transcribed the cases presented to capture the words in Robert Eisele's (2007) screenplay. In the scene she chose, the specific question under debate was *Should southern white colleges be integrated?*

> *Debater 1* (con): And because of racism, it would be impossible for a Negro to be happy in a southern white college today. If someone is unhappy, it is impossible to see how they could receive a proper education. Yes, a time will come when Negroes and whites will walk on the same campus, and we will share the same classrooms. But, sadly, that day is not today.

> *Debater 2* (pro): As long as schools are segregated, Negroes will receive an education that is both separate and unequal. By Oklahoma's own reckoning, the state is currently spending five times more for the education of a white child than it is spending to educate a colored child. That means better textbooks for that child than for that child. Oh, I say that's a shame, but my opponent says today is not the day for whites and coloreds to go to the same college, to share the same campus, to walk in the same classroom. Well, would you kindly tell me when is that day gonna come? Is it gonna come tomorrow? Is it gonna come next week? In a hundred years? Never? No, the time for justice, the time for freedom, and the time for equality is always, is always, right now.

During the first reading, Mrs. Allen asked her students to read the transcription to find out what each of the texts was saying. Students were able to articulate that both were about segregation in southern colleges, with each taking a different position on the subject. For a second reading, Mrs. Allen asked students to identify what each debater was claiming or arguing and what evidence supported their claims. For a third reading, she asked them to identify the persuasive techniques used by each debater.

After lots of discussion following each reading, Mrs. Allen provided a different kind of close reading experience by playing the video clip from the movie. Students were asked to closely "read" the video as they listened and watched for verbal and nonverbal persuasive techniques. Again, lots of discussion followed this viewing.

To conclude the experience, Mrs. Allen asked students to use both the written and the viewed texts to write a response identifying which debater had done the better job of presenting his argument, Debater 1 or Debater 2. She tasked students with identifying the evidence that supported their impressions and to also analyze whether they relied on both the written and viewed versions of the text to support their responses. Many of the students' responses were similar to Keith's response. He said that the passionate presentation made by Debater 2 was just as obvious in his words as in his oral argument. Karina summed it up by saying the power of the argument should be built into the written argument, which will make the oral argument even stronger.

Through this close reading, Mrs. Allen was teaching her students to analyze the components of two arguments presented through two different formats. Within the content discipline of Humanities, she addressed a bundle of Common Core standards for reading, speaking and listening, and language:

> **RL.6.1.** Cite textual evidence to support analysis of what the text says explicitly as well as inferences drawn from the text.

> **RL.6.4.** Determine the meaning of words and phrases as they are used in a text, including figurative and connotative meanings; analyze the impact of a specific word choice on meaning and tone.

> **RL.6.7.** Compare and contrast the experience of reading a story, drama, or poem to listening to or viewing an audio, video, or live version of the text, including contrasting what they "see" and "hear" when reading the text to what they perceive when they listen or watch.

RL.6.9. Compare and contrast texts in different forms or genres (e.g., stories and poems; historical novels and fantasy stories) in terms of their approaches to similar themes and topics.

SL.6.2. Interpret information presented in diverse media and formats (e.g., visually, quantitatively, orally) and explain how it contributes to a topic, text, or issue under study.

SL.6.3. Delineate a speaker's argument and specific claims, distinguishing claims that are supported by reasons and evidence from claims that are not.

L.6.5. Demonstrate understanding of figurative language, word relationships, and nuances in word meanings.

This bundling of standards emphasizes all of the language processing Mrs. Allen's students engaged in within a single lesson.

Close Reading in Science

In science, the Common Core can be interpreted through a lens of inquiry, investigation, and problem solving, which are the foundational elements of the Next Generation Science Standards (NGSS Lead States, 2013) and of any well-constructed science curriculum. Students are now expected to plan and carry out investigations, construct explanations, and design solutions (Achieve et al., 2013). Clearly, such tasks cannot be accomplished without background knowledge built through informational reading.

Consider Common Core Reading Informational Text Standard 8, which focuses on evaluating arguments. The 6th grade version of this anchor standard states, "Trace and evaluate the argument and specific claims in a text, distinguishing claims that are supported by reasons and evidence from claims that are not" (RI.6.8). When scientists read information, they naturally look for supporting pieces of evidence that advance an idea or theory. When students are taught to identify the author's supporting points or documented data, they are seeking to identify evidence that can be later applied to a design project or a laboratory investigation. A close reading of an informational science text (e.g., a journal article, a firsthand account of a natural event, or a news story documenting recent research), offered with appropriate text-dependent questions, can further a mindset that questions, predicts, designs, and investigates. Science readers read to determine credible evidence. They evaluate data. They interpret graphs and charts. And they draw conclusions.

When students reach 9th and 10th grade, Reading Informational Text Standard 8 expects them to "delineate and evaluate the argument and specific claims in a text, assessing whether the reasoning is valid and the evidence is relevant and sufficient; identify false statements and fallacious reasoning" (RI.9–10.8). This standard asks that students delve deeply to identify illogical or inappropriate evidence and to note relevant, sufficient evidence. To accomplish this, multiple readings are required. Consider the online text from the National Oceanic and Atmospheric Administration (NOAA): *What Is Ocean Acidification?* (n.d.). Within it, NOAA notes the chemistry behind the increasing acidity of the oceans and then looks at the biological and global impacts. Science readers might respond to a progression of text-dependent questions that guide them to identify and evaluate reasoning and evidence at a deep level. Links in the NOAA text take students to correlated research papers that might help them determine the relevance and credibility of noted evidence. Students need guided practice when it comes to this type of evaluation. When students chat after each close reading, the teacher has the opportunity to listen in to formatively assess progress. Strategic text-dependent questions (e.g., *Where does the author find evidence? Is the evidence sufficient? Is the evidence relevant to the topic?*) help to establish the practice of evidence evaluation.

In 11th grade, students are continuing to read complex texts as they "delineate and evaluate the reasoning in seminal U.S. texts, including the application of constitutional principles and use of legal reasoning" (RI.11–12.8). While this standard may look like it applies to social studies and history texts only, science has its share of seminal texts that could be addressed—Rachel Carson's *Silent Spring,* for example, or James Watson's *The Double Helix.* To address this standard, students might first engage in a cold read to determine the general sense of the text. The second reading might focus them on data tables, charts, and documented evidence to determine trends. For the third reading, the teacher might ask them to evaluate the studies and research to determine credibility of the data generated. All these pieces of text evidence would work together to support a particular author point.

Reading a science text is clearly different from reading a historical account or a short story. It involves the mental accumulation of evidence and the simultaneous collection of data represented in graphic form, included as a support for the written text. Science readers commonly go back and forth between a graph and a part of the text to determine correlations and connections. They identify scales on graphs and charts. They determine cause/effect relationships. They look for patterns in data. They interpret models that represent real-world phenomena. And they identify and investigate systems. All these elements show up in science texts, and the expert reader must know how to discern them and how to interpret them. Close reading provides the instructional means to develop these skills.

Close Reading in the Social Sciences

The Common Core standards for grades 6–12 do more than simply recommend literacy practices for social studies instruction. As Shennan Hutten (2013) observes, "The Common Core standards . . . emphasize thinking skills, primary sources, evidence, analysis, point of view or perspective, and argument. These are not merely, or even primarily, English/Language Arts skills. They are closely related to historical inquiry, a process of helping students to act as historians" (p. 6). It's worth underlining that there is close alignment between the literacy standards for history/social studies and the College, Career, and Civic Life (C3) Framework for Social Studies State Standards (National Council for the Social Studies, 2013).

Close reading in social studies classes will look different from close reading in language arts classes in terms of (1) the types of complex texts used, (2) the instructional purposes, and (3) the teaching points addressed. Informational texts should represent 55 percent of middle school students' reading experiences across the school day and 70 percent of high school students' reading; social studies is a logical place to include those texts.

The Common Core standards specifically require that students

- Read, comprehend, and analyze complex history/social studies texts.
- Engage with primary and secondary sources.
- Integrate the analysis of charts and research data in print or digital texts.
- Evaluate multiple data sources from information presented in diverse formats and media.

According to Rich Cairn (2012), primary sources are at the heart of the Common Core State Standards. He notes, "Primary sources provide authentic materials for students to practice the skills required by the [Common Core]. Encouraging students to grapple with the raw materials of history, such as photographs, newspapers, film, audio files, government documents, and economic data, provides opportunities for them to practice critical thinking, analysis skills and inquiry" (p. 2).

For example, during a unit on westward expansion, an 11th grade American History teacher might engage students in a close reading of a visual primary source text like Emanuel Leutze's *Westward the Course of Empire Takes Its Way*, a painting that appears as a mural in the U.S. Capitol building. For the first encounter with this text, the teacher might distribute copies of the mural study and ask students to carefully review it, moving from left to right, identifying the narrative storyline of the painting and noticing how the artist used light and dark to create mood. Students could then discuss the storyline they have constructed, the changes in mood, and what those changes represent, citing evidence for their views. For the second encounter with the text, students might work in pairs to identify visual evidence supporting the artist's argument that the conquest of the West is Manifest Destiny—divinely ordained. Following analysis and conversation, students could write a short essay comparing and contrasting the depiction of Manifest Destiny in this painting with that provided in John Gast's 1872 painting *American Progress*, which appears in their textbook.

The Common Core has also triggered a shift in the instructional objectives for close reading within social studies instruction. In grade 6, for example, the literacy version of Reading Standard 1 in history/social studies requires that students "cite specific textual evidence to support analysis of primary and secondary sources" (RH.6–8.1). By grades 9–10, they are expected to cite similar evidence while "attending to such features as the date and origin of the information" (RH.9–10.1). By grades 11–12, they are to cite evidence while "connecting insights gained from specific details to an understanding of the text as a whole" (RH.11–12.1).

As you can see, the standard requires progressively more critical thinking as students advance from grade to grade, and it places particular emphasis on argument and comparison of sources and accounts of events. In grades 6–8, for example, students are expected to distinguish among facts, opinions, and reasoned judgments (RH.6–8.8). By grades 9–10, they must "assess the extent to which the reasoning and evidence in a text support the author's claims" (RH.9–10.8), and by grades 11–12, they must "evaluate an author's premises, claims, and evidence by corroborating or challenging them with other information" (RH.11–12.8). Using the previous example of teaching analysis of *Westward the Course of Empire Takes Its Way*, a teacher might engage students in reading Helen Hunt Jackson's *A Century of Dishonor*. Jackson's text, originally published in 1881, documents the mistreatment of Native Americans at the hands of the U.S. government; it was a call to action that was largely ignored in its time. Students could closely read this text, considering how it might challenge the premises of the aforementioned painting in terms of Manifest Destiny and what that policy meant to Native Americans.

Close Reading in Mathematics

In math classes, students must read exemplar problems or complicated textbook explanations loaded with technical language, symbols, and concise, to-the-point sentences. Bear in mind, too, that the Common Core State Standards for Mathematics focus on specific skills at each grade level (e.g., students in grade 7 concentrate on understanding and applying proportional relationships, performing operations with rational numbers, and working with expressions and linear numbers; students in grade 10 look at structures in expressions and work on arithmetic with polynomials and rational functions, among other topics). How can we merge the demands of content math learning with the focus on reading informational text called for by both sets of Common Core standards—math and ELA/literacy?

At the intersection of these two areas of instructional need are math texts that include problem-solving information and number data in real-world contexts. When students encounter texts that introduce a math-related concept (e.g., data about the connection between habitat destruction and the decrease in particular animal populations) or math word problems that ask them to determine the difference in time of arrival for two different trains traveling at given speeds, some are overwhelmed by the mix of numerals and words. As one 8th grader told us, "It's hard to pull out what information I need and figure out what equations to use." A close reading with well-crafted text-dependent questions can help focus students by directing their thinking, in a progressive manner, to the appropriate parts of the text that provide clues to math problem solving or data/number analysis.

Although the kinds of problems that students will solve in a math class may differ from potential tasks embedded within a math-related informational text that connects math to the real world, many of the skills needed to solve both tasks could be taught through a close reading. Consider this paragraph from a *Time* magazine article called "Families: Pulling the Plug on TV" (Cornell, 2000):

> Fun isn't the only benefit of going TV-less. Television gobbles up 40 percent of Americans' free time. Doing without TV allows people to do lots of positive things. More than 80 percent of nearly 500 children in the survey play

sports. Four-fifths of TV-free children have above-average reading skills: 41 percent read an hour or more a day. Nine of 10 families eat dinner together at least four times a week. Overall, they average nearly an hour a day of meaningful conversation. "It seems like such a simple solution," says Brock.

Notice how the text is strewn with numbers—percentages, raw numbers, and ratios. To glean meaning from this data, a reader must negotiate both phrase meaning and numerical data. It is a skill that is characteristic of math reading—and something that adept math readers do seamlessly. A student engaging in a first read of this text would undoubtedly garner a general understanding that the text is about the effects of turning off the TV. A second reading might be focused by a text-dependent question that asks the reader what math terms or ideas the author uses to provide evidence for the claim being made. A third reading could involve a response to a text-dependent question that homes in on assessment of a claim (e.g., "What do you think of the data the author provides to support her claim?"). With each subsequent reading, the student goes deeper, considering the statistics, the claim, and the value of the numbers.

⇥ ♦ ⇤

Through close reading experiences in all of the disciplines, students will develop the skills they need to effectively master the wide array of disciplinary literacy skills they will need to succeed in college and the workplace. With the help of effective teachers, student mastery of these skills can become a reality. In Chapter 5, we use scenarios to illustrate some of the speaking, listening, and writing practices that these teachers so naturally apply to close reading practice.

CHAPTER 5

SUPPORTING ACADEMIC COMMUNICATION ABOUT CLOSELY READ TEXTS

There is power in having the language you need to communicate your ideas effectively. In her memoir, United States Supreme Court Justice Sonia Sotomayor notes that facility with language provides the self-confidence necessary to converse with a wide array of people across many situations: "It occurred to me that if I was going to be a lawyer—or, who knows, a judge—I had to learn to speak persuasively and confidently in front of an audience. I couldn't be a quivering mess of nerves" (2013, p. 85).

Developing this facility with language takes time. For some students, opportunities to engage in meaningful conversation around myriad school-related topics begin long before coming to school (Hart & Risley, 1995). Children of college-educated parents often have an advantage here. Their home language experiences, which support the development of vocabulary and the skillful use of language, prosody, syntax, grammar, and rules of conversation, provide the foundation for academic success. It is therefore not surprising that so many of the Common Core's ELA/literacy standards address students' use of language—in speaking, in listening, and in writing—with the intent that all students, and especially English language learners, receive enhanced language opportunities.

As the introduction to the ELA/literacy standards document notes, students acquire language proficiency across the disciplines as they "read purposefully and listen attentively to gain both general knowledge and discipline-specific expertise. They refine and share their knowledge through writing and speaking" (NGA Center & CCSSO, 2010a, p. 7). Although the individual's interaction with the text is an essential process of close reading, the ability to communicate about what is read is a major component of it as well. Being able to succeed with text investigations and collaborate effectively during a close reading encounter develops the language functions of speaking, listening, and writing. In turn, being able to read, discuss, and then write about a text facilitates deeper understanding of the information and language that text contains.

If we expect students to communicate about the texts they are reading, and the ideas and information those texts contain, we must teach them how to do so. To become proficient communicators, students need supported practice speaking and writing about all kinds of topics in the disciplines of mathematics, science, art, literature, social studies (history, geography, civics), and technical subjects; it must be a significant component of instruction. In this chapter, we focus on various ways to provide students with opportunities to communicate about a text before they begin a close reading, throughout the close reading, and as they collaborate and share ideas through oral and written discourse after a close reading. While there are multiple standards identified within each ELA/literacy strand of the Common Core, we will address only those that pertain to communication relevant to a close reading. It is through this kind of communication that insights about issues are both shared and expanded.

Language for Speaking and Listening

The Common Core ELA/literacy standards contain a strand focused on speaking and listening and a strand focused on language. While speaking and language are obviously related, each has distinct features. Speaking involves verbally communicating through (1) *language*, which has vocabulary and rules related to grammar, syntax, and use (register), and (2) *pragmatics*, which involves the context and relationship of speaker and listener. Martin Joos (1967) identifies five language registers—styles of using language—that people employ during various language-based interactions:

- *Frozen register*—language that remains fixed, such as the Lord's Prayer, the Pledge of Allegiance, and patriotic songs.
- *Formal or academic register*—language used for "proper" public speaking and classroom talk or discourse. The tone of formal language is serious, and the message is shared through complete sentences and specific theme- or discipline-related words.

- *Consultative register*—A formal type of language used in workplace situations, typically for speaking with or asking for assistance from a supervisors or employer. A consultative register is also what teachers use when greeting their students: *Good morning. I hope your day is off to a terrific start and you are ready to move forward with our study of vectors. To begin, let's look at a demonstration of the interdependence of magnitude and direction.*
- *Casual (informal) register*—language used when talking with friends or family in a casual setting: *Hey Mom, what's for dinner? Hi Jack, what's up?*
- *Intimate register*—language shared privately in love relationships. A good example is a parent speaking with a child: *How's my little sweetie pie?*

"Language power" comes from knowing when and with whom to use each register. Speaking, listening, and language unite as speakers attempt to convey a verbal message within each register. The more proficient students are at using the formal or academic register of a language, the essential register of the classroom, the better they will be at both retrieving information during a close reading and conveying information through speaking and writing so that it will be understood by the listener or the reader.

Clearly, the question is how to help students develop the language power they need to communicate effectively in close reading sessions. Before discussing instructional practices that support language development for close reading, though, let's first consider the Common Core's anchor standards for both language and speaking and listening. The outcomes they aim for are closely related when it comes to communicating about texts verbally and in writing.

The Common Core's Language Standards

There are six Common Core language anchor standards organized under three headings: Conventions of Standard English, Knowledge of Language, and Vocabulary Acquisition and Use.

Conventions of Standard English

Language Standard 1 and **Language Standard 2** fall under this heading; both emphasize knowing the conventions of grammar, punctuation, and spelling, and when and how to use these skills in creating a text:

> **CCRA.L.1.** Demonstrate command of the conventions of standard English grammar and usage when writing or speaking.

CCRA.L.2. Demonstrate command of the conventions of standard English capitalization, punctuation, and spelling when writing.

This kind of competence is essential during text annotation, collaborative conversations, and the writing that students do during and after a close reading. The reference to "standard English" indicates that speakers must be prepared to address a wider audience than their casual register may allow. Both of these standards remind us of how significantly students' language proficiency or the lack thereof affects their school experiences.

Knowledge of Language

The process of close reading requires students to grapple with language in various contexts, including the different genres of texts and registers students use to talk and write about them. As students read across the disciplines they will be exposed to the loaded language of history, the ethos and pathos of rhetoric, and the fact-driven stances of science. As illustrated in the classroom scenarios in this chapter, close reading and collaborative conversation provide students with authentic opportunities to be introduced to, grapple with, and gain the power of the language of each discipline. These goals align clearly with **Language Standard 3:**

CCRA.L.3. Apply knowledge of language to understand how language functions in different contexts, to make effective choices for meaning or style, and to comprehend more fully when reading or listening.

Vocabulary Acquisition and Use

Language Standards 4, 5, and **6** illustrate the precision with language students need to have in order to select just the right words to convey ideas during a collaborative conversation or to generate writing in response to information gleaned while reading closely:

CCRA.L.4. Determine or clarify the meaning of unknown and multiple-meaning words and phrases by using context clues, analyzing meaningful word parts, and consulting general and specialized reference materials, as appropriate.

CCRA.L.5. Demonstrate understanding of figurative language, word relationships, and nuances in word meanings.

CCRA.L.6. Acquire and use accurately a range of general academic and domain-specific words and phrases sufficient for reading, writing, speaking, and listening at the college and career readiness level; demonstrate independence in gathering vocabulary knowledge when encountering an unknown term important to comprehension or expression.

The language chosen to communicate an idea is every bit as important as the decision to communicate. It's essential that students realize, as Philip Roth put it, that "language is a form of communication! Conversation isn't just crossfire where you shoot and get shot at! Where you've got to duck for your life and aim to kill! Words aren't only bombs and bullets—no, they're little gifts containing *meanings*" (2004, pp. 221–222). The conversations that students have as part of the close reading process are essential for expanding their understanding of the topical concepts and clearing up misconceptions. For this reason, teachers in every discipline must devote time to developing students' language skills in ways that support close reading and the ability to communicate the insights and questions that close reading raises.

The Common Core's Speaking and Listening Standards

The Common Core's speaking and listening standards also offer many possibilities to expand students' ownership of language through the extended discussions related to a text that is being closely read.

There are six Common Core speaking and listening anchor standards organized under two headings: Comprehension and Collaboration, and Presentation of Knowledge and Ideas.

Comprehension and Collaboration

Speaking and Listening Standards 1, 2, and **3** address the ability to communicate successfully in a range of situations and with a range of partners, as when students communicate about a text they are closely reading:

CCRA.SL.1. Prepare for and participate effectively in a range of conversations and collaborations with diverse partners, building on others' ideas and expressing their own clearly and persuasively.

CCRA.SL.2. Integrate and evaluate information presented in diverse media and formats, including visually, quantitatively, and orally.

CCRA.SL.3. Evaluate a speaker's point of view, reasoning, and use of evidence and rhetoric.

Presentation of Knowledge and Ideas

Speaking and Listening Standards 4, 5, and **6** focus on the ability to organize and present information, part of which is understanding which register an author is using in a text and which register to use oneself in different information-sharing contexts:

CCRA.SL.4. Present information, findings, and supporting evidence such that listeners can follow the line of reasoning and the organization, development, and style are appropriate to task, purpose, and audience.

CCRA.SL.5. Make strategic use of digital media and visual displays of data to express information and enhance understanding of presentations.

CCRA.SL.6. Adapt speech to a variety of contexts and communicative tasks, demonstrating command of formal English when indicated or appropriate.

Combined, these standards underscore the power of understanding language well enough to "interrogate" a text and glean the author's purpose or intent and of being able to use language precisely enough to ask questions and convey a stance or argument. When readers interact with a text during a close reading, this is exactly what they are doing: using language skills to conduct and convey an in-depth analysis. They need language proficiency both to comprehend the key ideas of the text and to scrutinize how the author uses language in order to identify additional ideas and details intended to promote an opinion or argument, share information, or entertain.

Supporting Effective Communication About Close Reading

The following instructional approaches and examples illustrate ways to support students' language use as they speak, listen, and write during and after a close reading. English language learners and their classmates have opportunities to "try on" both academic language and the language of the disciplines as they engage in these instructional routines. Each of these examples relates to Reading Anchor Standard 1, *Read closely to determine what the text says explicitly and to make logical inferences from it; cite specific textual evidence when writing or speaking to support conclusions drawn from the text.* To illustrate the connections among close reading and language, speaking, and listening, in each scenario we have identified the related Common Core speaking and listening and language standards.

Oral Strategies for Developing and Communicating Understanding

To quote Vygotsky (1978), "By giving our students practice in talking with others, we give them frames for thinking on their own" (p. 19).

Partner talk and small-group conversation. Participating effectively in conversation is a learned practice, and students must have opportunities to converse if they are to become more proficient in it. If the teacher doesn't take steps to nurture participation, the "whole-class discussions" of closely read texts can turn into a conversation between the teacher and a handful of students who are answering the teacher's questions.

A great first step toward avoiding that outcome is to invite partner talk or small-group conversation before students share their findings and ideas as a whole class. Speaking to only one or a few others builds speaking confidence in students who might initially feel uncomfortable speaking to the entire class. Text-dependent questions (*What was the main idea of the text? Where exactly did you find that information? What in the text made you think that? What language did the author use to contrast the two claims being made in the text?*) can provide the focus and the structures student pairs or small groups need for such conversation. As students engage in partner talk and collaboration, they are addressing Speaking and Listening Standard 1: *Prepare for and participate effectively in a range of conversations and collaborations with diverse partners, building on others' ideas and expressing their own clearly and persuasively* (CCRA.SL.1).

You can teach "school talk," the language and behavior of the academic register, through a Fishbowl setting where you first engage with a few students and model how to participate in a small-group or partner discussion (see pp. 145–147). Through regular participation in conversations about information gleaned from close text reading and the use of awareness-boosting tools like the "Assessing My Speaking" guide shown in Figure 5.1, students learn the behaviors associated with academic communication, and it becomes a habit for them to use evidence to support their text interpretations. In doing, so, they are addressing Speaking and Listening Anchor Standard 4: *Present information, findings, and supporting evidence such that listeners can follow the line of reasoning and the*

Figure 5.1 | **A Student Self-Assessment for Academic Communication**   ⬇ Download

Assessing My Speaking

When it was my turn to speak . . .

☐   I used a clear voice.

☐   I made eye contact with listeners.

☐   I stated information clearly and concisely.

☐   I shared text-based support for the ideas I shared.

☐   I invited questions.

☐   I listened to questions before responding.

☐   I invited and supported the participation of others.

☐   I asked others what they thought.

☐   I provided clarification or additional information when others asked me to.

☐   I brought up points others had made.

☐   I offered summary statements when appropriate.

Throughout the conversation . . .

☐   I paid attention to the speaker.

☐   I encouraged the speaker by nodding my head and looking pleasantly engaged.

☐   I asked appropriate questions.

☐   I challenged ideas in a respectful way.

☐   I asked the speaker to verify information using polite language.

☐   I allowed others a chance to participate.

☐   I gained insights from others.

☐   I shared confirming or alternate positions.

☐   I provided text-based support for my thinking.

☐   I encouraged the conversation through my responses and attention to the speaker(s).

organization, development, and style are appropriate to task, purpose, and audience (CCRA.SL.4) .

Purposeful partner talk supported with sentence frames. *Turn to your partner and . . .* is a very common phrase in close reading instruction—an alert to students that they are to discuss information they have encountered in the text or answer a question posed or perhaps brainstorm ideas in preparation for a follow-up writing activity. Generally speaking, today's students have become very good at turning to a peer and talking; whether they stick to the topic at hand rather than discuss their weekend, recess plans, or the latest video game is another question. Furthermore, although the intent of partner talk is to build responsive and collaborative language exchanges, the practice of partner talk can easily turn into students waiting to be heard rather than focusing on the partner's message. They can spend more time thinking about what they are going to say when their partner has (finally!) finished talking than truly listening to their partner's ideas.

Sentence frames, like those shown in Figure 5.2, can support focused and purposeful partner talk in which students extend, question, justify, or build on their partner's responses to a teacher's question. Amy Miles, who teaches 6th grade science and English, regularly places laminated sets of sentence frames on her students' desks. When she wants them to focus on listening and conversing during partner talk about a text or topic that is being closely read, she refers them to a chart containing the kind of information shown in Figure 5.3 (see p. 143)—a combination of sentence frames and close reading annotations. This chart serves as a reference for students, both as they partner-talk about the annotations they have made during a close reading and as they write about their ideas after a close reading. Purposeful partner talk addresses Language Standard 1: *Demonstrate command of the conventions of standard English grammar and usage when writing or speaking* (CCRA.L.1).

Four Corners. This kinesthetic strategy, which gets students up and out of their seats to discuss their thoughts and ideas in different parts of the classroom, supports language learning and development. It is a good way to teach argumentation while fostering engaged, purposeful, and productive conversation.

Here's an illustration. After leading his class in a close reading and large-group discussion of Anna Quindlen's essay "A Quilt of a Country," a Common Core text exemplar for grades 9–10, History teacher Jim Dunn displayed the following statement on the document camera: *The real America is deeply unified.* He

Figure 5.2 | **Sentence Frames for Close Reading Conversations**

To Share Insight

• "I believe the text is about _____ because on page ___, the author says,

_____."

• "I notice that on page _____, the author used the word(s) _____ to help us see _____."

To Disagree

• "I understand that you are saying _____, but I think _____ because on page ___, it says _____

_____."

• "You and I differ on this point. You said _____, and I think _____ because on page ___, it says

_____."

To Agree

• "We are saying similar things. I believe that _____, and you believe that _____."

• "We both interpreted the information on page ___ in the same way."

To Question

• "As I read the text, I thought _____, and I wondered why _____."

• "I agree with the author that _____, but I question the idea on page ___ that says _____."

• "I'm wondering if _____ (character name) is feeling _____ because of the description on page _____."

invited his 11th grade students to think about this statement while reflecting on information they had learned while reading the text. Then he asked them to move to one of the four corners of the room he had marked with signs reading Strongly Agree, Agree, Disagree, and Strongly Disagree. Once there, students discussed why they responded as they had to the statement and also listened to others' ideas. They shared lines from the text to support their thinking. After several minutes of corner discussion, each small group "defended" its position to the rest of the class. Then, when all four groups had been heard from, students were free to move to a different corner if they had been persuaded by another group's case.

Figure 5.3 | **Visual Support for Purposeful Partner Talk**

Close Reading Annotations

Highlight = major points   **Circle** = confusing or unknown words/phrases
! = What surprises you   **?** = Questions you have

Make a Prediction

I think that _____ because _____.
I believe _____.
I predict _____.
I infer from this passage that _____,
which causes me to predict _____.
This information leads me to predict _____.

Ask a Question

I wonder _____.
How did _____?
What does the author mean when he/she
mentions _____.
Why does the author discuss _____?
What words did the author use to _____?
Why is it important to know _____?

Don't forget your margin notes!

Put It in Your Own Words

What _____ says is _____.
The author is basically saying _____.
The author mentions _____.
The gist of this passage/chapter/paragraph is
_____.
In short, this text is about _____.
In short, this _____ tells us _____.
From this passage, we learn _____.
The main idea of this passage is _____.

Clarify It

When the author states _____, he/she is
trying to _____.
The word _____ is used to _____.
When the author mentions _____, it tells
us _____.
The word _____ means _____.
To clarify, the author is saying that the difference
between _____ and _____
is _____.

Courtesy of Amy Miles.

The conversation and argumentation that ensues from a Four Corners activity is a great way to build the academic language used in the texts students are closely reading and discussing. In this example, it provided a way for Mr. Dunn's 11th grade students to address Reading Standard 8 for Literacy in History/Social Studies: *Evaluate an author's premises, claims, and evidence by corroborating or challenging them with other information* (RH.11–12.8).

Inside Outside Circles. Used at the conclusion of a close reading session, this strategy provides a great way for students to develop their academic language use. Begin by asking the students to stand up and form two large circles—an inner circle and an outer circle. Those in the inner circle face outward, those in the outer circle face inward, and students "partner" with the peer they are immediately facing. Once the stage is set, ask a text-dependent question focused on the meaning of the text. The inner-circle partner speaks first, and then the outer-circle partner. Once pairs of students have shared their ideas, the inner-circle students take a step to the right or left and share with a new partner.

Here's an example of how Inside Outside Circles was used in a 7th grade English classroom to develop both language and listening and speaking skills in concert with close reading instruction. Gerilyn Drake's 7th grade language arts students were closely reading Robert Frost's "The Road Not Taken," a Common Core text exemplar. After the final reading, she asked everyone to grab their annotated copy of the poem and get into the Inside Outside Circles formation. When students were set, facing their first partner, she posed this question: "What is Frost's attitude about the road that was chosen, and what lines from the poem best show these feelings?" After a few minutes of conversation, she asked the students to rotate to new partners and then repeated the question. Mrs. Drake had anticipated that some pairs might not be able to infer the poet's attitude, even after the extensive discussion that preceded the activity, so she deliberately chose a classroom strategy that would allow them to talk with multiple partners and expose them to various levels of insight.

Assessing what she was hearing from students during the conversations allowed Mrs. Drake to conclude that the 7th graders were deepening their understanding of the content each time they conversed with a new partner. Some of the students who were not secure initially became more so with each rotation. All of her students were elaborating on their responses and identifying exactly which lines in the poem supported their interpretations. The collaborative conversations that occur as a part of close reading offer a powerful way to expand students' comprehension of the text and also their security in talking about the text. This language activity provided Mrs. Drake's 7th graders students a way to address Speaking and Listening Standard 1 and its first subcomponent: *Engage effectively in a range of collaborative discussions (one-on-one, in groups, and teacher-led) with diverse partners on grade 7 topics, texts, and issues, building on others' ideas and expressing their own clearly* (SL.7.1) and *Come to discussions prepared, having read or researched material under study; explicitly draw on that preparation by referring to evidence on the topic, text, or issue to probe and reflect on ideas under discussion* (SL.7.1.a).

Gallery Walk. This structured activity is a good way to promote discussion of particular aspects of a topic, image, or text following a close reading or viewing. It involves using a wall or desk space to display "works of art" and having students travel in groups to each station and discuss what they see. While at the stations, students might talk about questions that are posed, jot and post ideas on sticky notes, or watch a video clip and add notes to a Foldable®.

Here's an example. Eleventh grade English teacher Brian Arnez set up 15 posters around his classroom, each showing slang terms and phrases used in American English in various past decades. While leading a close reading and discussion of Amy Tan's essay "Mother Tongue," which addresses the language variations and slang expressions often spoken as a part of one's home or casual register, Mr. Arnez had discovered that his students didn't know much about historical slang. Although his text-dependent questions had sent his students back to the text to analyze Tan's use of slang, Mr. Arnez decided that a subsequent lesson would expand their knowledge for future conversations and readings. So, at each gallery stop, he asked students to pause for several minutes to discuss the meanings of each decade's slang and how the terms and phrases resembled or differed from those used in other decades. For example, what did they make of the fact that both the 1900s (*killer*) and the 1990s (*da bomb*) used "violent" words to mean "something or someone excellent or outstanding"? At each station, Mr. Arnez also set up an iPad where students could play videos featuring slang throughout the decades, which allowed them to see and hear the terms they were reading being used in context. By assessing the discourse he heard during close reading, Mr. Arnez was able to plan instruction that furthered his students' understandings of language use, evolution, and nuance, and prepared them for future reading. As students engaged in this activity, they were addressing the grades 11–12 version of Language Standard 3: *Apply knowledge of language to understand how language functions in different contexts, to make effective choices for meaning or style, and to comprehend more fully when reading or listening* (L.11–12.3).

Fishbowl. This is another effective way for students to learn about and practice effective collaborative conversation about close reading. During a Fishbowl, most of the class sits in a large circle. A few (4–6) students sit in a small, inner circle; they are the primary voice during the discussion. As the inner-circle students speak, those in the outer circle listen to the conversation, record main points, and write down questions of their own. You might include an empty chair in the inner circle so students can voluntarily come into the Fishbowl, offer an idea, and quickly return to the outer circle, freeing up the inner-circle chair for another student.

Here's an example to consider. Immediately following a close reading of "Eleven" by Sandra Cisneros, Elisa Brown asked her 8th graders to gather in a Fishbowl to talk more about the author's writing style. Ms. Brown knew that several students understood the author's writing style better than others. She chose some of these students to sit in the inner circle to talk about the evidence that demonstrated Cisneros's use of poetic, succinct, and clear language. To push them a little further, she asked guiding questions that focused them on comparing the language and style in "Eleven" with J. D. Salinger's writing style in *The Catcher in the Rye*, which they had read earlier in the year: *What language did these authors use that gave you clues about their writing style? Did they use similar approaches?* With these questions as the stepping-off point, the students went on to ask questions of one another, clarify misconceptions, and support ideas with detailed evidence. Here is a sample of the insights and questions Sarah and Yaredi generated when they were in the Fishbowl:

> *Sarah:* I think Cisneros chose the words *stupid, mama's lap,* and *need to cry* to give us some ideas about how Rachel was feeling. She also used other phrases, like *the way you grow old is kind of like an onion,* which is figurative and sounds like poetic language. Then she ends one of the paragraphs with *Maybe she's feeling three,* which is so short, simple, and clear. You know exactly what Rachel is feeling.

> *Yaredi:* You say that Cisneros is using a short, succinct, clear language, but it's very powerful, too. I don't think I'd call it "simple." That phrase about the onion is pretty complex and really makes sense. I can imagine peeling away layers, like years of our lives. So you aren't saying Cisneros has a simple writing style, are you?

As students engaged in this lesson, they were addressing a key subcomponent of the 8th grade version of Speaking and Listening Standard 1: *Pose questions that connect the ideas of several speakers and respond to others' questions and comments with relevant evidence, observations, and ideas* (SL.8.1.c).

To ensure that a Fishbowl discussion will provide beneficial models of both productive conversation and productive conversation about complex texts, it's a good idea to practice ahead of time with the members of the inner circle. You can also invite other members of the class to ask questions of the "fish." This encourages everyone to share documented ideas, using academic language to do so.

Writing Strategies for Developing and Communicating Understanding

Students also need to become well-versed in the various ways in which they can use writing to document their thinking as they respond to a closely read text. Often they struggle with incorporating appropriate evidence in a logical, academic-sounding manner. The following instructional approaches and examples illustrate ways to support students' written responses to closely read texts.

Generative Sentences. This strategy can be used to help focus students on extracting and documenting evidence from a text to support their comprehension and thinking. Teachers can ask students to work with partners to *generate,* or create, sentences that focus on particular key words or on finding evidence from the text. For example, a teacher might ask students who are reading an informational text to work with a partner to write a sentence that includes a specific key word, like *retina* when reading about the structure of eyes, or *gibbous* when reading about lunar phases. When students seek out evidence from the text on an area related to a key word, they are being directed to center their thinking on main ideas. In this way, student-created sentences like *The retina is located at the back of the eye and is sensitive to light*, and *The gibbous moon appears a little less fully lit than a full moon* reveal student understanding.

To incorporate academic language and to take student thinking to a deeper level, a teacher might next ask partners to write a sentence in which they incorporate particular academic language. The academic language can be strategically chosen to guide student attention to a particular part of the text. For instance, a middle school teacher who wants students to better understand the function of the retina might ask student partners to generate a sentence that uses this academic language: *According to the text, the function of the retina* _____ or *Based on my understanding of the text, the role of the retina* _____. A sentence built using one of these frames (e.g., *According to the text, the function of the retina is to translate light into nerve signals*) can show evidence that students have gone back to the text to identify key ideas. As the middle schoolers engage in this learning experience, they address two subcomponents of Writing Standard 2 for Literacy in History/Social Studies, Science, and Technical Subjects: *Develop the topic with relevant, well-chosen facts, definitions, concrete details, quotations, or other information and examples* (WHST.6–8.2.b) and *Use precise language and domain-specific vocabulary to inform about or explain the topic* (WHST.6–8.2.d).

GIST. Another way to get students to record both their thinking and the ideas generated from conversations they participate in between consecutive close reads is to have them work with partners or small teams using the GIST strategy (Cunningham, 1982). Here, students focus on the *who, what, where, when, why,* or *how* (5Ws and 1H) of a piece of text. They write a 20-word *GIST*—a summary or explanation that addresses one or more of the 5Ws or the H. Students can create their GISTs individually and then collaborate to synthesize their ideas into one joint GIST.

What's particularly valuable about the GIST strategy is that in order for students to pare down their ideas to only 20 words, they must reflect on what is most important—what is essential—to answering their W or H question. It is oftentimes through peer conversations during close reading that students come to an understanding of central ideas. Clearly, this strategy holds the potential to link peer conversations to writing. As students engage in this writing experience, they are addressing Writing Standard 9: *Draw evidence from literary or informational texts to support analysis, reflection, and research* (CCRA.W.9).

Writing as a Close Reading Connection

Like speaking, writing is both an expressive language process and a means of communication—a way to tell stories and share information, positions, experiences, insights, and ideas. The purpose of sharing written discourse with an intended, but often unknown, audience provides the frame for the text. Instead of writing for the teacher alone or for "no one in particular," students are asked to write for a blog audience, for a community board, to readers of a newspaper, to a member of Congress, for members of a nonprofit organization, and on and on. All writing is produced with a purpose in mind, and the process of writing for a specific audience can help to clarify that purpose for the author. This authorial intent provides a frame for the reader's understanding.

The Common Core's writing standards map the progress of skill development a student needs to graduate high school capable of communicating across disciplines with varied audiences for myriad purposes. The 10 anchor standards address writing to inform, explain, convey experiences both real and imagined, and, from grade 6 onward, present a well-documented stance and argue its merits.

How is writing a dimension of a close reading experience? The most succinct response to this question is that each time students return to the text to more deeply analyze an author's message or intent, they are navigating the language choices that author has made. Identifying these choices supports critical analysis not just of the message but also of how language has been employed to convey that message. Acquiring such insights furthers students' growth as writers as they "develop the capacity to build knowledge on a subject through research projects and to respond analytically to literary and informational sources" (NGA Center & CCSSO, 2010a, p. 18). Perhaps most significantly for teachers of history/social studies, science, and technical subjects, the process of writing articulated in the Common Core develops students' ability to evaluate, critique, and communicate their comprehension of the texts they read.

The Common Core's Writing Standards

The 10 anchor standards for writing are grouped under four headings: Text Types and Purposes, Production and Distribution of Writing, Research to Build and Present Knowledge, and Range of Writing. Let's explore the anchor standards under each heading, and also take a look at the versions of them as presented within the literacy standards for history/social studies, science, and technical subjects. As we did with the speaking and listening and language standards, we focus on these writing standards to illustrate the powerful relationship that exists between close text reading and writing, and then look at instructional examples that promote writing as it relates to communicating about a text.

Text Types and Purposes

The three standards under the Text Types and Purposes heading identify the three types of written texts that students should be able to produce (arguments, informative/explanatory texts, narratives):

> **CCRA.W.1.** Write arguments to support claims in an analysis of substantive topics or texts using valid reasoning and relevant and sufficient evidence.

CCRA.W.2. Write informative/explanatory texts to examine and convey complex ideas and information clearly and accurately through the effective selection, organization, and analysis of content.

CCRA.W.3. Write narratives to develop real or imagined experiences or events using effective technique, well-chosen details and well-structured event sequences.

Each of these standards also clearly specifies why there is value in being able to share ideas and information through multiple formats. Arguments, for example, are written to support a claim being made; informative/explanatory texts are written to convey complex ideas and information across many topics; and narratives are crafted in ways that share real and imagined events or experiences.

Writing Standard 1: Argumentative writing. The decision to make this kind of writing the focus of the first writing standard suggests just how important it is in college readiness. Writing Standard 1's call for students to engage in evidence-based, text analysis makes it a natural partner with close reading instruction, and so we want to give it a particularly thorough examination.

Here is how the writers of the Common Core intend this standard to be addressed in history/social studies, science, and technical subjects in grades 6–12: *Write arguments focused on discipline–specific content* (WHST.6–12.1). This general expectation is followed by a set of lettered components that describe the attributes of satisfactory discipline-focused argumentative writing at each of the three grade-level bands. You can find these on page 64 of the ELA/literacy standards document, available at corestandards.org, and we've provided the full middle and high school versions in Figure 5.4.

Writing Standard 1 gives teachers in all disciplines a clear mandate: Students must be taught to write a cogent, content-focused argument within each discipline at each grade level, and students need plenty of ongoing practice to develop this skill. In science, that might mean having students prepare written arguments that support or deny the need to reduce carbon emissions. In social studies, they might make written arguments that support or condemn the nuclear bombing of Hiroshima and Nagasaki. In computer science, they might argue in writing for or against greater online privacy protections. Any content important enough to include in your curriculum is important enough for students to explore through well-documented argumentative writing. Argument writing begins in kindergarten, as children are called on to state an opinion and

Figure 5.4 | **The Progression of Writing Standard 1 for History/Social Studies, Science, and Technical Subjects: Argumentative Writing in the Disciplines**

Grades 6–8	Grades 9–10	Grades 11–12
WHST.6–8.1. Write arguments focused on *discipline-specific content.* a. Introduce claim(s) about a topic or issue, acknowledge and distinguish the claim(s) from alternate or opposing claims, and organize the reasons and evidence logically. b. Support claim(s) with logical reasoning and relevant, accurate data and evidence that demonstrate an understanding of the topic or text, using credible sources. c. Use words, phrases, and clauses to create cohesion and clarify the relationships among claim(s), counterclaims, reasons, and evidence. d. Establish and maintain a formal style. e. Provide a concluding statement or section that follows from and supports the argument presented.	**WHST.9–10.1.** Write arguments focused on *discipline-specific content.* a. Introduce precise claim(s), distinguish the claim(s) from alternate or opposing claims, and create an organization that establishes clear relationships among the claim(s), counterclaims, reasons, and evidence. b. Develop claim(s) and counterclaims fairly, supplying data and evidence for each while pointing out the strengths and limitations of both claim(s) and counterclaims in a discipline-appropriate form and in a manner that anticipates the audience's knowledge level and concerns. c. Use words, phrases, and clauses to link the major sections of the text, create cohesion, and clarify the relationships between claim(s) and reasons, between reasons and evidence and between claim(s) and counterclaims. d. Establish and maintain a formal style and objective tone while attending to the norms and conventions of the discipline in which they are writing. e. Provide a concluding statement or section that follows from or supports the argument presented.	**WHST.11–12.1.** Write arguments focused on *discipline-specific content.* a. Introduce precise, knowledgeable claim(s), establish the significance of the claim(s), distinguish the claim(s) from alternate or opposing claims, and create an organization that logically sequences the claim(s), counterclaims, reasons, and evidence. b. Develop claim(s) and counterclaims fairly and thoroughly, supplying the most relevant data and evidence for each while pointing out the strengths and limitations of both claim(s) and counterclaims in a discipline-appropriate form that anticipates the audience's knowledge level, concerns, values, and possible biases. c. Use words, phrases, and clauses as well as varied syntax to link the major sections of the text, create cohesion, and clarify the relationships between claim(s) and reasons, between reasons and evidence, and between claim(s) and counterclaims. d. Establish and maintain a formal style and objective tone while attending to the norms and conventions of the discipline in which they are writing. e. Provide a concluding statement or section that follows from or supports the argument presented.

explain to the reader why this is their opinion. As children do so, they are learning to take a stance and support it with reasons. This early preparation with position-taking and documentation lays the foundation for writing and supporting well-structured arguments across the disciplines when students reach the middle and high school years.

Figure 5.5 provides more detail on the subtle differences between writing opinion pieces (the persuasive writing students focus on in elementary school) and crafting arguments (the argumentative writing they first attempt in 6th grade

Figure 5.5 | **A Comparison of Persuasive Writing and Argumentative Writing**

Persuasive Writing	Argumentative Writing
Purpose: To convince reader of a point of view.	**Purpose:** To convince reader that the stance taken is a supported position worthy of consideration.
Author's Position: Shares one emotional or impassioned position with the intent of convincing reader to agree.	**Author's Position:** Acknowledges that there may be multiple perspectives on a topic but uses data to show that there is only one stance or conviction that is worthwhile to believe.
Audience: An identified audience the author is attempting to persuade.	**Audience:** No specific audience needs to be identified. The author is attempting to share a viable position on a topic.
Composing Technique: The author combines some fact with emotion in an attempt to convince.	**Composing Technique:** The author combines well-documented facts, evidence, connections or warrants, counterclaims, and rebuttals to present a position of substance.
Writing Process: The author identifies a position within a topic and shares an emotionally driven justification to gain the reader's agreement.	**Writing Process:** The author researches a topic thoroughly; makes a claim/takes a stance; supports the claim with evidence; examines a counterclaim; creates the bridging link, or warrant, between the claim and the evidence and shares a rebuttal to refute the counterclaim in support of the original stance; and summarizes the claim.

and develop throughout the secondary grades). Notice how the skills associated with persuasive writing are applied in argumentative writing.

When providing instructional guidance to students, there are a number of key terms to stress. First, effective written argument includes a *claim,* which is a conclusion that the writer makes based on *evidence,* which are the facts that he or she has identified. The *warrant* is the logical bridge connecting the claim and the evidence. *Counterclaims* offer an alternative position that the student or writer should discredit with additional evidence. In Figure 5.6, we share a progression of sentence frames to support students' efforts at argumentative writing.

For further clarification on the difference between presenting a written opinion and making a written argument, consider the following student response, generated after a close reading of a text on the global effects of fishing on biodiversity:

Fishing too much can hurt the ocean environment. In paragraph two of our article, it says that we need different kinds of fish to have a healthy ocean. Big fish eat little fish, and if some of the little fish are gone, the big ones won't have food. If people catch the big fish, there will be too many little fish. This could affect the food web in the ocean. I think that people need to stop fishing so much. We need to keep the coral reefs and other parts of the ocean full of many different kinds of fish.

Figure 5.6 | **Step-by-Step Sentence Frames for Argumentative Writing**

Step 1: Take a stance/*make a claim.*

• Because of evidence found on page ___ suggesting that _____, I believe that _____. Therefore my claim, or stance, is _____.

Step 2: Provide *evidence* to support your claim.

• I believe my position is worthwhile because _____. Other evidence to support my analysis is that _____. This information promotes my belief that _____.

Step 3: Acknowledge a *counterclaim.*

• While _____ believes _____, I remain convinced that _____, because _____.

• An alternate position might be _____, but I maintain that _____, because _____.

Step 4: Provide a *warrant* (a commonsense bridge between the claim and the evidence).

• I believe _____ (claim), because _____ (evidence) and _____ (commonsense warrant).

• Based on my observation that _____ (evidence) and the facts that suggest _____ (evidence), I believe _____ (claim). Furthermore, _____ (commonsense warrant) suggests that _____ (claim).

• However, _____ (counterclaim), but the facts—namely, _____ (evidence)—support my original stance that _____ (claim).

Step 5: *Summarize* your claim.

• To conclude, I maintain that _____. This is a reasonable stance because evidence that _____ and _____ overwhelmingly support the conclusion that _____.

This is persuasive writing, generated by a 5th grader; it's a statement of opinion that contains some text-based facts. Now, consider how this text might look if the writer were a 6th grader tasked with writing an argument. See if you can spot the claim, the presentation of the counterclaim, the documentation, and the writer's final stance:

Overfishing can hurt the marine environment. We need a variety of fish in the ocean to have biodiversity. If we don't, that's a problem. A report by the United Nations says that commercial fish populations of cod, hake, and flounder are lower now, by 95 percent, in the North Atlantic Ocean. Some people think that we shouldn't worry about overfishing because people need to fish for food. Two hundred million people fish. Lots of them are in poor countries. Some people think that if we stop them from fishing by making rules about how much you can catch, they won't have food. Even though this might be true, a bigger problem is overfishing. If we overfish, soon we won't have any fish. We need biodiversity—lots of different kinds of fish in the ocean—to have a healthy environment.

Although teachers may set out to design learning experiences to address one particular standard, it is highly probable that other standards will be involved at the same time. As the instructional context changes from a partner chat during a close reading to a topical debate and then to a written response, different standards can be integrated to support language skill development across grades and situations. In the writing samples above, the 5th grader is reacting to a reading by developing an opinion based on an informational text, an activity that addresses the 5th grade version of Writing Standard 1:

W.5.1. Write opinion pieces on topics or texts, supporting a point of view with reasons and information.

a. Introduce a topic or text clearly, state an opinion, and create an organizational structure in which ideas are logically grouped to support the writer's purpose.

b. Provide logically ordered reasons that are supported by facts and details.

c. Link opinion and reasons using words, phrases, and clauses (e.g., *consequently, specifically*).

d. Provide a concluding statement or section related to the opinion presented.

The 5th grader is reporting on the article and evaluating information to develop an opinion. Now consider the 6th grade writing sample, which shows that the student is moving more toward making a claim that is supported by evidence from the text. The writing style is more formal, credible evidence is introduced, and the student even verges on addressing a counterclaim. The 6th grader is addressing the 6th grade version of Writing Standard 1:

W.6.1. Write arguments to support claims with clear reasons and relevant evidence.

a. Introduce claim(s) and organize the reasons and evidence clearly.

b. Support claim(s) with clear reasons and relevant evidence, using credible sources and demonstrating an understanding of the topic or text.

c. Use words, phrases, and clauses to clarify the relationships among claim(s) and reasons.

d. Establish and maintain a formal style.

e. Provide a concluding statement or section that follows from the argument presented.

Additionally, students, as they engage in partner talk centered around the informational texts that support this writing, may also be addressing Speaking and Listening Standard 4 in both its 5th and 6th grade versions:

SL.5.4. Report on a topic or text or present an opinion, sequencing ideas logically and using appropriate facts and relevant, descriptive details to support main ideas or themes; speak clearly at an understandable pace.

SL.6.4. Present claims and findings, sequencing ideas logically and using pertinent descriptions, facts, and details to accentuate main ideas or themes; use appropriate eye contact, adequate volume, and clear pronunciation.

In essence, close reading instruction that engages students in partner talk for the purpose of writing will inevitably move students through several different Common Core State Standards.

Writing Standard 2: Informative/explanatory writing. The second writing standard also merits a bit of special attention. After all, it focuses on the familiar "research report" writing that is a staple of secondary classrooms and has traditionally been most common in history and social studies. The Common Core aims to reinforce the value of informative writing, which requires critical thinking and helps students to solidify, deepen, and expand their knowledge of all kinds of topics, and encourage the use of informative writing across all disciplines.

The literacy version of Writing Standard 2 is phrased as follows for grades 6–12: *Write informative/explanatory texts, including the narration of historical events, scientific procedures/experiments, or technical processes* (WHST.6–12.2).

You can find the detailed components articulating the grade-level expectations on page 65 of the ELA/literacy standards document and in Figure 5.7.

Informative/explanatory writing experiences in grades 6–12 might include students explaining how a bill becomes a law (social studies), how cell division occurs (science), or how a computer application works (technical subjects).

Figure 5.7 | **The Progression of Writing Standard 2 for History/Social Studies, Science, and Technical Subjects: Informative/Explanatory Writing in the Disciplines**

Grades 6–8	Grades 9–10	Grades 11–12
WHST.6–8.2. Write informative/explanatory texts, including the narration of historical events, scientific procedures/experiments, or technical processes. a. Introduce a topic clearly, previewing what is to follow; organize ideas, concepts, and information into broader categories as appropriate to achieving purpose; include formatting (e.g., headings), graphics (e.g., charts, tables), and multimedia when useful to aiding comprehension. b. Develop the topic with relevant, well-chosen facts, definitions, concrete details, quotations, or other information and examples. c. Use appropriate and varied transitions to create cohesion and clarify the relationships among ideas and concepts. d. Use precise language and domain-specific vocabulary to inform about or explain the topic. e. Establish and maintain a formal style and objective tone. f. Provide a concluding statement or section that follows from and supports the information or explanation presented.	**WHST.9–10.2.** Write informative/explanatory texts, including the narration of historical events, scientific procedures/experiments, or technical processes. a. Introduce a topic and organize ideas, concepts, and information to make important connections and distinctions; include formatting (e.g., headings), graphics (e.g., figures, tables), and multimedia when useful to aiding comprehension. b. Develop the topic with well-chosen, relevant, and sufficient facts, extended definitions, concrete details, quotations, or other information and examples appropriate to the audience's knowledge of the topic. c. Use varied transitions and sentence structures to link the major sections of the text, create cohesion, and clarify the relationships among ideas and concepts. d. Use precise language and domain-specific vocabulary to manage the complexity of the topic and convey a style appropriate to the discipline and context as well as to the expertise of likely readers. e. Establish and maintain a formal style and objective tone while attending to the norms and conventions of the discipline in which they are writing. f. Provide a concluding statement or section that follows from and supports the information or explanation presented (e.g., articulating implications or the significance of the topic).	**WHST.11–12.2.** Write informative/explanatory texts, including the narration of historical events, scientific procedures/ experiments, or technical processes. a. Introduce a topic and organize complex ideas, concepts, and information so that each new element builds on that which precedes it to create a unified whole; include formatting (e.g., headings), graphics (e.g., figures, tables), and multimedia when useful to aiding comprehension. b. Develop the topic thoroughly by selecting the most significant and relevant facts, extended definitions, concrete details, quotations, or other information and examples appropriate to the audience's knowledge of the topic. c. Use varied transitions and sentence structures to link the major sections of the text, create cohesion, and clarify the relationships among complex ideas and concepts. d. Use precise language, domain-specific vocabulary and techniques such as metaphor, simile, and analogy to manage the complexity of the topic; convey a knowledgeable stance in a style that responds to the discipline and context as well as to the expertise of likely readers. e. Provide a concluding statement or section that follows from and supports the information or explanation provided (e.g., articulating implications or the significance of the topic).

Writing Standard 3: Narrative writing. Understandably, teaching narrative writing is not required in history/social studies, science, or technical subjects. It remains a feature of the ELA classroom, of course, and arguably, in disciplines like history and science, occasional narrative writing tasks can increase students' engagement in course content and even increase their sensitivity to and appreciation of the narrative techniques employed by authors of both fiction and literary nonfiction.

Production and Distribution of Writing

The three standards under this heading address the skills involved in planning, writing, and then publishing text. The very carefully developed process of writing a text is influenced by that text's purpose and intended audience—factors that students focus on explicitly during a close reading. Here are the standards.

> **CCRA.W.4.** Produce clear and coherent writing in which the development, organization, and style are appropriate to task, purpose, and audience.

Writing Standard 4 has the same phrasing throughout the middle and high school grades, reinforcing the idea that every piece of writing across the grades and disciplines should be focused, organized, and written to accommodate an identified audience.

> **CCRA.W.5.** Develop and strengthen writing as needed by planning, revising, editing, rewriting, or trying a new approach.

Writing Standard 5 calls for more instructional scaffolding in the middle school grades and less in the high school grades. Across the disciplines, students are called on to reflect on authorial purpose and audience with increasing sophistication, as you can see here:

- *Grades 6–8:* With some guidance and support from peers and adults, develop and strengthen writing as needed by planning, revising, editing, rewriting, or trying a new approach, focusing on how well purpose and audience have been addressed (WHST.6–8.5).
- *Grades 9–12:* Develop and strengthen writing as needed by planning, revising, editing, rewriting, or trying a new approach, focusing on addressing what is most significant for a specific purpose and audience (WHST.9–12.5).

Notice also that independence is expected of writers during the high school years. Middle school teachers in the various disciplines will need to factor in time to provide support, explicitly providing time for partner and peer work.

CCRA.W.6. Use technology, including the Internet, to produce and publish writing and to interact and collaborate with others.

We find it interesting that, as noted in **Writing Standard 6,** the Common Core identifies collaboration via the Internet as a dimension of both the production of text and its publication. Take a look at the expectation for skill development in history/social studies, science, and technical subjects throughout the three secondary grade bands:

- *Grades 6–8:* Use technology, including the Internet, to produce and publish writing and present the relationships between information and ideas clearly and efficiently (WHST.6–8.6).
- *Grades 9–10:* Use technology, including the Internet, to produce, publish, and update individual or shared writing products, taking advantage of technology's capacity to link to other information and to display information flexibly and dynamically (WHST.9–10.6).
- *Grades 11–12:* Use technology, including the Internet, to produce, publish, and update individual or shared writing products in response to ongoing feedback, including new arguments or information (WHST.11–12.6).

As students conclude a close reading experience, it's common practice to ask them to share an extension of their learning and response through writing. Writing Standard 6 promotes the idea that these extensions should be supported by online connections, calls on schools to provide the necessary technology, and calls on us to offer guidance. As Diane and her colleagues have noted, "There is no question about it, our students have adopted a digital ecosystem bursting with opportunities. What we make of these opportunities is key. Give students a pencil and paper, and they will write an essay. Provide students access to social media, and they will give you a viral online campaign" (Lapp, Fisher, Frey, & Gonzalez, 2014, p. 183).

Research to Build and Present Knowledge

The three standards under this heading focus on the skills associated with researching, analyzing, validating, and reflecting on topically related sources of information. Let's consider the skill progression of each standard for literacy in history/social studies, science, and technical subjects. First, though, a reminder about the how the standards are structured, in the words of the standards document itself:

> The reading and writing standards in grades 6–12 are divided into two sections, one for ELA and the other for history/social studies, science, and technical subjects. This division reflects the unique, time-honored place of ELA teachers in developing students' literacy skills while at the same time recognizing that teachers in other areas must have a role in this development as well. (NGA Center & CCSSO, 2010a, p. 4)

Because our focus in this text is close reading across the disciplines, we are looking specifically at the progression of writing standards across the disciplines of history, science, and technical subjects. As students complete a close reading in each of these disciplines and share their written reflections, arguments, and extensions, they will be addressing the discipline-specific versions of the writing standards.

Let's begin with **Writing Standard 7:**

> **CCRA.W.7.** Conduct short as well as more sustained research projects based on focused questions, demonstrating understanding of the subject under investigation.

Notice that the skill development this standard calls for is generally addressed across the secondary school disciplines and parallels the skill development needed for the precise and concise writing done by scientists and historians as they write lab reports, empirical reports, or historical accounts. This is also the type of writing students must generate when they write a text summary or response to a text they have just closely read.

Here are the specific expectations for Writing Standard 7 in the disciplines, from middle school through high school:

- *Grades 6–8:* Conduct short research projects to answer a question (including a self-generated question), drawing on several sources and generating additional related, focused questions that allow for multiple avenues of exploration (WHST.6–8.7).
- *Grades 9–10:* Conduct short as well as more sustained research projects to answer a question (including a self-generated question) or solve a problem; narrow or broaden the inquiry when appropriate; synthesize multiple sources

on the subject, demonstrating understanding of the subject under investigation (WHST.9–10.7).

- *Grades 11–12*: Conduct short as well as more sustained research projects to answer a question (including a self-generated question) or solve a problem; narrow or broaden the inquiry when appropriate; synthesize multiple sources on the subject, demonstrating understanding of the subject under investigation (WHST.11–12.7).

On to **Writing Standard 8:**

> **CCRA.W.8.** Gather relevant information from multiple print and digital sources, assess the credibility and accuracy of each source, and integrate the information while avoiding plagiarism.

Again, the skill is intended to be developed across the disciplines in a way that parallels the practical skills scientists and historians need to produce analytical and accurate writing that consolidates information found in multiple and multi-formatted documents and reports:

- *Grades 6–8:* Gather relevant information from multiple print and digital sources, using search terms effectively; assess the credibility and accuracy of each source; and quote or paraphrase the data and conclusions of others while avoiding plagiarism and following a standard format for citation (WHST.6–8.8).
- *Grades 9–10:* Gather relevant information from multiple authoritative print and digital sources, using advanced searches effectively; assess the usefulness of each source in answering the research question; integrate information into the text selectively to maintain the flow of ideas, avoiding plagiarism and following a standard format for citation (WHST.9–10.8).
- *Grades 11–12:* Gather relevant information from multiple authoritative print and digital sources, using advanced searches effectively; assess the strengths and limitations of each source in terms of the specific task, purpose, and audience; integrate information into the text selectively to maintain the flow of ideas, avoiding plagiarism and overreliance on any one source and following a standard format for citation (WHST.11–12.8).

The last of the writing standards under the Research to Build and Present Knowledge heading, **Writing Standard 9** is phrased exactly the same in all its formats: as an ELA anchor standard, as grade-level ELA standards, and as grade-level disciplinary literacy standards: *Draw evidence from literary or informational texts to support analysis, reflection, and research.* As with the other standards under the Research to Build and Present Knowledge heading, Writing Standard 9 highlights the skill and stamina necessary to write well-researched and well-documented texts of varying lengths. The kind of in-depth analysis of complex texts that students engage in during close reading serves them well as they investigate and evaluate sources—informational and literary, print and digital—as part of their writing experiences.

Range of Writing

Although there is only one standard under the Range of Writing heading, it is a comprehensive one. **Writing Standard 10** encourages students' regular engagement in writing tasks that promote the ability to write many text types of alternate lengths with multiple purposes and for an array of audiences:

> **CCRA.W.10.** Write routinely over extended time frames (time for research, reflection, and revision) and shorter time frames (a single sitting or a day or two) for a range of tasks, purposes, and audiences.

The phrasing of Writing Standard 10 is the same in the disciplinary literacy section of the standards document (WHST.6–12.10) as it is in the ELA section, and it is uniform throughout the middle and high school grades. One intention explicit in Writing Standard 10 is that writing be done routinely and for longer spans of time so that it becomes an expected component of instruction within every discipline.

Strategies for Supporting Understanding of Written Language Use

Students learn about written language by observing how authors use it to inform, entertain, and persuade. It's important to build into close reading sessions a variety of listening, speaking, and writing activities that draw students' attention to the craft of writing. Here are some tools for doing so.

Writer's Reference Notebooks. Before beginning a close reading, invite students to create a personal Writer's Reference Notebook where they can keep track of how authors use language to convey information, to entertain, to convince and persuade, and so on. You can have students use labeled dividers to create separate sections focusing on different aspects of the authors' language use: "Word Choices," "Unique Text Features," "Imagery," and so on.

In close reading, the multiple returns to a text that help students acquire a deeper understanding of its information also give them the opportunity to explore the author's use of language. To encourage such rereading, ask students to go back to the text for specific, language-focused purposes, such as to identify which words make them "see" or "hear" the author's voice. They can record their findings in the "Word Choices" section of their Writer's Reference Notebook along with other words, phrases, and sentences that they feel were artfully used.

For example, in the piece "Amusement Park Physics," a grades 9–10 Common Core text exemplar, author Jearl Walker (1983) describes the motion of a roller coaster this way:

> When the coaster reaches the bottom of the valley and starts up the next hill, there is an instant when the cars are symmetrically distributed in the valley. The acceleration is zero. As more cars ascend, the coaster begins to slow, reaching its lowest speed just as it is symmetrically positioned at the top of the hill. (p. 162)

When physical sciences teacher Kendra Peters engaged her students in a close reading of this text, she had them comment in their notebooks about how the language the author used made the text more accessible, interesting, and informative for them. She shared that Walker's phrase *there is an instant when the cars are symmetrically distributed in the valley* conjured for her an image of stillness, with the roller coaster cars frozen in a "U" shape along the bottom of the curving track. During a rereading, Ms. Peters asked students to return to the text to spot techniques the author used to share ideas. She reminded them to note words and phrases that stood out to them as well as the aspects of science writing they had discussed under "Unique Text Features" in their Writer's Reference Notebook, being sure to indicate where in the text each was located. In the conversation that followed, Andre pointed out that the author was using contrastive analysis—a common feature of science writing that he'd already recorded in his notebook—to talk about energy transformation. Nadia pointed out that when Walker writes *When the chain hauls the cars to the top of the first hill, it does work on the cars, endowing them with gravitational potential energy,* his use of the word *endowing* reminded her of endowments—big monetary gifts or donations. "That's a vivid way of explaining how the roller coaster cars gain energy," she added.

Students should be encouraged to use the evidence they gather in these notebooks to support their discussions of the text and further their own writing techniques. Because science concepts are sometimes abstract and hard to visualize, authors and researchers may employ vivid language, including metaphors and analogies, to clarify meaning and connect abstractions to more tangible or familiar concepts. As students create their notebooks, they are addressing the grades 11–12 version of Writing Standard 4 for History/Social Studies, Science, and Technical Subjects: *Produce clear and coherent writing in which the development, organization, and style are appropriate to task, purpose, and audience* (WHST.11–12.4).

Socratic Circles. Socrates was a famous champion of using artful discussion to logically examine the validity of an idea. Instruction that supports such dialogue is referred to as a Socratic Circle (Copeland, 2005).

When students in Deborah Bartalucci's 8th grade science class were investigating factors that have contributed to the rise in global temperatures over the past century, they developed research-based questions derived from ideas shared in two texts selected by Miss Bartalucci: "Climate Panel Cites Near Certainty on Global Warming," an article from the *New York Times* by Justin Gillis (2013), and "Geologist Connects Regular Changes of Earth's Orbital Cycle to Changes in Climate," a research report published on *Science Daily* (2010). Based on their close reading of these two texts, students posed and discussed questions (e.g., *To what degree could fossil fuel combustion and other human activity contribute to global warming? What's the connection between levels of gases in the air, like carbon dioxide and methane, and the rate of human activities, like building cars and running factories? What's the connection between Earth's orbit and climate change?*). Miss Bartalucci wanted this conversation to help students develop insights that would support a better understanding of the texts. Then she divided the students into inner and outer circles and prompted those in in the inner circle to pose and discuss open-ended questions about the text, thinking about the text closely so they could establish opinions rooted in evidence. Students in the outer circle listened, took notes, jotted down questions, and later shared the additional insights about the text they had acquired from observing the discussion.

Following the Socratic Circle discussion, Miss Bartalucci asked students to work with partners to develop a critique of the articles in which they established their own ideas and understandings based on an in-depth discussion of the factors that might cause global temperature changes and possible correlation to

human activity. She provided these language frame options and then asked partners to incorporate at least two of them into their writing:

Despite the fact that _____, we believe _____.

Considering the evidence, _____.

We do not agree that _____ because _____.

The data shows that _____.

Through this activity, Miss Bartalucci's students gained experience in all of the
following: (1) the consideration of multiple perspectives of an issue through the
reading of two texts; (2) discussion in an in-depth, inquiry-based manner; and
(3) writing experience based on the close reading of two texts and informed by
analytical conversations. In addition, many students were inspired to seek out
more information, going online to *ScienceDaily*, the website of the National Geo-
graphic Society, and various other sites to find other articles focused on how
human activity is influencing climate change. The language and writing experiences that students engaged in during and after this close reading experience
addressed Speaking and Listening Standard 4—*Present information, findings,
and supporting evidence such that listeners can follow the line of reasoning and
the organization, development, and style are appropriate to task, purpose, and
audience* (CCRA.SL.4)—and Writing Standard 9 for History/Social Studies, Science, and Technical Subjects, which is *Draw evidence from informational texts to
support analysis, reflection, and research* (WHST.6–12.9).

Depth of Knowledge–based questioning. Depth of Knowledge (DOK) is
a process for analyzing the complexity of standards and assessments that was
created by Norman Webb (see Webb et al., 2005) and is widely used by educators to help students to access content in more profound ways. The DOK levels
are Recall (Level 1), Skill or Concept (Level 2), Strategic Thinking (Level 3), and
Extended Thinking (Level 4). Strategically developed text-dependent questions
can help drive the reader to increasingly higher DOK levels:

- Level 1 questions might ask the student to *identify the main idea* or to *list
  key ideas.* Answers to these types of questions help manifest a foundational
  understanding of the text.
- Level 2 questions might require that the student *summarize the events* or
  interpret data from a chart or *graph.* Questions from this level guide students

to home in on specific areas of a text so that they can note ways in which language is used to show how events progressed, show how evidence and ideas are connected to form patterns, or show particular events in a certain situation.

- Level 3 questions might move the reader to *form conclusions based on multiple forms of data presented* or to *cite evidence to help formulate an understanding of a key term like "civil disobedience"* or even to *identify how the author constructed his or her argument or perspective using different pieces of evidence.* These questions drive students to think more deeply as they identify potential research questions or investigations or as they create models to help understand a problem or situation.
- Level 4 questions ask readers to go even further, into the realm of extended thinking.

Here is what DOK-based questioning looks like in the classroom. Jose Monticello had his 11th grade students closely read Gordan Kane's "The Mysteries of Mass," a Common Core text exemplar. To move his students from Level 1 (text-dependent recall questions) to Level 2 to Level 3 (text-dependent strategic thinking questions) over the course of three readings, Mr. Monticello asked them to engage in three close readings of several key pages. With each close reading, students responded to text-dependent questions that drove them progressively deeper into the text. Once Mr. Monticello was satisfied that his students had a deep understanding of the content, he moved them toward DOK Level 4 by requiring them to work with partners to develop a plan to study an aspect of mass that they had read about in the text or had become interested in as a result of having read the text (e.g., particle accelerators or the Higgs boson).

Mr. Monticello provided an example, telling his students that he had recently read an article discussing the effect of gravity on light. The article made him curious to find out how light behaves when it passes by a black hole, and he developed a series of questions he wanted answered: *How does light travel near something that is very massive? Does it go in a straight line? Or bend? And why does it behave in certain ways?* These questions, he explained, would guide his further reading and research. Then Mr. Monticello got his students started on the first step of their extended thinking task by brainstorming research questions related to their reading of "The Mysteries of Mass." Roberto and Maria wanted to investigate the Higgs field. Lupe and Santiago were determined to study why different atoms have different masses. Ultimately, mini research studies grew out of these questions, and the student-made posters illustrating their creative plans for study were displayed around the classroom. During these learning experiences, students were addressing bundles of standards, including the grades 11–12 version of Writing Standard 7 for History/Social Studies, Science, and Technical Subjects—*Conduct short as well as more sustained research projects to answer a question (including a self-generated question) or solve a problem; narrow or broaden the inquiry when appropriate; synthesize multiple sources on the subject, demonstrating understanding of the subject under investigation* (WHST.11–12.7)—and Speaking and Listening Standard 4—*Present information, findings, and supporting evidence such that listeners can follow the line of reasoning and the organization, development, and style are appropriate to task, purpose, and audience* (CCRA.SL.4).

DOK Level 4 questions are great springboards to writing that occurs post-reading. Here are a few examples of other tasks at Level 4 DOK that students might engage in after a close reading:

- Generate additional questions that connect the content to real-world, relevant issues. Then use additional resources to seek answers to the questions and determine a user group that could benefit from the information. Share the information in various formats—a podcast, a skit, a poster, a graphic cartoon, and so on.
- Analyze a problem mentioned in the text and create a solution (by building a product, writing a proposal, etc.).
- Critique a current solution to a real-world situation, identify areas of weakness and areas of strength, and design a revised plan.
- Apply concepts learned to create and design a solution/product/service to address a real-world problem or issue.

Karen Hess (2009) created a chart correlating Bloom's taxonomy (Bloom et al., 1956) with Webb's Cognitive Matrix—otherwise known as the Depth of Knowledge. It's a good resource for supporting students' deep inquiry into text, and is available online at http://static.pdesas.org/content/documents/M1-Slide_22_DOK_Hess_Cognitive_Rigor.pdf.

Power Writing. Close reading demands that students return to a text numerous times to conduct deeper and deeper analysis. This requires focus, stamina, and a well-developed understanding of language use. To build this kind of stamina (and promote language fluency), Fearn and Farnan (2001) advocate power writing, a daily "structured free-write where the objective is quantity alone" (p. 501). In power writing, either the teacher or a student offers a topic in the form of a word (e.g., *magnets, football, stars*) or phrase (e.g., *sugar is good and bad, new shoes, at the zoo*). Students have one minute to write as much as they can, as well as they can. When time is up, each student counts the number of words he or she has written and records it in the page margin. Then the cycle repeats twice: two more one-minute writing sessions on different topics, with the documentation of the number of words written. At the conclusion of the third cycle, students return to each writing sample to circle and correct any words they believe they misspelled; the number of errors made and caught provides assessment information on the students' self-monitoring ability. Students convert the word counts into a visual documentation of their developing fluency, charting the longest response of the day over a series of days and eventually pasting a graph into their notebooks as a private record of their progress. As they engage in this learning, they are addressing Writing Standard 5: *Develop and strengthen writing as needed by planning, revising, editing, rewriting, or trying a new approach* (CCRA.W.5).

Writing RAFTs. The RAFT writing strategy (Santa & Havens, 1995) is an effective tool for helping students grasp the point of view of a character in a text they are reading closely, for calling their attention to how perspective functions in literature, and for focusing them on how both audience and format can shape the message of a written text. When writing a RAFT, students must consider the following:

> *Role of the Writer:* What perspective/voice are you assuming? (a pilgrim, a citizen, a piece of chocolate)
> *Audience:* To whom are you writing? (a turkey, a member of Congress, the digestive system)
> *Format:* What form will the message take? (a speech, a letter, a poem)
> *Topic:* What is the topic of the message? (celebrations, taxes, eating habits)

For example, after closely reading David Macaulay's *Cathedral: The Story of Its Construction*, a Common Core text exemplar for grades 6–8, students might create a RAFT response in which R = a visitor to the cathedral, A = the carpenter who constructed the cathedral, F = a thank-you letter, and T = regarding the building design and construction. Similarly, after 7th graders conduct a close reading of Nikki Giovanni's "A Poem for My Librarian, Mrs. Long," a Common Core text exemplar for grades 6–8, exploring the author's style and word choices, they might write a RAFT from the perspective of the author herself—a new poem about another favorite person, in which R = Nikki Giovanni, A = 7th grade reader (essentially, an audience like themselves), F = a poem, and T = a person who has made a positive difference, big or small.

Having students write from the perspective of another character, author, or person they have just explored in a close reading is a way to assess their writing proficiencies and also learn a great deal about their comprehension of the text. When students create RAFTs after a close reading, they are addressing Writing Standard 4: *Produce clear and coherent writing in which the development, organization, and style are appropriate to task, purpose, and audience* (CCRA.W.4).

Writing Scavenger Hunts. Writers search their minds and notes for the right detail, the perfect setting, and the ideal character description. Authors choose their words very carefully, and one way for students to examine such powerful language is to participate in a writing scavenger hunt. During this engaging task, students return to closely read text to find a "list of items." For example, Sarah Fink, 6th grade teacher, created a "list of items" for her students to find while closely reading the play *Sorry, Wrong Number* by Lucille Fletcher, a Common Core text exemplar. As you can see in Figure 5.8, Mrs. Fink designed the questions to help her students understand how authors use language to shape the reader's impression of a character.

Jen Koyamatsu engaged her 10th grade history students in a writing scavenger hunt of a different kind. After her students did a close reading of Elie Wiesel's Nobel Peace Prize acceptance speech, "Hope, Despair and Memory," a Common Core text exemplar published in *Nobel Lectures in Peace 1981–1990*, she directed them to Nobelprize.org to listen to a recording of the speech, reasoning that hearing the passion in Wiesel's voice would give students a clearer understanding of why he was awarded the prize. She also directed them to History. com to closely read *Remembering the Holocaust* (2014), a collection of photographic images taken during the Holocaust, and asked them to search through them, scavenger-hunt style. The list she provided is also shown in Figure 5.8. Ms. Koyamatsu's 10th graders searched and analyzed this largely visual text and generated written responses. They compared their scavenger hunt answers and had a rich discussion about the Holocaust, based on evidence from the speech, photos, and captions.

Figure 5.8 | **Two Lists for Writing Scavenger Hunts**

Mrs. Fink's List of Items for Fletcher's *Sorry, Wrong Number*

☐ Words that describe the setting, telling us about Mrs. Stevenson's character.
☐ Examples of things that Mrs. Stevenson does that tell us she is irritated.

   Supporting evidence:

☐ Explanation of what the lighting directions tell us about the characters:

   Supporting evidence:

☐ The number of times Mrs. Stevenson dials her husband's number:

   What this tells us about her:

   Supporting evidence:

Writing Task: Based on what you know about Mrs. Stevenson, how might this character evolve or change as the drama continues? ·

Ms. Koyamatsu's List of Items Related to History.com's *Remembering the Holocaust*

☐ The photo you found most disturbing:

   Explain why:

☐ The photo that has increased your understanding of the Holocaust the most:

   Explain why:

☐ The photo that best helps you visualize how concentration camp prisoners felt:

☐ Which words in the caption contribute to this photo's effect?

Writing Task: What do the concentration camps, gas chambers, and crematorium tell you about the treatment of the prisoners?

Students will develop and learn to use academic language when they are invited and taught to do so. As Miller and Calfee (2004) note,

> [An] individual may experience great internal delight after struggling with a message and finally "getting it." But how can external observers (teachers and researchers) tap into this experience, assuming a good reason for such an attempt? The most direct and comprehensive approach is to ask the individual to present the results of the activity, by retelling, summarizing, applying, critiquing, extending, transforming, and so on—in brief, by composing some sort of response. (p. 229)

As students participate in scavenger hunts as a dimension of close reading, they will be addressing Language Standard 3: *Apply knowledge of language to understand how language functions in different contexts, to make effective choices for meaning or style, and to comprehend more fully when reading or listening* (CCRA.L.3).

≡◆≡

The Common Core State Standards give us hope that the interrelated processes of language, writing, and reading will be taught as such. As identified in this chapter, close reading, the analytic discussion it involves, and the follow-up activities and projects it can lead to provide an excellent context for developing these proficiencies, which will, in turn, enhance students' ability to learn from texts. In Chapter 6, we'll examine how teachers, during a close reading, can assess students for the purpose of making informed and helpful "next step" decisions about instruction.

CHAPTER 6

ASSESSING TO SUPPORT MEANING MAKING DURING CLOSE READING

How do we assess students' performance during close reading? To begin to answer this question, pause and think about how you assess the performance of your students on any instructional task. Then think about *why* you assess their performance.

Wise teachers assess student performance and progress not just to assign grades but also to identify strengths and needs as related to the accomplishment of an identified learning purpose or objective. They know that assessment isn't a single event that takes place at the end of a lesson or unit; it's a process of collecting data to inform decisions about the best next step to support student learning, given students' growing strengths and changing needs (Lapp, Fisher, Flood, Cabello, 2001).

This process—the recursive cycle of using evidence of student understanding to adjust instructional practice—is what Popham (2008), Frey and Fisher (2011), and others describe as *formative assessment.* It has become increasingly familiar in today's classrooms, and the explanation for this is simple: formative assessment helps to improve student learning because it provides teachers with insights regarding their students' learning progress toward well-defined goals. Students who are in the classrooms of teachers who employ formative assessment practices outperform students in other classes. After conducting a comprehensive review of the research related to formative assessment practices, Black and Wiliam (1998) concluded, "Innovations that include strengthening the practice of formative assessment produce significant and often substantial learning gains" (p. 140). Hattie and Timperley (2007) found a 29 percent gain in achievement for students in classrooms with teachers who employed a formative assessment cycle; this was almost double the gains made by students in classrooms where teachers employed other, more traditional forms of assessment.

The gathering of performance-based insights through formative assessment is a very critical feature of close reading instruction, as these insights provide an ongoing means of supporting a student's comprehension growth. Here's how it plays out. Once a teacher has determined the purpose for closely reading a selected passage during the instructional planning stage and has identified the related performance task(s), he or she can assess the understanding students are sharing through their annotations, partner and whole-class collaborations, and written responses. Students' responses also offer insights about their developing self-awareness as close readers. The mental and written notes collected while listening in, observing, and discussing a text with students are data a teacher uses to inform subsequent instructional decisions.

Formative assessment during instruction is an ongoing process—and this is no less the case when it's done in conjunction with close reading. The growth that occurs through this process of formatively assessing student performance as related to identified standards and adjusting instruction to address students' identified strengths and needs prepares them for the PARCC and Smarter Balanced summative assessments that are also aligned with the Common Core standards (see Chapter 1).

In this chapter, we examine the cycle of formative assessment as a pathway to gather insights about the comprehension that is occurring for students as they engage in a close analysis of texts across the disciplines. Our purpose is to emphasize how formative assessment supports teachers as they observe student performance, and then, working from these observed behaviors, provide instructional scaffolds to further students' growth as readers who understand how to deeply analyze texts. We also illustrate how the scaffolded instruction that occurs as a result of formative assessment can be aligned with the Common Core standards that are measured by the PARCC and Smarter Balanced summative assessments.

An Overview of the Formative Assessment Cycle

Formative assessment is an ongoing process that asks teachers to *identify* standards, *plan* related instruction, *teach, assess* student performance, *analyze* collected information to identify patterns of student need, and *plan* forward steps or revisions to instruction that will address the perceived needs. The goal is to use continually collected performance data to plan additional instruction and interventions to help all students achieve the identified standards.

For a classroom teacher, the cycle of formative assessment begins with identifying the lesson purpose; making note of the standards that will serve as the foundation for the lesson; and plotting instruction in logical, purposeful segments that will advance students, step by step, toward the achievement of those standards. Although an initial, big-picture pre-assessment may help a teacher identify teaching points that, when addressed, will help students achieve identified standards, this is just the beginning of a formative assessment cycle. At predetermined points within the lesson, the teacher takes a measure of student progress, quickly analyzes data gathered, and alters instruction and instructional tasks as needed to continue moving all students toward the learning goal.

Guided instruction occurring during the *we do it* phase of the Gradual Release of Responsibility model (Fisher & Frey, 2014a; Lapp, Grant, Moss, & Johnson, 2013; Pearson & Gallagher, 1983), in which a teacher works closely with students, provides excellent opportunities for formatively assessing how well individual students are learning information that will help them reach each learning target. Teachers can also gather formative assessment data by monitoring students' verbal responses to direct questions, partner-talk conversations, lab reports, collaborative participation, quizzes, exit and entry slips, response logs, graphic organizers, presentations, writing samples, self-assessments, and any other work samples that provide evidence regarding current learning.

In short, formative assessment provides the path needed to connect national and grade-level standards, learning targets, instruction, and continuous insights. It's a way to identify how well you are teaching and how well your students are learning. Well-planned formative assessment provides very precise information that will allow you to effectively scaffold instruction in order to address your students' different needs, build on their strengths, and provide each of them better access to challenging curriculum.

Formative Assessment and Close Reading

The formative cycle of teaching and assessment starts with the teacher identifying standards-related learning targets that contain well-articulated, identifiable measures of success. It continues with the teacher identifying "assessment points"—the places within the lesson where he or she will gather, formally or informally, data about the learning that is occurring and use that data to make an instructional adjustment.

As illustrated in Figure 6.1, the formative assessment cycle informs close reading instruction in much the same way. The identified lesson purpose is the goal for the close reading—and it generally includes Common Core Reading Anchor Standard 1 in addition to whatever disciplinary standards may be

Figure 6.1 | **Formative Assessment Within Close Reading Instruction**

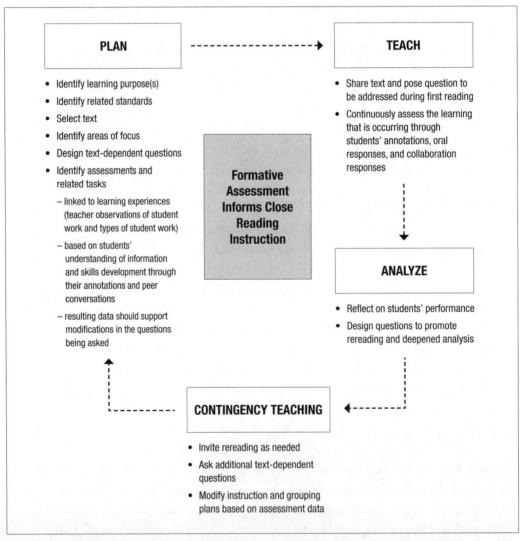

involved. The assessment points can be mapped to the various readings, teaching points, or features of the text, and the assessment tools include observation of students' annotations and independent reading behaviors, student comments in their partner talks/discussions, student responses to direct questioning, student self-assessments (like the one in Figure 5.1; see p. 140), students' written follow-up work, and students' behaviors during reading. The instructional adjustments are often revisions to the planned text-dependent questions, but they can also be new instructional modes/groupings or instructional sessions to backfill knowledge or vocabulary.

Formative Assessment in a 10th Grade Science Class

The following scenario provides an example of how a 10th grade science teacher, Mrs. Karina Ramirez, revised her instruction as a result of information gleaned while listening to the students as they engaged in conversation about a text they were closely reading—the Common Core informational text exemplar *Circumference: Eratosthenes and the Ancient Quest to Measure the Globe* by Nicholas Nicastro (2008). The standard guiding this close reading session was the Common Core's Reading Standard 1 for Literacy in Science in grades 9–10:

> **RST.9–10.1.** Cite specific textual evidence to support analysis of science and technical texts, attending to the precise details of explanations or descriptions.

Students were also beginning the work that would ultimately allow them to address a Next Generation Science Standard focused on Earth and Space Sciences (and, more specifically, on understanding the universe and its stars):

> **HS-ESS1-4.** Use mathematical or computational representations to predict the motion of orbiting objects in the solar system.

At this point, Mrs. Ramirez wanted students to consider how scientists of the past have utilized engineering, design, and tools to learn about Earth and celestial objects in space. Here is the purpose she sets: *Students will understand how tools and technological devices have helped us to learn about Earth.*

Mrs. Ramirez always begins her close reading lessons by asking students to do the first reading independently, and she always prepares them for possible struggle by saying something like this: "I know that you will encounter new words and unfamiliar phrases. Remember that you should persist—keep going, keep reading. With each new reading of this text, you will gain more understanding. You will also have the chance to chat with your classmates. Through your conversations, you will work together to gain insights about the text."

For this first reading of *Circumference*, Mrs. Ramirez had all students focus on the text-dependent question about the text's overall meaning: *What big ideas did you get from this text?* She encouraged them to highlight the sentences or phrases that supported their interpretation. After all students had finished reading and annotating the text, Mrs. Ramirez directed them to turn to their elbow partners to share their responses to the first question, accurately quoting lines from the text as evidence. She listened in as Evie talked with Iman:

> *Evie:* I think this is about how people used to make measurements with a thing called an astrolabe. And there's information about circumference and star measurements.
>
> *Iman:* I saw that too. Look at this line: *This image, which was typically etched on a brass plate, was inserted into a round frame (the* mater*) whose circumference was marked in degrees or hours. Over the plate was fitted a latticework disk, the rete, with pointers to indicate the positions of major stars.*
>
> *Evie:* I'm trying to picture an astrolabe, but it's hard because I don't know what this brass plate really looks like. Like, how big is it? Is it a piece of metal in a square or round shape?

To Mrs. Ramirez, Evie's struggle to visualize the device was a concern. She decided her next text-dependent question would require students to look at the details regarding the design of the astrolabe and refocus them on how the device was used—a point that was central to understanding the text. She also made a note to look for an illustrated partner text that would *show* an astrolabe as well as discuss it. Using the information she gathered from listening to students talk, Mrs. Ramirez asked students to read the text a second time: "Closely read with this key detail question in mind: *How did the design of the astrolabe help scientists measure angular height of mountaintops and stars?* Be sure you continue to annotate the text and jot down questions in the margins."

Following the second close reading, Mrs. Ramirez again asked students to turn to their partners to chat about the key detail question. Mariah told Miguel that she sketched a picture in the margin of the text to help her understand the astrolabe better. Moving toward Evie and Iman, Mrs. Ramirez heard Evie say again that she thought the astrolabe was too hard and confusing to picture. It was time for a direct intervention. She leaned in, pointed to a sentence, and asked Evie to reread it aloud.

> *Evie: The fundamental innovation underlying the astrolabe was the projection of an image of the sky (usually the northern hemisphere, centered on Polaris) on a plane corresponding to the Earth's equator.*

> *Mrs. Ramirez:* What is the innovation of the astrolabe, according to that sentence? Read it once again to yourself. I'll wait.

> *Evie: . . .* The innovation must be that it has an image of stars in the sky. I know Polaris is a star. We learned that.

> *Mrs. Ramirez:* OK, good. Now let's look at the next sentence. What does it tell you about what an astrolabe might look like?

> *Evie: This image, which was typically etched on a brass plate, was inserted into a round frame (the mater) whose circumference was marked in degrees or hours. Over the plate was fitted a lattice-work disk, the rete, with pointers to indicate the positions of major stars. . . .* I think there might be a picture of the night sky on a round piece of metal. The metal could be marked like a protractor with degrees. I think there's a pointer . . . like the hand of a clock. Is that right?

> *Mrs. Ramirez:* Yes, terrific thinking. You stuck with this complex description and developed a mental image of the device. Good work!

While Mrs. Ramirez was pleased that Evie was able to picture an astrolabe, she was even happier that Evie had persevered—had worked through complex, language-intensive text featuring unfamiliar vocabulary without giving up. Mrs. Ramirez did not supply Evie with the information she needed; rather, she used questions to prompt Evie to reread to find and analyze the information herself and come to an understanding.

It was now time to make some larger connections. Glancing down at the clipboard holding her prepared set of text-dependent questions and notes, Mrs. Ramirez turned to the rest of the class and said, "For the next close reading, I'd like you to focus on the technical innovations of the astrolabe. As you've noted, the author states that the astrolabe has been called the world's first personal computer. How does the author support this statement?" Identifying supporting evidence is an essential part of reading in science. This text-dependent question was strategically offered to help students connect the idea of evidence to statements or claims. After the third close reading, Mrs. Ramirez listened in on Mariah and Miguel's discussion.

> *Mariah:* How can an old instrument be like a computer? A computer is high tech. I'm not really sure about this.

> *Miguel:* Right? Computers do so much, and this astrolabe is basically just a piece of metal. . . .

Again, Mrs. Ramirez stepped in to provide clarification through questioning.

> *Mrs. Ramirez:* How do we use computers in our lives? How do you use them for school, for example?

> *Mariah:* Well, I use mine for writing assignments, like to write essays and reports and poems. I look things up. I research topics . . . and I check my grades online. Oh, and sometimes, I put my school science data on them. I make tables for that. I use computers lots of ways. I even take tests for some of my classes on a computer.

> *Mrs. Ramirez:* Perfect. Now look again at the text. Do astrolabes help us—help people—in similar ways? Do they help us do work? Do they help us to figure things out? Reread and think about it.

> *Mariah:* . . . OK, yes! Here the author talks about all the things an astrolabe can do. It can find the times of sunrise and sunset, predict eclipses, find stars or constellations, and it can measure the height of objects on Earth and the circumference of the Earth.

> *Miguel:* And it collects measurements, which are data. A computer collects data, too.

> *Mariah:* I think I've got it now. An astrolabe and a computer make collecting information easier.

Through her use of formative assessment during close reading and guided instruction, Mrs. Ramirez was able to address the specific learning needs of individual students. She was able to stem confusion and misconceptions, hone their evidence-finding skills, and move them toward a deeper understanding of the text. As you can see in this example, when a lesson's learning targets are explicit, the teacher can design instruction and then assess throughout the lesson to continuously identify the extent of the learning that is occurring for each student. As problems arise due to unfamiliar language, unknown concepts, lack of background knowledge, or lack of reading proficiency, the teacher can ask additional questions or refocus a student's attention to information in the text that can support comprehension. When these supports are not sufficient during the close reading instruction, the teacher may need to convene a smaller group of students and provide instruction that addresses the problem areas.

Formative Assessment in a 10th Grade English Class

Here's another example that illustrates how a teacher can continuously observe students' performance and make the necessary instructional adjustments that will help them accomplish the lesson purpose. In Robert Jackson's 10th grade English class, students were getting ready to closely read an excerpt from Chapter 4 of Maya Angelou's *I Know Why the Caged Bird Sings,* a Common Core text exemplar. Before starting the reading, Mr. Jackson wanted to provide an opportunity for students to build background knowledge about the use of metaphor that would help them better grasp the inspiration and context for Angelou's work He announced the lesson purpose (for students to understand how metaphor is used as a communication device), and began class by asking them to listen to an audio reading of Paul Laurence Dunbar's "Sympathy" (1889), the poem that provided Angelou with the title of her memoir, *I Know Why the Caged Bird Sings.* "I'm passing out copies of the poem now," Mr. Jackson told his students. "I want you to read along with the recording, and I want you to use your colored pencils, please, to highlight the big ideas that Dunbar, the poet, is sharing."

When the audio recording ended, he asked students to chat in partner pairs about the big ideas they had identified and to pinpoint the language that helped them find those big ideas. As Mr. Jackson listened in, here's what he heard.

> *Tameka:* At first the poem sounded nice: *the wind stirs soft through the springing grass/And the river flows like a stream of glass.* That's a pretty scene. But I don't get why the poem starts to sound sad. Like when it says, *the caged bird beats his wing/Till its blood is red on the cruel bars.* That sounds horrible!
>
> *Tony*: Why would a bird beat his wings till he bleeds? That's pretty weird, huh?

After a few minutes of listening to student conversations and observing student actions, Mr. Jackson realized that he needed to provide more instruction.

> *Mr. Jackson:* OK, everybody, let's pause and think back to when we read Langston Hughes's poem "Mother to Son." Remember when we drew our images of the stairs that the mother had to climb?
>
> *Tanisha:* It was a stairway with tacks and splinters, not like a real stairway. It was a metaphor.
>
> *Mr. Jackson:* Exactly: a metaphor. I want everybody to think about the concept of a metaphor as you read and listen to "Sympathy" again. And think about this question: *What words does the poet use to let you know how the bird feels in his cage?*

After the second close reading and round of notation, Mr. Jackson again checked in on partner conversations.

> *Christina:* I think line 12 tells us how the bird feels: *And a pain still throbs in the old, old scars.* He's hurt. He's sad.
>
> *Daniel:* Yeah. And look at line 18: *It is not a carol of joy or glee,/But prayer that he sends from his heart's deep core,/But a plea.* The bird wants to be free, right?

Satisfied his students were moving toward an understanding of the metaphor, Mr. Jackson announced, "We're going to listen one more time. This time think about this question: *What was the poet's purpose in writing this poem?*" Again, students listened and made annotations to record their thinking. During the partner talk about this question, Mr. Jackson heard a comment from Marcus that he asked Marcus to share with the whole class: "The poet wrote this because he wanted to talk about freedom and how it feels if you don't have it. I think this is not really about a bird, but about people who feel trapped, like they're in a cage." At this point, Mr. Jackson was confident his students were ready to take on Maya Angelou's text.

Let's look at what Mr. Jackson did here. During his planning, he determined that his students' rudimentary knowledge of metaphor would hinder their investigation of Angelou's text. But rather than provide a lesson on metaphor, he had his students engage in a close reading of an alternate, less difficult text—Dunbar's poem. Through this close reading, he scaffolded their developing knowledge that authors use metaphor to make implied comparisons between things that may be very different but do have some common characteristics, and he got them used to thinking metaphorically. Mr. Jackson also provided access to this less difficult text in an alternate format—a recording of a fluent reader that allowed them to listen as well as read. By asking text-dependent questions about Dunbar's poem and listening to the resulting discussion, Mr. Jackson was able to guide his students to knowledge they would need to engage with *I Know Why the Caged Bird Sings*, grasp its author's use of metaphor, and unlock its complex meanings.

As we mentioned in Chapter 1, one misconception about close reading is that teachers give students a complex text and then leave them alone to struggle their way to understanding. While we do advocate limiting the frontloading of information at the start of close reading sessions so that students have the opportunity to gain independent insight, little is gained by throwing students into the lion's den of a text that is simply too difficult for them. If there are huge language or background knowledge gaps separating students from understanding, the close reading session will almost certainly lead to frustration or failure. This is the scenario envisioned by those who wonder if the use of close reading will produce a generation of students who hate to read. We must reiterate that incorporating close reading is not about leaving students alone with extremely difficult texts that they cannot understand because they don't have sufficient topic knowledge or reading proficiency or don't understand the text's language, structure, or features. On the contrary, as we have illustrated, close reading instruction offers teachers the opportunity to teach their students a process they can use to access deep meaning. By leveraging what they do know and understand, by asking questions, by reading and rereading, they learn to unpack texts that are complex but within their reach.

Formative Assessment in an 11th Grade Science Class

Here's an additional scenario that illustrates how formative assessment supports the continual improvement of teaching and learning through the construction of scaffolds that move all students' learning forward and help them attain lesson purposes and meet standards.

In Rachel Golding's 11th grade class, students were studying radiation in a unit linked to both a Next Generation Science Standard focused on waves and their applications in technologies for information transfer and a Common Core standard for reading in science and technical subjects:

HS-PS4-4. Evaluate the validity and reliability of claims in published materials of the effects that different frequencies of electromagnetic radiation have when absorbed by matter.

RST.11–12.4. Determine the meaning of symbols, key terms, and other domain-specific words and phrases as they are used in a specific scientific or technical context relevant to grades 11–12 texts and topics.

In the early stages of the unit, Ms. Golding had provided her students with experiences to help them understand the electromagnetic spectrum. They participated in a jigsaw activity in which they researched and then shared information about the characteristics and behaviors of electromagnetic waves at different frequencies. They built spectroscopes on meter sticks and used gas tubes glowing in power supplies to study and measure light frequencies. They also read texts about the uses of electromagnetic waves and about the effects of exposure to electromagnetic fields, including a document posted by the World Health Organization.

At this point, the stage was properly set. Students were prepared with the background knowledge they needed to engage in a close reading of a complex text on the topic of radiation. To begin, Ms. Golding asked the whole class to closely read "Radiation Sickness—Symptoms," an online text authored by the Mayo Clinic Staff (2014) that provides specific facts about radiation exposure. After an initial reading and partner chat that asked the students to identify the general information in the passage, she asked them to closely read it again and respond to this question: *What's the relationship between the time of onset for symptoms and the amount of radiation exposure?*

For two minutes, students examined this short article, which contained a chart, and noted the relationship between data presented in the chart and discussed in the text. After this round of reading and annotating, Ms. Golding asked students to chat in pairs about the features they discovered and to identify where the information had been found. She listened in.

> *Dave:* There's a big decrease in the time of onset of symptoms with an increase in the amount of radiation exposure. You can see it on the chart. As the absorbed amount of radiation increases by two to four grays [the unit for absorption], the time of symptom onset decreases by a really big amount.

Ms. Golding noted Dave's astute comment and how he connected it to the data. She moved on to partners Amad and Chloe.

> *Amad:* Sorry, I'm not getting these numbers. Maybe it's my English? I don't get how a gray connects to radiation. I've only ever heard of gray as a color! This is so confusing.

> *Chloe:* A gray is a measurement you use with radiation, like you use a degree when talking about temperature. See there in the second paragraph? *The absorbed dose of radiation is measured in a unit called a gray (Gy). Diagnostic tests that use radiation, such as an X-ray, result in a small dose of radiation—typically well below 0.1 Gy, focused on a few organs or small amount of tissue.*

Amad, still looking puzzled, put his head on the desk. It was clear to Ms. Golding that she would need to take a differentiated approach in order to help both struggling students, like Amad, and students ready for extended challenge, like Chloe and Dave, to continue to move their learning forward.

The next day, she divided the class into small groups and sent them to various learning stations for hands-on exploration. Station 1 had an investigation tool—a cloud chamber activity that allowed students to look at the footprints of radiation. At this station, students were directed to use a premade cloud chamber and a flashlight to see "trails" coming from a simulated source of radiation. (This required the lights in the classroom to be turned off periodically.) Students recorded observational data in their science notebooks. At Station 2, students reviewed a document from NASA that detailed the risks and symptoms of radiation exposure. Station 3 had students examining how radiation is measured. Station 4 was the teacher station. There, Ms. Golding met with Amad and three other English language learners to look at how data in charts, like the one they had examined in the initial reading, could be used to represent real-world science phenomena. To foster better understanding, Ms. Golding asked the group to analyze another chart in an online article at BBC.com that related similar data using a related unit of measure called a sievert. She conducted a think-aloud, articulating how she viewed the chart. Then she asked the students in this small group to think aloud with partners to describe what they noticed about the numbers and the amount of danger to humans.

As evidenced in this scenario, Ms. Golding and the entire 11th grade class were engaged in an exploration of the topic of electromagnetic radiation absorption. She often involved the class in whole-group activities as a way to promote conversation and collaboration. During the students' initial conversations about the Mayo Clinic article and its chart, she determined that she needed to tailor her instructional plans to accommodate her students' varying strengths and needs, so she moved from whole-group to small-group instruction. Her actions illustrate very well the processes of using formative assessment during close reading instruction.

Using Formative Assessment to Build Close Reading Skill

As we know, close reading involves students returning to a text passage to study language and ideas presented at the word, sentence, paragraph, and passage levels. This demands sustained interest and energy on the part of the reader. Of course, closely reading a text also empowers the reader to comprehend, critique, and evaluate ideas within and across texts. This results in the acquisition of an informed base of knowledge that the reader can use to take a stance and present an enlightened argument.

This is the goal we are working toward, of course, but students develop this facility over time and at different paces, and the teacher has a vital role to play in scaffolding students' close reading efforts in order to support forward momentum. As Vygotsky (1978) reminds us, the scaffolding of instruction by a knowledgeable teacher helps a learner build new or extended knowledge from that learner's existing base of knowledge. The scaffolds we provide should be temporary, and as the knowledge of the learner increases, so should learning independence. The overall goal of scaffolding is to help students to become independent, self-regulating learners and problem solvers who understand how to advance their own learning.

Think now about how closely this goal parallels the goal of teaching students to analyze complex texts. Teaching them to closely read a text means teaching them to think deeply about the text message by engaging in dialogue or conversation with the author as a means to determine the message and the author's intent in sharing it. It empowers students to be critical thinkers and independent seekers of understanding.

Building Close Reading Skill in 6th Grade Social Studies

Let's look at an example of how 6th grade teacher Jamie Yee developed his students' close reading skills, pushing them back into a complex text to identify the author's intent. The text was *This Land Was Made for You and Me: The Life and Songs of Woody Guthrie*, a Common Core exemplar for grades 6–8 written by Elizabeth Partridge (2002). The class session began with Mr. Yee identifying the lesson's purpose: for students to get a better understanding of how cultural phenomena—including art, books, poetry, and music—often reflect events in history.

Using Partridge's text as a starting point, Mr. Yee asked this general understanding question: *In what ways did Woody Guthrie expose himself to different forms of music?* Students read and annotated with that question in mind, marking personal copies of the text with colored pencils as Mr. Yee had taught them to do. Cedella used a blue pencil to underline the phrase *He'd stick out his thumb and hitchhike, swing onto moving freight trains, and hunker down with other traveling men* and then drew a line to the margin and wrote, "traveled this way." After the first reading, Mr. Yee paused for partner chats, saying, "Talk with your tablemates about ways that Woody Guthrie exposed himself to different forms of music."

> *Robert:* It says right here that *he moved restlessly from state to state, soaking up some songs: work songs, mountain and cowboy songs, sea chanteys, songs from the southern chain gangs.*

> *Cedella:* And he also heard music from his family and neighborhood friends and stuff: *He added them to the dozens he already knew from childhood.*

None of the students Mr. Yee observed pointed out the evidence that Guthrie was influenced by the events of the Great Depression. Maybe they weren't familiar with it, and didn't pick up on the text's mention of Hoovervilles? To help spotlight the Great Depression, Mr. Yee asked the students to develop Frayer cards (see Figure 6.2 for an example), using online dictionaries and information from a website to guide their work.

With 15 minutes of class still remaining, Mr. Yee returned the students to the Partridge text with this text-dependent question focused on finding key details: *Is there any evidence that lets you know when Woody Guthrie began writing songs?* Now that students had the background vocabulary knowledge they needed, they reread the text for evidence.

Figure 6.2 | **Frayer Word Card Used in Close Reading of Partridge's**
This Land Was Made for You and Me

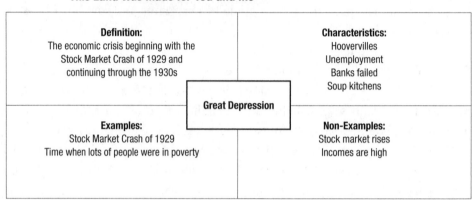

Zach: Look at this part: *hunker down with other traveling men in flophouses, hobo jungles, and Hoovervilles across Depression America.*

Connor: So he began writing songs during the Great Depression. That's how this reading connects to history.

Based on this student conversation, Mr. Yee was satisfied that they understood the concept of the Great Depression. He sent students back into the text to reread independently and address the final text-dependent question: *Does the author provide evidence to show how Guthrie used his experiences of the Great Depression to compose his songs?*

As students continued reading and annotating, Mr. Yee noticed that Cedella was numbering her evidence, writing notes above each line of the text that supported the notion that Guthrie wrote songs that reflected the times and his experiences. During the follow-up chat session with her tablemates, she clearly outlined her evidence: "The author tells us that Woody wrote *hard-bitten, rough-edged songs that told it like it was, full of anger and hardship and hope and love.*" She added, "Based on what this says, I bet Woody saw all those things on his travels and wrote about those feelings in his songs."

As this scenario illustrates, even 6th graders are able to critique the contents of informational text to seek substantial evidence to support a concept or opinion if they are provided with scaffolded instruction that emerges from continuous formative assessment during the instructional sequence. For students who struggle with the reading level or the length of the text, repeated readings, interspersed with strategically crafted text-dependent questions and occasional scaffolding tasks like the creation of a Frayer card, may be warranted. Mr. Yee's questions prompted his students to think deeply about the language the author used. Although students applied existing knowledge—and some newly acquired knowledge of the Great Depression—to answer his questions, Mr. Yee cautioned them to think about the author's position and not let their prior knowledge obscure the author's take. What they needed to do, he reminded them, was seek out text-based evidence. With such a sophisticated academic foundation, Mr. Yee's students will be ready for the increased demands of close reading and argumentative essay writing as they move through middle school and into high school.

A Closer Look at Adjusting Close Reading Instruction in Light of Formative Data

Consider the following example of how teacher insights acquired through teacher-and-student conversations during close reading can lead to beneficial instructional adjustments that help achieve learning goals. Notice specifically how the whole-class questions relate so closely to the teachers' identified learning target. Also notice the individual discussion moves that the teachers make through the questions they ask and the prompts and clues they offer to both individual students and the whole class. In doing so, they backfill the language and background information students need to read successfully.

Instructional Adjustment in 7th Grade Social Studies

Two 7th grade social studies teachers, Michelle Valdez and Andrew Conley, coplanned a close reading session focused on a passage from Chapter 1 of Jim Murphy's (1995) literary nonfiction book *The Great Fire*, a Common Core exemplar for grades 6–8:

> Chicago in 1871 was a city ready to burn. The city boasted having 59,500 buildings, many of them—such as the Courthouse and the Tribune Building—large and ornately decorated. The trouble was that about two-thirds of all these structures were made entirely of wood. Many of the remaining buildings (even the ones proclaimed to be "fireproof") looked solid, but were actually jerrybuilt affairs; the stone or brick exteriors hid wooden frames and floors, all topped with highly flammable tar or shingle roofs. It was also a

common practice to disguise wood as another kind of building material. The fancy exterior decorations on just about every building were carved from wood, then painted to look like stone or marble. Most churches had steeples that appeared to be solid from the street, but a closer inspection would reveal a wooden framework covered with cleverly painted copper or tin.

The situation was worst in the middle-class and poorer districts. Lot sizes were small, and owners usually filled them up with cottages, barns, sheds, and outhouses—all made of fast-burning wood, naturally. Because both Patrick and Catherine O'Leary worked, they were able to put a large addition on their cottage despite a lot size of just 25 by 100 feet. Interspersed in these residential areas were a variety of businesses—paint factories, lumberyards, distilleries, gasworks, mills, furniture manufacturers, warehouses, and coal distributors.

Wealthier districts were by no means free of fire hazards. Stately stone and brick homes had wood interiors, and stood side by side with smaller wood-frame houses. Wooden stables and other storage buildings were common, and trees lined the streets and filled the yards. (pp. 18–19)

Each teacher's classroom had a similar composition of students, with a range of language and proficiency levels. Both teachers were addressing the Common Core's Reading Anchor Standard 1—specifically the 7th grade version for literacy in social studies, which states that students should be able to *cite specific textual evidence to support analysis of primary and secondary sources* (RH.6–8.1).

In their pre-planning, Mrs. Valdez and Mr. Conley established the following as their lesson purpose: *Understand why Chicago was a city ready to burn, based on its description in the text.* As you can see in Figure 6.3's side-by-side comparison of the teachers' instructional plans, they agreed on a common set of text-dependent questions. But as you can also see, Mrs. Valdez went on to make significant adjustments to her instruction in light of the formative assessment data she collected during the actual close reading session. While asking text-dependent questions and listening closely to student responses, she determined that some of the questions she and Mr. Conley had planned could be eliminated because her students didn't need them as a scaffold to support their understanding. For example, when asked, "What evidence does the author provide to back up his argument that Chicago is a city ready to burn?" students responded with specifics:

Figure 6.3 | **A Comparison of Formative Assessment Adjustments During a Close Reading**

Mrs. Valdez's Plan		Mr. Conley's Plan	
Reading	**Text-Dependent Questions**	**Reading**	**Text-Dependent Questions**
First Reading: Students Read Independently	1. What is this passage about?	**First Reading:** Students Read Independently	1. What is this passage about?
Second Reading: Students Read Independently *Skip question because students shared specific words to describe the structures after the question above. This question wasn't needed.*	2. What evidence does the author provide to back up his argument that Chicago is "a city ready to burn"? 3. What words does the author use to describe the structures in Chicago?	**Second Reading:** Students Read Independently	2. What evidence does the author provide to back up his argument that Chicago is "a city ready to burn"? 3. What words does the author use to describe the structures in Chicago?
Third Reading: Students Read Independently *Skip question 4 because students understand how businesses contributed to the fire's spread.*	4. How do the Chicago businesses contribute to the city being ready to burn? 5. What is a distillery, and how did the "human element" factor into this tragedy?	~~**Third Reading:** Students Read Independently~~ *Read the text aloud because students' comprehension is breaking down due to their disfluent reading.* *Added a question because students needed to focus on specific examples.*	4. How do the Chicago businesses contribute to the city being ready to burn? 5. What is a distillery, and how did the "human element" factor into this tragedy? *6. Think about the businesses in paragraph 2. How do the paint factories and lumberyards contribute to fire risk?*

Sam: He says in paragraph 1 that *two-thirds of all these structures were made entirely of wood*—even the ones that didn't look like wood had wood underneath.

Isabella: The wooden buildings were close together—*cottages, barns, sheds, and outhouses* crammed into really small lots.

Carly: In the neighborhoods, where you had all those buildings in small lots, there were also businesses filled with flammable stuff. It says that in paragraph 2: *paint factories, lumberyards, distilleries, gasworks, mills, furniture manufacturers, warehouses, and coal distributors.*

Mrs. Valdez realized that she didn't need to ask any other text-dependent questions connecting the author's descriptions to the city's flammable state.

By contrast, what Mr. Conley heard in his students' responses to the very first text-dependent question helped him determine that all of his planned text-dependent questions would be useful; they would provide direction and support that his students needed with a text that turned out to be very challenging for them—a true stretch. He even added a new question because it was clear from students' pattern of responses that they would benefit from another specific example of why the author called Chicago "a city ready to burn." Mr. Conley had the students reread the paragraphs a few more times than he'd planned and even stepped in to read the text aloud at a certain point, when it was clear that a significant number of students were unable to stay focused during independent reading. Both the multiple rereadings and hearing the descriptions they were reading on the page were valuable scaffolds.

Formative assessment involves attending not just to what students say in response to text-dependent questions but also to whether and how well students manage to attend to the text. Off-task behaviors and text margins filled with doodles rather than on-task notes should also be indicators that provide insights about the appropriate instructional path for each student.

Beyond Classroom Assessment of Close Reading: Summative and Formative Measures in the Common Core Assessments

As noted in the Introduction, at press time, plans are in place for students in most of the United States to be tested on their mastery of the Common Core standards via assessments developed by one of two Common Core assessment consortia: the Smarter Balanced Assessment Consortium or the Partnership for Assessment of Readiness for College and Careers. Both consortia plan to assess students in grades 3–8 and in grade 11 using an online assessment that includes a variety of item types: selected responses, constructed responses, and complex performance tasks. These assessments will be administered in the final weeks of the school year, and will employ both electronic and human scoring, and it is projected that teachers will receive their students' results within two weeks of test administration.

The results of the Common Core assessments are intended to serve as a summative assessment of the year's learning and provide teachers, students, and families with valid and reliable data on student proficiency levels. Many states have announced plans to use the summative data as a measure of teacher effectiveness, and individual teachers might also use these results to reflect on the effectiveness of their teaching practices and help them identify focus areas for the following year. Educators will also be able to compare student proficiency levels and achievement growth among schools, districts, and states.

Both Smarter Balanced and PARCC also plan to provide optional interim assessments that can be administered throughout the year to generate formative data teachers can use to plan more effective instruction. They can examine student scores to determine which standards need more attention and which areas of instruction need more explicit teaching and scaffolding. The idea is that if a teacher's students do not do well on assessment items that ask them to use details from the text to support answers, the teacher needs to explicitly teach the processes of revisiting text, annotating it, and using a graphic organizer to become more proficient at identifying text-supported evidence.

One of the major differences between the two consortia is that PARCC uses a fixed-form delivery, while Smarter Balanced uses adaptive delivery, meaning students will see individually tailored sets of items and tasks. The adaptive delivery system presents the student with the next assessment question based on the response to the question just answered. Students who answer satisfactorily will get more challenging questions or move on to different aspects of the assessment. Students who answer unsatisfactorily will get more questions at the same level of challenge or less. The intention is that all students, through the answering of text-dependent questions, will be building a base of knowledge, language, and reading skill that will allow the complexity of the texts they read to increase. This adaptive system is a form of formative assessment in that the series of questions to which a student responds is individualized based on his or her responses.

Starting in 2015–2016, PARCC assessments will also include a locally scored, non-summative speaking and listening test intended to provide students opportunities to demonstrate skills they need to perform successfully at school and will later need in workplace situations. Students will show off their speaking and listening prowess through both real-time engagement and assessments for which they can do advanced preparation. The Real-Time performance assessments, administered in grades 3, 5, 7, 9, and 11, will involve students in listening to prerecorded speeches and media productions and then responding to related questions. The Advanced Preparation assessments, administered in grades 4, 6, 8, 10, and 12, will give students time to conduct research on authentic topics and then require them to give a formal spoken presentation of their findings (assessing speaking skills) and respond spontaneously to questions from the audience (assessing both listening and speaking skills). The teachers who will be scoring these speaking and listening assessments will be cautioned to be sensitive to presentations by English language learners and students with disabilities; dialects or "mispronunciations" that diverge from the standard academic register are not to be viewed as errors. In addition to using the data from these interim assessments in a formative manner to inform decisions about the speaking and listening instruction and opportunities students will receive in classrooms, teachers might also use them in assigning grades. The instructional scenarios included in Chapter 5 provide examples that can help you support the speaking and listening skill development of your students.

Both assessment consortia pledge to provide information that is helpful in determining school effectiveness, directions for teaching, learning and program improvement, and individual student college and career readiness.

Making "Big" Summative Assessments Useful in the Classroom

Teachers have often been concerned that their students' scores on state and national assessments do not connect to their classroom instruction, either because the data from these assessments do not reach teachers in a timely fashion or because the data are in a format that does not identify the specific areas in which a student needs support. This concern has not gone unnoticed. The SAT, a high-stakes summative college admissions assessment, is being redesigned to more closely reflect what is being taught in schools. According to David Coleman, president of the College Board, the present reading and writing items on the SAT will be replaced with source materials "important for educated Americans to know and understand deeply" and test items that require students to provide evidence and justification for their responses (Balf, 2014, p. 31).

The historical lack of usefulness of national test results highlights a mismatch between the intent of the assessments and teachers' intended uses of the results. Teachers generally want assessment data they can use to focus on student response as a way to monitor and further plan instruction. This is what formative assessment data collected during any type of instruction, including close reading instruction, has the potential to give us: immediate and continual feedback on students' ability to analyze complex text and access the content of the discipline. This information is extremely useful in daily instructional planning. When you are creating an assessment task to use in association with a close reading session or formulating the text-dependent questions you plan to use, always ask yourself this key question: *How will students' responses inform my instructional planning, reveal the progress they are making, and point me toward the instructional interventions I may need to make?*

That said, summative assessment items on large-scale assessments can also be useful in instructional planning. We recommend taking a look at the large depository of sample assessment items and performance tasks that Smarter Balanced provides at http://sampleitems.smarterbalanced.org/itempreview/sbac/ELA.htm. These items are sortable by grade bands and content focus, and evaluation rubrics are also provided.

Analyzing items associated with the grade or grades you teach not only is a great way to gain insight about the skills that are being assessed and the kind of instruction you need to provide; it also drives home how close reading will help students develop the skills and stamina they need to read test items critically and analytically.

For example, a Smarter Balanced sample performance task for evaluating Writing Standard 3, called "The Invasion of Kudzu" (Item 43016), asks students in grades 9–12 to read "an excerpt from a student's report," look for extraneous details, and then identify sentences that should be cut and explain why those sentences are not necessary. In order to accomplish this writing task, students must read the paragraph closely enough to note key details, understand which information is necessary to support the overall message and meaning of the text, recognize extraneous information that is not, and express this case in writing. This assessment example illustrates the type of reading and writing skills and strategies that students will need to be taught in order to respond accurately to multistep assessments when these appear on future assessments.

Remember, too, that the Common Core State Standards offer learning progressions for each identified anchor standard—including Reading Anchor Standard 1, which focuses on closely reading literary and informational texts. Although these progressions are not based on research data, Pearson (2013), in communication with the developers of the Common Core, documented that these progressions are based on a consensus of expert opinion regarding how the identified skills develop. In our view, using an authoritative body of experts to make such decisions is a valid way of establishing such a progression. In fact, as we mentioned in the Introduction, this is pretty similar to how basal reader skill progressions have been established for decades. In Figure 6.4, we share the progression of Reading Anchor Standard 1 from grades 6–12, along with a few

Figure 6.4 | Reading Anchor Standard 1: Progression of Instruction and Assessment, Grades 6–12

CCR.R.1. Read closely to determine what the text says explicitly and to make logical inferences from it; cite specific textual evidence when writing or speaking to support conclusions drawn from the text.

Grade-Level Standard*	Area of Focus—Instructional Possibilities	Examples of Assessment
Grade 6 **RI.6.1.** Cite textual evidence to support analysis of what the text says explicitly as well as inferences drawn from the text. **RL.6.1.** Cite textual evidence to support analysis of what the text says explicitly as well as inferences drawn from the text. **RH.6–8.1.** Cite specific textual evidence to support analysis of primary and secondary sources. **RST.6–8.1.** Cite specific textual evidence to support analysis of science and technical texts.	By the time students are in 6th grade, they should be able to identify evidence to support the inferences they are making while reading both fiction and informational text. *Sample Informational Text Question:* If you had been asked to rebuild homes after the Chicago fire, what materials would you have used? Use text information to support your thinking.	1. What did the author mostly likely mean by the phrase "Chicago in 1871 was a city ready to burn" (Murphy, *The Great Fire*)? Support your answer with evidence from the text. 2. What factors in both the wealthy and poor districts of Chicago contributed to the homes and buildings being destroyed in the fire of 1871? Use evidence from the text to support your answer. 3. Look at the newspaper article from 1871 and the text from Murphy's *The Great Fire* to identify similar facts regarding the causes of the Great Chicago Fire from each source. 4. What materials were least fire resistant? (Click all that apply.) A. "shingle roofs" B. "wood frames" C. "stone or brick" D. "flammable tar" E. "painted copper or tin"
Grade 7 **RI.7.1.** Cite several pieces of textual evidence to support analysis of what the text says explicitly as well as inferences drawn from the text. **RL.7.1.** Cite several pieces of textual evidence to support analysis of what the text says explicitly as well as inferences drawn from the text. **RH.6–8.1.** Cite specific textual evidence to support analysis of primary and secondary sources. **RST.6–8.1.** Cite specific textual evidence to support analysis of science and technical texts.	By grade 7, students should be able to support their analysis of a text by citing several pieces of information. *Sample Informational Text Question:* What words and phrases did Winston Churchill use to indicate his feelings regarding war?	**Part A** Which of these inferences about the author's point of view is best supported by Winston Churchill's "Blood, Toil, Tears and Sweat" speech to Parliament? A. The author believes that he was joining his men on the front lines for battle. B. The author believes that the war should not be ended until it is won. C. The author believes that there was a justification for the war. D. The author believes that the war will end quickly. **Part B** Which sentence from the text supports your answer in Part A? A. "It is victory. Victory at all costs—Victory in spite of all terrors." B. "Come then, let us go forward together with our united strength." C. "We have before us an ordeal of the most grievous kind." D. "I have nothing to offer but blood, toil, tears, and sweat."

Grade 8 **RI.8.1.** Cite the textual evidence that most strongly supports an analysis of what the text says explicitly as well as inferences drawn from the text. **RL.8.1.** Cite the textual evidence that most strongly supports an analysis of what the text says explicitly as well as inferences drawn from the text. **RH.6–8.1.** Cite specific textual evidence to support analysis of primary and secondary sources. **RST.6–8.1.** Cite specific textual evidence to support analysis of science and technical texts.	Notice the specificity of the type of evidence that students should be able to cite by 8th grade. It is the evidence that *most strongly* supports inference making. *Sample Informational Text Question:* What descriptions does author Elizabeth Partridge share about Guthrie that help you get a better understanding of him as a songwriter?	1. What conclusions can be drawn about Partridge's impressions of Woody Guthrie in "Ramblin Round?" Support your answer with details from the text. 2. Which sentence from the text best reveals how Partridge feels about Guthrie's music? A. "He moved restlessly from state to state, soaking up some songs." B. "It was an easy song that people could sing the first time they heard it, remember, and sing it again later." C. "He added to songs he already knew." D. "He always had fifteen to twenty songs running around in his mind."
Grades 9–10 **RI.9–10.1.** Cite strong and thorough textual evidence to support analysis of what the text says explicitly as well as inferences drawn from the text. **RL.9–10.1.** Cite strong and thorough textual evidence to support analysis of what the text says explicitly as well as inferences drawn from the text. **RH.9–10.1.** Cite specific textual evidence to support analysis of primary and secondary sources, attending to such features as the date and origin of the information. **RST.9–10.1.** Cite specific textual evidence to support analysis of science and technical texts, attending to the precise details of explanations or descriptions.	By grades 9 and 10, the type of evidence that students are asked to note must be very thorough in nature. Notice that in history, thoroughness of evidence includes adding the date and location that contextualizes the text. In science, thoroughness includes details and explanations. *Sample Informational Text Question:* What details about art does author Phillip Isaacson help us to understand through his description of the pyramids? *Sample Informational Text Question:* Why does author Annie J. Cannon refer to the rainbow as "Nature's most glorious demonstration that light is composed of many colors"?	1. Which three phrases in *A Short Walk Through the Pyramids and Through the World of Art* that the author uses to refer to "spirit harmony" help clarify the meaning of the term? (Choose 3.) A. "… cordial companion for a simple, logical, pleasing shape …" B. "… the stone and the shape are so comfortable with each other …" C. "…sitting in their field is breathtaking …" D. "…too perfect to have been formed by nature …" E. "… their broad proportions, the beauty of the limestone …" F. "… its components – complement one another …" G. "… not solid enough to be attached to the sand …" **Part A** Use evidence from the text "Classifying the Stars" by Annie J. Cannon to explain how Fraunhofer expanded the original understanding of the sun as presented by Newton. **Part B** Which detail from the article best supports the answer to Part A? A. "… the multiple spectral tings, ranging from delicate violet to deep red were crossed by hundreds of fine dark lines." B. "… sunlight and starlight are composed of waves of various lengths …" C. "… light is composed of many colors." D. "… sunbeams passing through rain drops are transformed into the myriad-tinted rainbow."

Continued ↑

Figure 6.4 | **Reading Anchor Standard 1: Progression of Instruction and Assessment, Grades 6–12 (cont'd.)**

Grade-Level Standard*	Area of Focus—Instructional Possibilities	Examples of Assessment
Grades 11–12 **RI.11–12.1.** Cite strong and thorough textual evidence to support analysis of what the text says explicitly as well as inferences drawn from the text, including determining where the text leaves matters uncertain. **RL.11–12.1.** Cite strong and thorough textual evidence to support analysis of what the text says explicitly as well as inferences drawn from the text, including determining where the text leaves matters uncertain. **RH.11–12.1.** Cite specific textual evidence to support analysis of primary and secondary sources, connecting insights gained from specific details to an understanding of the text as a whole. **RST.11–12.1.** Cite specific textual evidence to support analysis of science and technical texts, attending to important distinctions the author makes and to any gaps or inconsistencies in the account.	By grades 11 and 12, the specificity of what students are asked to do increases dramatically. They are now expected to document their inferences with specific information from one or more sources and also to identify inconsistencies or informational gaps. *Sample Informational Text Question:* Now that we've read some of Elon Musk's ideas regarding how to revolutionize space exploration, how do you think his thinking might be further informed by reading Gordon Kane's "The Mysteries of Mass"?	1. As Kane notes, scientists are hunting for the Higgs field. What questions might be answered if it is located? What questions regarding mass will still remain unanswered?

related areas of instructional focus and sample assessment items that are similar to those created by Smarter Balanced and PARCC (where applicable) and available in Appendix B of the Common Core ELA/literacy standards document.

What becomes obvious from reviewing the progression of Reading Standard 1 and the test items designed to assess it at the various grade levels is that students are being asked to move beyond the identification of information and to think about and analyze what they are reading. They are being asked to look deeply at a text and to think about what they are reading by explicitly and implicitly considering the language, author intent, text structure, and context.

≡◆≡

Teaching every student to "read like a detective and write like [an] investigative reporter" (Coleman, 2011, p. 11) implies a move to the upper quadrants of Bloom's taxonomy and greater emphasis on analyzing, hypothesizing, and critical evaluation. As Petrilli and Finn (2010) note, "Standards describe the destination that schools and students are supposed to reach, but by themselves have little power to effect change" (para. 4). The instruction you provide between the identification of the standard and student performance on the new and challenging Common Core assessments is a key determiner of how well your students will perform. By engaging students in close reading, you're helping them develop the skills and stamina they need to succeed. Through the process of formative assessment that we have shared in this chapter, you can focus on the immediate performance of your students during close reading and, based on what you observe, provide them with the instructional scaffolds they need to be able to read and learn from a complex text.

CONCLUSION

Like you, we realize that implementing the Common Core State Standards is a major undertaking that requires a reexamination of instruction. The ideas and examples presented in this text are shared to help you better understand what's involved in teaching your students to closely read a text and to support you in accommodating this added feature of instruction within your already crowded instructional day.

Just think for a minute about all that you already know about how to teach your students to read and communicate about texts. Don't let go of this information! Now add to those many research-supported practices one new practice—engaging your students in closely reading a short text or text segment.

As you have come to realize through your close reading of this book, the practice of close reading gets students involved in analyzing text-based information at a word, phrase, paragraph, or whole-passage level. While they are doing so, they make decisions about how all of the information fits together. They determine the central themes, ideas, contrasting perspectives, validity of arguments, and why the author chose this specific language to present the information. The thinking that students engage in during a close reading parallels the thinking we all do to succeed in daily life, as we're barraged with information from a wide variety of sources. What should be believed, repeated, studied, investigated, challenged, or disregarded? We can only make these decisions if we are able to think analytically.

Close reading instruction provides you the opportunity to teach your students to analyze complex text. Your questions cause them to return to the message of the text to determine its important ideas, and the facts and documentation supporting those ideas. Your questions help them to note similarities and differences across texts, to synthesize information, to evaluate the veracity of an author's claim, and to grasp the power of language. With your perseverance, they can learn to think deeply about information shared in the messages they receive in both written and spoken forms. With practice in attending to these details, your students will eventually be able to engage in closely reading texts and doing all of this analysis independently. Just as you taught them the content of their disciplines, you will now teach them to closely read the difficult text. The skills of analysis they gain from close text scrutiny will also empower their written and spoken discourses as they study an issue from multiple perspectives, and then share and support a well-grounded stance.

As a teacher, you are committed to providing the best possible instruction for each of your students. You continually add new practices to your instructional toolbox. Close reading instruction is one such practice. It can and should be used in all subject areas, and in all kinds of instructional configurations, both whole class and small group. It's a complex undertaking with a simple-to-describe format: Students purposefully read a complex text multiple times, guided by text-dependent questions and subsequent discussions that take them deeper into the text, where they develop a nuanced understanding of the text's information and language, as well as the author's intent. As you continue to implement the practice of close reading over time, you will see your students becoming increasingly able to tackle more difficult texts on their own. You will have given them vital tools that will serve them well as they move through the middle and high school grades and beyond—into college and careers and the next steps of their lives.

We hope we have helped you gain a better understanding of the process of close reading, its purpose, and all that students have to gain from its use. Give close reading a try in your classroom, and you'll be amazed, as we were, at how it will empower the thinking and communicating your students do.

APPENDIX A

A GUIDE FOR ADMINISTRATORS

How to Support Whole-School Implementaton of Close Reading

- Become informed about text complexity and close reading by learning what the Common Core standards say about these important topics.
- Schedule and attend workshops for your teachers that demonstrate how to analyze texts for text complexity and how to do close reading.
- Give teachers time for whole-school planning for close reading, identifying key goals and coordinating (1) what texts will be used at different grade levels in different content areas and (2) how close reading will be integrated into English language arts, social studies, science, mathematics, and other technical subjects.
- Give teachers time for planning for close reading to determine schedules for close reading experiences during each school day.
- Work with teachers to decide upon schoolwide, grade-level, or departmental annotations so students do not need to relearn annotation markings each year.
- Provide coaching for teachers as they "try on" close reading in their classrooms.
- Support teachers' efforts to implement close reading by arranging opportunities for peer observation and feedback.
- Use an observation form that parallels the planning they are doing for close reading instruction. An example follows on pages 202–204.

A CLOSE READING OBSERVATION GUIDE

Teacher: _____ Observer: _____

Grade: _____ Date: _____ Time: _____

Text Title: _____ ○ Whole Group ○ Small Group

- ○ Purpose statement is posted and explained.
- ○ Short complex passage is used.
- ○ Passage is numbered.
- ○ Annotation chart is posted, and students are annotating text.
- ○ Passage is read multiple times, as indicated below. Rereading the text 3–4 times is typical, but not required.

- ○ Frontloading is limited.
- ○ Teacher asks text-dependent questions.
- ○ Student talk is used.
- ○ Writing or closing task extends meaning or is used for assessment purposes.

	1st read	2nd read	3rd read	4th read
Teacher				
Students				

Questions to Consider:

- Is the purpose addressed throughout the lesson?
- What text-dependent questions are asked?

- How is student talk used to enhance students' understanding?
- Are insights gained from students' responses used to scaffold follow-up questions, discussion, and instruction?

1st Reading Notes/Comments:

2nd Reading
Notes/Comments:

3rd Reading
Notes/Comments:

**4th Reading
Notes/Comments:**

**Focus Forward
Notes:**

Resources for Learning More

Online

- EngageNY (http://engageny.org) is a comprehensive website for educators from the New York State Education Department that contains videos, professional development modules and resources, information for students and parents, and more.
- EduCore: Tools for Teaching the Common Core (http://educore.ascd.org/) from ASCD contains resources for teachers and administrators that include evidence-based strategies, videos, and supporting documents designed to support educators as they transition to the Common Core State Standards.
- The National Association of Secondary School Principals (NASSP) has a section of their website (www.nassp.org/knowledge-center/topics-of-interest/common-core-state-standards) featuring resources for teachers and administrators related to the Common Core, including professional articles and action briefs designed to provide information about the standards.
- The International Literacy Association (www.reading.org) has numerous resources related to implementation of the Common Core English language arts/literacy standards that include webinars featuring experts in literacy instruction.
- The Text Project (http://textproject.org/library/professional-development/) contains Common Core–related resources for teachers and administrators, including information on text complexity and free webinars on a range of topics related to the standards.

Books

- Blau, S. (2003). *The literature workshop.* Portsmouth, NH: Heinemann.
- Burke, J. (2013). *The Common Core companion: The standards decoded, grades 6–8: What they say, what they mean, how to teach them.* Thousand Oaks, CA: Corwin Press.
- Burke, J. (2013). *The Common Core companion: The standards decoded, grades 9–12: What they say, what they mean, how to teach them.* Thousand Oaks, CA: Corwin Press.

- Calkins, L., Ehrenworth, M., & Lehman, C. (2012). *Pathways to the Common Core: Accelerating achievement.* Portsmouth, NH: Heinemann.
- Fisher, D., & Frey, N. (2015). *Text-dependent questions: Pathways to close and critical reading (6–12).* Thousand Oaks, CA: Corwin.
- Fisher, D., Frey, N., & Lapp, D. (2012). *Text complexity: Raising rigor in reading.* Newark, DE: International Reading Association.
- Gallagher, K. (2004). *Deeper reading.* Portland, ME: Stenhouse.
- Lapp, D., Wolsey, T. D., Wood, K., & Johnson, K. (2015). *Mining complex texts: Using and creating graphic organizers to grasp content and share new understandings (6–12).* Thousand Oaks, CA: Corwin.
- Papert, S. (1980). *Mindstorms: Children, computers, and powerful ideas.* New York: Basic Books.
- Snow, C., & O'Conner, C. (2013, September 13). *Close reading and far-reaching classroom discussion: Fostering a vital connection.* (A Policy Brief from the Literacy Research Panel of the International Reading Association). Newark, DE: International Reading Association.
- Wessling, S. B., Lillge, D., & VanKooten, C. (2011). *Supporting students in a time of core standards: Grades 9–12.* Urbana, IL: National Council of Teachers of English.

APPENDIX B

COMMON CORE TEXT EXEMPLAR LOCATOR

You can find (and read) excerpts of the Common Core text exemplars discussed in this book in Appendix B to the Common Core State Standards for English Language Arts & Literacy in History/Social Studies, Science, and Technical Subjects. This document is available online at **http://www.corestandards.org/assets/ Appendix_B.pdf.**

The excerpts are the perfect length for close reading.

Title & Author	Location in the CCSS Appendix B	Text Type & Genre	Grade Band	Subject
1776; David McCullough	p. 176	Informational Text: Literary nonfiction	11–CCR	HST
"1941 State of the Union Address"; Franklin Delano Roosevelt	p. 124	Informational Text: Argumentative text	9–10	ELA/HST
"Address to Students at Moscow State University"; Ronald Reagan	p. 128	Informational Text: Argumentative text	9–10	HST
The Adventures of Tom Sawyer; Mark Twain	p. 77	Literature: Historical fiction	6–8	ELA
The American Reader: Words That Moved a Nation; Diane Ravitch (Ed.)	p. 175	Literature and Informational Text: Multiple genres	11–CCR	HST
America's Constitution: A Biography; Akhil Reed Amar	p. 176	Informational Text: Literary nonfiction	11–CCR	HST
"Amusement Park Physics"; Jearl Walker	p. 136	Informational Text: Expository text	9–10	SMT
Billy Budd, Sailor; Herman Melville	p. 147	Literature: Story	11–CCR	ELA
Black, Blue and Gray: African Americans in the Civil War; Jim Haskins	p. 131	Informational Text: Literary nonfiction	9–10	HST

Subject Key: ELA = English language arts; HST = history/social studies; SMT = science, mathematics, and technical subjects

Continued ➜

Title & Author	Location in the CCSS Appendix B	Text Type & Genre	Grade Band	Subject
Black Ships Before Troy: The Story of the Iliad; Rosemary Sutcliff	p. 81	Literature: Story	6–8	ELA/HST
"Blood, Toil, Tears and Sweat: Address to Parliament on May 13th, 1940"; Winston Churchill	p. 91	Informational Text: Argumentative text	6–8	HST
The Book Thief; Markus Zusak	p. 109	Literature: Historical fiction	9–10	ELA
Bury My Heart at Wounded Knee: An Indian History of the American West; Dee Brown	p. 130	Informational Text: Expository text	9–10	HST
Cathedral: The Story of Its Construction; David Macauley	p. 96	Informational Text: Expository text	6–8	SMT
Circumference: Eratosthenes and the Ancient Quest to Measure the Globe; Nicholas Nicastro	p. 137	Informational Text: Expository text	9–10	SMT
"Classifying the Stars"; Annie J. Cannon	p. 135	Informational Text: Expository text	9–10	SMT
Common Sense; Thomas Paine	p. 164	Informational Text: Argumentative text	11–CCR	ELA/HST
The Dark Is Rising; Susan Cooper	p. 79	Literature: Fantasy	6–8	ELA
"Demeter's Prayer to Hades"; Rita Dove	p. 163	Literature: Poetry	11–CCR	ELA
Democracy in America; Alexis de Tocqueville's	p. 172	Informational Text: Argumentative text	11–CCR	HST
The Diary of Anne Frank: A Play; Frances Goodrich and Albert Hackett	p. 83	Literature: Drama	6–8	HST
A Doll's House; Henrik Ibsen	p. 113	Literature: Drama	9–10	ELA
Don Quixote; Miguel de Cervantes	p. 140	Literature: Parody	11–CCR	ELA
Dragonwings; Laurence Yep	p. 80	Literature: Historical fiction	6–8	ELA
"Eleven"; Sandra Cisneros	p. 81	Literature: Realistic fiction	6–8	ELA

Title & Author	Location in the CCSS Appendix B	Text Type & Genre	Grade Band	Subject
"The Evolution of the Grocery Bag"; Henry Petroski	p. 98	Informational Text: Expository text	6–8	SMT
FedViews; Federal Reserve Bank of San Francisco	p. 177	Informational Text: Expository text	11–CCR	HST
Freedom Walkers: The Story of the Montgomery Bus Boycott; Russell Freedman	p. 95	Informational Text: Literary nonfiction	6–8	HST
Geeks: How Two Lost Boys Rode the Internet out of Idaho; John Katz	p. 97	Informational Text: Literary nonfiction	6–8	SMT
"Geology"; Rob Nagel (Ed.)	p. 98	Informational Text: Expository text	6–8	SMT
"Gettysburg Address"; Abraham Lincoln	p. 123	Informational Text: Argumentative text	9–10	ELA/HST
The Glass Menagerie; Tennessee Williams	p. 114	Literature: Drama	9–10	ELA
Google Hacks: Tips & Tools for Smarter Searching, 2nd Edition; Tara Calishnia and Rael Dornfest	p. 180	Informational Text: Expository text	11–CCR	SMT
The Grapes of Wrath; John Steinbeck	p. 105	Literature: Historical fiction	9–10	ELA/HST
The Great Fire; Jim Murphy	p. 94	Informational Text: Literary nonfiction	6–8	HST
The Great Gatsby; F. Scott Fitzgerald	p. 149	Literature: Historical fiction	11–CCR	ELA
Harriet Tubman: Conductor on the Underground Railroad; Ann Petry	p. 92	Informational Text: Biography	6–8	ELA/HST
"Hope, Despair, and Memory"; Elie Wiesel	p. 128	Informational Text: Argumentative text	9–10	ELA
The Hot Zone: A Terrifying True Story; Richard Preston	p. 136	Informational Text: Literary nonfiction	9–10	SMT
"I Am an American Day Address"; Learned Hand	p. 125	Informational Text: Argumentative text (persuasive speech)	9–10	ELA/HST

Continued ➜

Title & Author	Location in the CCSS Appendix B	Text Type & Genre	Grade Band	Subject
I Know Why the Caged Bird Sings; Maya Angelou	p. 128	Literature: Auto-biographical fiction	9–10	ELA
Innumeracy: Mathematical Illiteracy and Its Consequences; John Allen Paulos	p. 179	Informational Text: Literary nonfiction	11–CCR	SMT
Invasive Plant Inventory; California Invasive Plant Council	p. 99	Informational Text: Expository text	6–8	SMT
The Joy Luck Club; Amy Tan	p. 108	Literature: Contemporary novel	9–10	ELA
"Letter from Birmingham Jail"; Martin Luther King Jr.	p. 127	Informational Text: Argumentative text	9–10	ELA/HST
Life by the Numbers; Keith Devlin	p. 137	Informational Text: Expository text	9–10	SMT
The Longitude Prize; Joan Dash	p. 132	Informational Text: Literary nonfiction	9–10	HST
Math Trek: Adventures in the Math Zone; Ivars Peterson and Nancy Henderson	p. 97	Informational Text: Procedural text	6–8	SMT
Mirror of the World: A New History of Art; Julian Bell	p. 176	Informational Text: Literary nonfiction	11–CCR	HST
"Mother Tongue"; Amy Tan	p. 170	Informational Text: Argumentative text	11–CCR	ELA
"The Mysteries of Mass"; Gordon Kane	p. 180	Informational Text: Expository text	11–CCR	SMT
Narrative of the Life of Frederick Douglass, an American Slave, Written by Himself; Frederick Douglass'	p. 90	Informational Text: Autobiography	6–8	ELA/HST
"The Nose"; Nikolai Gogol	p. 102	Literature: Story	9–10	ELA
The Number Devil: A Mathematical Adventure; Hans Magnus Enzensberger	p. 96	Informational Text: Literary nonfiction	6–8	SMT
"O Captain! My Captain!"; Walt Whitman	p. 85	Literature: Poetry	6–8	ELA
"Ode on a Grecian Urn"; John Keats	p. 158	Literature: Poetry	11–CCR	ELA
The Odyssey; Homer	p. 101	Literature: Poetry	9–10	ELA

Title & Author	Location in the CCSS Appendix B	Text Type & Genre	Grade Band	Subject
Oedipus Rex; Sophocles	p. 110	Literature: Drama	9–10	ELA
Our Town: A Play in Three Acts; Thornton Wilder	p. 156	Literature: Drama	11–CCR	ELA
"Ozymandias"; Percy Bysshe Shelley	p. 117	Literature: Poetry	9–10	ELA
"Paul Revere's Ride"; Henry Wadsworth Longfellow	p. 83	Literature: Poetry (narrative)	6–8	ELA/HST
"The People Could Fly"; Virginia Hamilton	p. 80	Literature: Folktale	6–8	ELA
"A Poem for My Librarian, Mrs. Long"; Nikki Giovanni	p. 88	Literature: Poetry	6–8	ELA
"A Quilt of a Country"; Anna Quindlen	p. 129	Informational Text: Argumentative text	9–10	ELA
The Race to Save Lord God Bird; Phillip Hoose	p. 137	Informational Text: Literary nonfiction	9–10	SMT
"The Railway Train"; Emily Dickinson	p. 86	Literature: Poetry	6–8	ELA
"The Raven"; Edgar Allan Poe	p. 117	Literature: Poetry	9–10	ELA
"The Road Not Taken"; Robert Frost	p. 87	Literature: Poetry	6–8	ELA
Roll of Thunder, Hear My Cry; Mildred D. Taylor	p. 80	Literature: Historical fiction	6–8	ELA
A Short Walk Around the Pyramids and Through the World of Art; Phillip M. Isaacson	p. 93	Informational Text: Expository text	6–8	HST
Society and Solitude; Ralph Waldo Emerson	p. 167	Informational Text: Argumentative text	11–CCR	ELA
"Song of Myself"; Walt Whitman	p.159	Literature: Poetry	11–CCR	ELA
"The Song of Wandering Aengus"; William Butler Yeats	p. 87	Literature: Poetry	6–8	ELA
"Sonnet 73"; William Shakespeare	p. 116	Literature: Poetry	9–10	ELA
Sorry, Wrong Number; Lucille Fletcher	p. 82	Literature: Drama	6–8	ELA
"Space Probe" in *Astronomy and Space: From the Big Bang to the Big Crunch;* Philis Engelbert	p. 98	Informational Text: Expository text	6–8	SMT

Continued ➜

Title & Author	Location in the CCSS Appendix B	Text Type & Genre	Grade Band	Subject
The Story of Art, 16th Edition; E. H. Gombrich	p. 131	Informational Text: Expository text	9–10	HST
The Story of Science: Newton at the Center; Joy Hakim	p. 137	Informational Text: Literary nonfiction	9–10	SMT
Their Eyes Were Watching God; Zora Neale Hurston	p. 150	Literature: Historical fiction	11–CCR	ELA
Things Fall Apart; Chinua Achebe	p. 107	Literature: Story	9–10	ELA
This Land Was Made for You and Me: The Life and Songs of Woody Guthrie; Elizabeth Partridge	p. 94	Informational Text: Literary nonfiction	6–8	ELA/HST
The Tipping Point: How Little Things Can Make a Big Difference; Malcolm Gladwell	p. 179	Informational Text: Literary nonfiction	11–CCR	SMT
To Kill a Mockingbird; Harper Lee	p. 107	Literature: Historical fiction	9–10	ELA
"Untangling the Roots of Cancer"; W. Wayt Gibbs	p. 182	Informational Text: Expository text	11–CCR	SMT
Vincent Van Gogh: Portrait of an Artist; Jan Greenberg and Sandra Jordan	p. 94	Informational Text: Biography	6–8	HST
"What to the Slave Is the Fourth of July? An Address Delivered in Rochester, New York, 5 July 1852"; Frederick Douglass	p. 173	Informational Text: Argumentative text	11–CCR	HST
"Working Knowledge: Electronic Stability Control"; Mark Fischetti	p. 181	Informational Text: Expository text	11–CCR	SMT
A Wrinkle in Time; Madeleine L'Engle	p. 79	Literature: Fantasy	6–8	ELA

REFERENCES

Achebe, C. (1994). *Things fall apart*. New York: Anchor Press. (Original work published 1958).

Achieve, College Summit, National Association of Secondary School Principals [NASSP] & National Association of Elementary School Principals [NAESP]. (2013). *Implementing the Common Core State Standards: The role of the secondary school leader*. Retrieved from http://www.achieve.org/files/RevisedSecondaryActionBrief_Final_Feb.pdf

ACT. (2006). *Reading between the lines: What the ACT reveals about college readiness in reading*. Iowa City, IA: Author. Available: http://www.act.org/research/policymakers/pdf/reading_summary.pdf

Adams, M. J. (2010–2011, Winter). Advancing our students' language and literacy: The challenge of complex texts. *American Educator, 34*(4), 3–12.

Adler, M. J., & Van Doren, C. (1972). *How to read a book*. New York: Touchstone. (Original work published 1940).

Anderson, R. C., & Pearson, P. D. (1984). A schema-theoretic view of basic processes in reading comprehension. In P. D. Pearson (Ed.), *Handbook of reading research* (pp. 255–291). New York: Longman.

Balf, T. (2014, March 9). The SAT is hated by . . . all of the above. *The New York Times Magazine*, 28–31, 48–51.

Bauerline, M. (2011, February). Too dumb for complex texts? *Educational Leadership, 68*(5), 28–33.

Black, P., & Wiliam, D. (1998). Inside the black box: Raising standards through classroom assessment. *Phi Delta Kappan, 80*(2), 139–148.

Blau, S. (2003). *The literature workshop*. Portsmouth, NH: Heinemann.

Bloom, B. S. (Ed.), Engelhart, M. D., Furst, E. J., Hill, W. H., & Krathwohl, D. R. (1956). *Taxonomy of educational objectives: The classification of educational goals. Handbook 1: Cognitive domain*. New York: David McKay.

Buell, D. (2009). *Classroom strategies for interactive learning* (3rd ed.). Newark, DE: International Reading Association.

Burke, J. (2013a). *The Common Core companion: The standards decoded, grades 6–8: What they say, what they mean, how to teach them*. Thousand Oaks, CA: Corwin Press.

Burke, J. (2013b). *The Common Core companion: The standards decoded, grades 9–12: What they say, what they mean, how to teach them*. Thousand Oaks, CA: Corwin Press.

Burkins, J., & Yaris, K. (2012, May 18). The centrality of text [blog post]. Retrieved from http://www.burkinsandyaris.com/the-centrality-of-text/

Cairn, R. (2012). Primary sources: At the heart of the Common Core State Standards. *The Teaching with Primary Sources Journal, 1*(2). Retrieved from http://www.loc.gov/teachers/tps/journal/common_core/article.html

California Invasive Plant Council. (2006, February). *California invasive plant inventory.* Retrieved from http://www.cal-ipc.org/ip/inventory/pdf/Inventory2006.pdf

Calkins, L., Ehrenworth, M., & Lehman, C. (2012). *Pathways to the Common Core: Accelerating achievement.* Portsmouth, NH: Heinemann.

Chall, J., & Jacobs, V. (2003, Spring). The classic study on poor children's fourth-grade slump. *American Educator.* Available: http://www.aft.org/periodical/american-educator/spring-2003/classic-study-poor-childrens-fourth-grade-slump

Chall, J., Jacobs, V., & Baldwin, L. (1990). *The reading crisis: Why poor children fall behind.* Cambridge, MA: Harvard University Press.

Cisneros, S. (1991). Eleven. In *Woman Hollering Creek and other stories.* New York: Random House.

Cody, A. (2013, November 16). Common Core standards: 10 colossal errors [blog post]. Retrieved from http://blogs.edweek.org/teachers/living-in-dialogue/2013/11/common_core_standards_ten_colo.html

Coleman, D. (2011, April 28). *Bringing the Common Core to life* [Webinar transcript]. Retrieved from http://usny.nysed.gov/rttt/resources/bringing-the-common-core-to-life.html

Coleman, D., & Pimentel, S. (2012). *Revised publishers' criteria for the Common Core State Standards in English language arts and literacy, grades 3–12.* Washington, DC: National Governors Association Center for Best Practices and Council of Chief State School Officers. Available: http://www.corestandards.org/assets/Publishers_Criteria_for_3-12.pdf

Common Core. (2012a). *The Common Core curriculum maps: English language arts grades 6–8.* San Francisco: Jossey-Bass.

Common Core. (2012b). *The Common Core curriculum maps: English language arts grades 9–12.* San Francisco: Jossey-Bass.

Common Core State Standards Initiative [CCSSI]. (2014). *Key shifts in English language arts.* Retrieved from http://www.corestandards.org/other-resources/key-shifts-in-english-language-arts/

Copeland, M. (2005). *Socratic circles: Fostering critical and creative thinking in middle and high school.* Portland, ME: Stenhouse.

Cornell, B. (2000, October 16). Families: Pulling the plug on TV. *Time.* Retrieved from http://content.time.com/time/magazine/article/0,9171,998244,00.html

Corry, N., Pruzinsky, T., & Rumsey, N. (2009). Quality of life and psychological adjustment to burn injury: Social functioning, body image, and health perspectives. *International Review of Psychiatry, 21*(6), 539–548.

Cunningham, J. (1982). Generating interactions between schemata and text. In J. A. Niles & L. A. Harris (Eds.), *New inquiries in reading research and instruction* (pp. 42–47). Washington, DC: National Reading Conference.

Duke, N. K. (2000). 3.6 minutes per day: The scarcity of informational texts in first grade. *Reading Research Quarterly, 35,* 202–224.

Duke, N. K., & Bennett-Armistead, S. (2003). *Reading and writing informational texts in the primary grades.* New York: Scholastic.

Duke, N. K., Caughlan, S., Juzwik, M., & Martin, N. (2011). *Reading and writing genre with purpose in K–8 classrooms.* Portsmouth, NH: Heinemann.

Duke, N. K., & Roberts, K. L. (2010). The genre-specific nature of reading comprehension. In D. Wyse, R. Andrews, & J. Hoffman (Eds.), *The Routledge international handbook of English, language and literacy teaching* (pp. 74–86). London: Routledge.

Dunbar, P. L. (1889). Sympathy. Retrieved from http://www.poetryfoundation.org/poem/175756

Duncan, A. (2014, January 27). Seize the day: Change in the classroom and the core of schooling. Remarks at the ASCD Leadership Institute Conference, Washington, DC. Available: http://www.ed.gov/news/speeches/seize-day-change-classroom-and-core-schooling

Eisele, R. (Screenwriter). (2007). First debate: Wiley College vs. Paul Quinn College. In D. Washington (Director), *The great debaters* [Motion picture]. United States: The Weinstein Company and Harpo Films.

Engelbert, P. (Ed.). (2009). Space probe. In *Astronomy and space: From the big bang to the big crunch.* Farmington Hills, MI: Gale Cengage Learning.

Fearn, L., & Farnan, N. (2001). *Interactions: Teaching writing and the language arts.* Boston: Houghton Mifflin.

Fisher, D., & Frey, N. (2014). *Better learning through structured teaching: A framework for the gradual release of responsibility* (2nd ed.). Alexandria, VA: ASCD.

Fisher, D., & Frey, N. (2013). *Common Core English language arts in a PLC at Work, grades 3–5.* Bloomington, IN: Solution Tree.

Fisher, D., Frey, N., & Lapp, D. (2012). *Text complexity: Raising rigor in reading.* Newark, DE: International Reading Association.

Frey, N., & Fisher, D. (2011). *The formative assessment action plan: Practical steps to more successful teaching and learning.* Alexandria, VA: ASCD.

Gallagher, K. (2004). *Deeper reading.* Portland, ME: Stenhouse.

Gast, J. (1872). American progress [Painting]. Retrieved from http://picturinghistory.gc.cuny.edu/item.php?item_id=180

Gillis, J. (2013, August 19). Climate panel cites near certainty on warming. *New York Times.* Retrieved from http://www.nytimes.com/2013/08/20/science/earth/extremely-likely-that-human-activity-is-driving-climate-change-panel-finds.html?pagewanted=all&_r=0

Grant, M., Lapp, D., Fisher, D., Johnson, K., & Frey, N. (2012). Purposeful instruction: Mixing up the "I," "we," and "you." *Journal of Adolescent & Adult Literacy, 56*(1), 45–55.

Guthrie, J. T., Schafer, W. D., Von Secker, C., & Alban, T. (2000). Contributions of integrated reading instruction and text resources to achievement and engagement in a statewide school improvement program. *Journal of Educational Research, 93,* 211–226.

Guthrie, J., & Wigfield, A. (2000). Engagement and motivation in reading. In M. Kamil, P. Mosenthal, D. Pearson, & R. Barr (Eds.), *Handbook of reading research* (pp. 518–533). Mahwah, NJ: Erlbaum.

Hakim, J. (2005). *The story of science: Newton at the center.* Washington, DC: Smithsonian Books.

Hakim, J. (2007). *A history of US: Liberty for all? 1820–1860. A history of US book five* (3rd rev. ed.). New York: Oxford University Press.

Hart, B., & Risley, T. (1995). *Meaningful differences in the everyday experience of young American children.* Baltimore, MD: Brookes.

Hattie, J., & Timperley, H. (2007). The power of feedback. *Review of Educational Research, 77*(1), 81–112.

Hess, K. K. (2009). *Hess' cognitive rigor matrix.* Dover, NH: National Center for Assessment. Retrieved from http://static.pdesas.org/content/documents/M1-Slide_22_DOK_Hess_Cognitive_Rigor.pdf

History.com. (2014). *Remembering the Holocaust* [Photo gallery]. Retrieved from http://www.history.com/topics/world-war-ii/the-holocaust/pictures

Hunt Institute. (2011, August 19). *Literacy in other disciplines* [Video file]. Retrieved from http://www.youtube.com/watch?v=1zHWMfg_8r0

Hutten, S. (2013). No fear! *The Source: California History-Social Science Quarterly Magazine, 5.* Retrieved from http://chssp.ucdavis.edu/source-magazine/teaching-the-common-core

Ivey, G. (2010, March). Texts that matter. *Educational Leadership, 67*(6), 18–23.

Jeong, J., Gaffney, J. S., & Choi, J. (2010). Availability and use of informational texts in second-, third-, and fourth-grade classrooms. *Research in the Teaching of English, 44*(4), 435–456.

Joos, M. (1967). *Five clocks.* New York: Harcourt, Brace, & World.

Kamil, M. (2004, August). *Reading to learn 2004.* Paper presented at the Reading to Learn Summer Institute, Escondido, California.

Kamil, M., & Lane, D. (1997). *Using information text for first grade reading instruction: Theory and practice.* Paper presented at the National Reading Conference, Scottsdale, Arizona.

Kuhn, M. R., & Stahl, S. A. (2000). *Fluency: A review of developmental and remedial practices.* Ann Arbor, MI: Center for the Improvement of Early Reading Achievement.

Lapp, D., & Fisher, D. (2009). It's all about the book: Motivating teens to read. *Journal of Adolescent & Adult Literacy, 52*(7), 556–651.

Lapp, D., Fisher, D., Flood, J., & Cabello, A. (2001). An integrated approach to the teaching and assessment of language arts. In S. R. Hurley & J. V. Tinajero (Eds.), *Literacy assessment of second language learners* (pp. 1–26). Boston: Allyn & Bacon.

Lapp, D., Fisher, D., Frey, N., & Gonzalez, A. (2014, November). Students can purposefully create information, not just consume it. *Journal of Adolescent & Adult Literacy, 58*(3), 182–188.

Lapp, D., Grant, M., Moss, B., & Johnson, K. (2013). Students' close reading of science texts: What's now? What's next? *The Reading Teacher, 67*(2), 109–119.

Lapp, D., Moss, B., Johnson, K., & Grant, M. (2012, Fall). Teaching students to closely read texts: How and when? (ILA E-ssentials, Rigorous Real World Teaching and Learning.) International Literacy Association. Retrieved from http://www.reading.org/general/Publications/e-ssentials/e8022

Lee, C. D., & Spratley, A. (2010). *Reading in the disciplines: The challenges of adolescent literacy.* New York: Carnegie Corporation of New York.

Leu, D., Castek, J., Hartman, D., Coiro, J., Henry, L., Kulikowich, J., & Lyver, S. (2005). *Evaluating the development of scientific knowledge and new forms of reading comprehension during online learning.* Final report presented to the North Central Regional Educational Laboratory/Learning Point Associates. Retrieved from http:// newliteracies.uconn.edu/ncrel-grant-project

Leutze, E. (1862). *Westward the course of empire takes its way* [Painting]. United States. Retrieved from http://www.aoc.gov/capitol-hill/other-paintings-and-murals/westward-course-empire-takes-its-way

Lincoln, A. (1863, November 19). Gettysburg address. Retrieved from http://www.abrahamlincolnonline.org/lincoln/speeches/gettysburg.htm

Lord, W. (2001). *Day of infamy: The classic account of the bombing of Pearl Harbor.* New York: Henry Holt.

Luke, A., & Freebody, P. (1999). A map of possible practices: Further notes on the four resources model. *Practically Primary, 4*(2), 5–8.

Marinak, B., & Gambrell, L. (2008). Intrinsic motivation and rewards: What sustains young children's engagement with text? *Literacy Research and Instruction, 47*(1), 9–26.

Mayo Clinic Staff. (2014). Radiation sickness: Symptoms. Retrieved from http://www.mayoclinic.org/diseases-conditions/radiation-sickness/basics/symptoms/con-20022901

McConachie, S. M., & Petrosky, A. R. (2010). *Content matters: A disciplinary literacy approach to improving student learning.* San Francisco: Jossey-Bass.

MetaMetrics. (2014a). Typical reader measures, by grade. Retrieved from http://www.lexile.com/about-lexile/grade-equivalent/grade-equivalent-chart

MetaMetrics. (2014b). Typical text measures, by grade. Retrieved from http://www.lexile.com/about-lexile/grade-equivalent/grade-equivalent-chart

Miller, R., & Calfee, R. (2004). Comprehending through composing: Reflections on reading assessment strategies. In S. Paris & S. Stahl (Eds.), *Children's reading comprehension & assessment* (pp. 215–233). New York: Routledge.

Mohr, K. (2006). Children's choices for recreational reading: A three-part investigation of selection preferences, rationales, and processes. *Journal of Literacy Research, 38*(1), 81–104.

Moss, B. (2002). Close up: An interview with Dr. Richard Vacca. *The California Reader, 36*, 54–59.

Moss, B. (2008). The information text gap: The mismatch between non-narrative text types in basal readers and 2009 NAEP recommended guidelines. *Journal of Literacy Research, 40*, 201–219.

Moss, B. (2011). Boost critical thinking: New titles for thematically based text sets. *Voices from the Middle, 19*(1), 46–48.

Moss, B., & Hendershot, J. (2002). Exploring sixth graders' selection of nonfiction trade books. *The Reading Teacher, 56*, 6–17.

Moss, B., Lapp, D., & O'Shea, M. (2011). Tiered texts: Supporting knowledge and language learning for English learners and struggling readers. *English Journal, 100*(5), 54–60.

Murphy, J. (1995). *The great fire.* New York: Scholastic.

National Council for the Social Studies. (2013). *The College, Career, and Civic Life (C3) Framework for Social Studies State Standards: Guidance for enhancing the rigor of K–12 civics, economics, geography, and history.* Silver Spring, MD: National Council for the Social Studies.

National Governors Association [NGA] Center for Best Practices & Council of Chief State School Officers [CCSSO]. (2010a). *Common Core State Standards for English language arts & literacy in history/social studies, science, and technical subjects.* Washington, DC: Authors. Retrieved from http://www.corestandards.org/assets/CCSSI_ELA%20Standards.pdf

National Governors Association [NGA] Center for Best Practices & Council of Chief State School Officers [CCSSO]. (2010b). *Common Core State Standards for English language arts & literacy in history/social studies, science, and technical subjects—Appendix B: Text exemplars and sample performance tasks.* Washington, DC: Authors.

National Oceanic and Atmospheric Administration [NOAA]. (n.d.). *What is ocean acidification?* Retrieved from http://www.pmel.noaa.gov/co2/story/What+is+Ocean+Acidification%3F

NGSS Lead States. (2013). *Next Generation Science Standards: For states, by states.* Washington, DC: The National Academies Press. Retrieved from http://www.nextgenscience.org/next-generation-science-standards

Nicastro, N. (2008). *Circumference: Eratosthenes and the ancient quest to measure the globe.* New York: St. Martin's Press.

Palincsar, A. S., & Duke, N. K. (2004). The role of text and text–reader interactions in young children's reading development and achievement. *The Elementary School Journal, 105*(2), 183–197.

Papert, S. (1980). *Mindstorms: Children, computers and powerful ideas.* New York: Basic Books.

Pappas, C. C. (1993). Is narrative "primary"? Some insights from kindergartners' pretend readings of stories and information books. *Journal of Reading Behavior, 25*, 97–129.

Partnership for Assessment of Readiness for College and Careers [PARCC]. (2012). *PARCC model content frameworks: English language arts/literacy grades 3–11.* Retrieved from http://www.parcconline.org/sites/parcc/files/PARCCMCFELALiteracyAugust2012_FINAL.pdf

Partridge, E. (2002). *This land was made for you and me: The life and songs of Woody Guthrie.* New York: Viking.

Pearson, P. D. (2004). The reading wars. *Educational Policy, 18*(1), 216–252.

Pearson, P. D. (2013). Research foundations of the Common Core State Standards in English language arts. In S. B. Neuman & L. B. Gambrell (Eds.), *Quality reading instruction in the age of Common Core standards* (pp. 237–262). Newark, DE: International Reading Association.

Pearson, P. D., & Gallagher, G. (1983). The gradual release of responsibility model of instruction. *Contemporary Educational Psychology, 8*, 112–123.

Petrilli, M. J., & Finn, C. E. Jr. (2010, October 20). Common Core standards: Now what? *Education Gadfly Weekly, 10*(39). Available: http://www.edexcellence.net/commentary/education-gadfly-weekly/2010/october-21/common-core-standards-now-what.html

Popham, W. J. (2008). *Transformative assessment.* Alexandria, VA: ASCD.

Ravitch, D. (2013, March 25). Should the Common Core standards have been field tested? [blog post]. Retrieved from http://dianeravitch.net/2013/03/25/should-the-common-core-standards-have-been-field-tested

Robb, L. (2002, May/June). The myth of learn to read/read to learn. *Scholastic Instructor, 111*(8), 23. Available: http://www.scholastic.com/teachers/article/myth-learn-readread-learn

Rosenblatt, L. M. (1978). *The reader, the text, the poem: The transactional theory of the literary work.* Carbondale, IL: Southern Illinois University Press.

Rosenblatt, L. M. (1995). *Literature as exploration* (5th ed.). New York: Modern Language Association.

Roth, P. (2004). *Portnoy's complaint.* New York: Vintage Books. (Original work published 1967).

Samuels, S. J. (2007). The DIBELS tests: Is speed of barking at print what we mean by reading fluency? *Reading Research Quarterly, 42*, 563–566.

Santa, C., & Havens, L. (1995). *Creating independence through student-owned strategies: Project CRISS.* Dubuque, IA: Kendall Hunt.

ScienceDaily. (2010, April 6). Geologist connects regular changes of Earth's orbital cycle to changes in climate. Retrieved from http://www.sciencedaily.com/releases/2010/04/100406133707.htm

Shanahan, T. (2009, September 28). Putting students into books for instruction [blog post]. Retrieved from http://www.shanahanonliteracy.com/2009/09/putting-students-into-books-for.html

Shanahan, T. (2012, June 18). What is close reading? [blog post]. Retrieved from http://www.shanahanonliteracy.com/2012/06/what-is-close-reading.html

Shanahan, T. (2013, August 11). Text dependency is too low a standard [blog post]. Retrieved from http://www.shanahanonliteracy.com/2013/08/text-dependency-is-too-low-standard.html

Shanahan, T., & Shanahan, C. (2008, Spring). Teaching disciplinary literacy to adolescents: Rethinking content-area literacy. *Harvard Education Review, 78*(1), 40–59.

Shanahan, T., & Shanahan, C. (2012, January/March). What is disciplinary literacy and why does it matter? *Topics in Language Disorders, 32*(1), 7–18.

Smith, M. W., & Wilhelm, H .D. (2002). *Reading don't fix no Chevys: Literacy in the lives of young men.* Portsmouth, NH: Heinemann.

Snow, C. (2001, February). *Improving reading outcomes: Getting beyond third grade.* Washington, DC: The Aspen Institute.

Snow, C., & O'Conner, C. (2013, September 13). *Close reading and far-reaching classroom discussion: Fostering a vital connection.* (A Policy Brief from the Literacy Research Panel of the International Reading Association). Newark, DE: International Reading Association.

Sotomayor, S. (2013). *My beloved world.* New York: Knopf.

Stenner, A. J., Koons, H., & Swartz, C. W. (2010). *Text complexity and developing expertise in reading.* Durham, NC: MetaMetrics.

Vygotsky, L. S. (1978). *Mind in society: The development of higher psychological processes.* Cambridge, MA: Harvard University Press.

Wade, S. E., & Moje, E. B. (2000). The role of text in classroom learning. In M. L. Kamil, P. B. Mosentha, P. D. Pearson, & R. Barr (Eds.), *Handbook of reading research, Vol. 3* (pp. 609–629). Mahwah, NJ: Erlbaum.

Walker, J. (1983, October). The amateur scientist: Thinking about physics while scared to death (on a falling roller coaster). *Scientific American, 249*(4), 162–169.

Webb, N., et al. (2005, July 24). WAT: Web alignment tool. Wisconsin Center of Educational Research, University of Wisconsin–Madison. Retrieved from http://www.wcer.wisc.edu/WAT/index.aspx

Wessling, S. B., Lillge, D., & VanKooten, C. (2011). *Supporting students in a time of core standards: Grades 9–12.* Urbana, IL: National Council of Teachers of English.

Williamson, G. L. (2006). *Aligning the journey with a destination: A model for K–16 reading standards.* Durham, NC: MetaMetrics.

Wineburg, S. S. (1991). On the reading of historical texts: Notes on the breach between school and academy. *American Educational Research Journal, 28,* 495–519.

Wineburg, S. S. (1998). Reading Abraham Lincoln: An expert/expert study in the interpretation of historical texts. *Cognitive Science, 22,* 319–346.

Wurman, R. S. (2001). *Information anxiety 2.* Indianapolis, IN: Que.

Zawilinski, L., & Leu, D. J. (2008, March 27). *A taxonomy of skills and strategies from verbal protocol of accomplished adolescent Internet users.* Paper presented at the American Educational Research Association Conference, New York.

Zygouris-Coe, V. (2012). Disciplinary literacy and the Common Core State Standards. *Topics in Language Disorders, 32*(1), 35–50.

INDEX

The letter *f* following a page number denotes a figure.

ABOUT THE AUTHORS

Barbara Moss, PhD, is a professor of literacy education at San Diego State University, where she teaches both preservice and graduate courses in literacy education. During her long career in the public schools, she taught reading or English language arts at the elementary, middle, and high school levels. In addition, she worked as a reading specialist, a reading supervisor, and a high school literacy coach. She has worked as a university professor in both Ohio and California. Her research interests focus on children's literature in the classroom, especially informational texts, disciplinary literacy, and teacher implementation of instructional strategies. Barbara has published widely in literacy journals including *The Reading Teacher, The Journal of Literacy Research,* and *Reading and Writing Quarterly.* She regularly presents at professional conferences on a range of topics, including children's literature, close reading, and the Common Core State Standards. She has served as the editor of *The Ohio Reading Teacher* and on the editorial board of *The Reading Teacher* and several other literacy journals. She has served as a staff developer for numerous school districts and done hundreds of professional presentations for teachers across the country, both face to face and online. She has authored, co-authored, or edited numerous books on topics including independent reading, classroom strategies for teaching informational texts, new literacies, and children's nonfiction trade books. Her most recently co-authored books include *35 Strategies for Guiding Readers Through Informational Texts* (Guilford Press) and *Not This but That: No More Independent Reading Without Support* (Heinemann). She also recently served as the Young Adult Literature column editor for *Voices in the Middle,* a publication of the National Council of Teachers of English. She can be reached at bmoss@mail.sdsu.edu.

Diane Lapp, EdD, is Distinguished Professor of Education in the Department of Teacher Education at San Diego State University (SDSU), where she teaches both preservice and graduate courses in literacy education. During her career, Diane has taught in elementary, middle, and high schools, and she has recently had the opportunity to return to the classroom to teach 6th grade English and Earth Science at Health Sciences Middle School in San Diego, where she is also an instructional coach at both the middle school and Health Sciences High and Middle College. Diane's major areas of research and instruction are issues related to struggling readers and writers, their families, and their teachers. Currently a co-editor of *Voices from the Middle*, published by the National Council of Teachers of English, Diane has authored, coauthored, and edited numerous articles, columns, texts, handbooks, and children's materials on reading, language arts, and instructional issues, including the Common Core State Standards. She has also chaired and cochaired several International Reading Association (IRA) and Literacy Research Association committees. A member of both the California and International Reading Halls of Fame, her many educational awards include being named as Outstanding Teacher Educator and Faculty Member in the Department of Teacher Education at SDSU, Distinguished Research Lecturer from SDSU's Graduate Division of Research, IRA's 1996 Outstanding Teacher Educator of the Year, and IRA's 2011 John Manning Award recipient for her work in public schools. Diane can be reached at lapp@mail.sdsu.edu. For additional information, please visit http://edweb.sdsu.edu/people/DLapp/DLapp.html.

Maria Grant, EdD, is an associate professor in secondary education at California State University, Fullerton (CSUF). She has authored numerous publications centered on close reading, Common Core State Standards, science literacy, formative assessment, and reading in the content areas, including articles in *Educational Leadership* and the *Journal of Adolescent & Adult Literacy*. Additionally, she is coauthor of *Reading and Writing in Science: Tools to Develop Disciplinary Literacy*, with Douglas Fisher, and *Teaching Students to Think Like Scientists: Strategies Aligned with Common Core and Next Generation Science Standards*, with Douglas Fisher and Diane Lapp. Her most recent work focuses on the Common Core State Standards for English Language Arts, concentrating on support for teachers working to implement the six shifts of ELA standards, move students toward reading more informational text, and use close reading in the classroom. Additionally, she works with teachers to implement key elements of the new Science Framework and the Next Generation Science Standards. Maria teaches courses in the credential and graduate programs at CSUF and conducts professional development with teachers at various schools across the country. She is currently director of the Intern Program and leads the Literacy Summer Seminar Series at CSUF. Maria can be reached at mgrant@fullerton.edu.

Kelly Johnson, PhD, a National Board–Certified teacher, is a Common Core support teacher in the San Diego Unified School District, where she works in classrooms with teachers modeling how to implement the Common Core strategies across the disciplines and grades. A faculty member in teacher education at San Diego State University, Kelly teaches reading methods, classroom management, and liberal studies. She received the California Reading Association's Constance McCullough Research Award for her study on assessment and diagnostic instruction. Kelly also received the International Reading Association's Celebrate Literacy Award, which honors educators for their significant literacy contributions. Kelly has published in *The Reading Teacher, The California Reader, The Reading Professor,* and *Literacy.* She has also coauthored several books: *Accommodating Differences Among English Language Learners: 75+ Literacy Lessons* (2nd and 3rd editions), *Designing Responsive Curriculum: Planning Lessons That Work,* and *Teaching Literacy in First Grade (Tools for Teaching Literacy).* Often referred to by her colleagues as a teacher's teacher, Kelly has appeared in many instructional videos on teacher modeling, assessment and instruction, effective grouping, and writing instruction. Her current focus is assessment and small-group instruction in secondary classrooms. Prior to her current secondary and postsecondary positions, Kelly taught grades 1–6 and worked as a peer coach and a reading intervention teacher. She can be reached at kjohnson@hshmc.org.

Related ASCD Resources

At the time of publication, the following ASCD resources were available (ASCD stock numbers appear in parentheses). For up-to-date information about ASCD resources, go to www.ascd.org.

ASCD EDge Group
Exchange ideas and connect with other educators interested in various topics, including "The Common Core in the Classroom," "English and Language Arts," and "Literacy, Language, Literature" on the social networking site ASCD EDge™ at http://edge.ascd.org/

Print Products
A Close Look at Close Reading: Teaching Students to Analyze Complex Texts, Grades K–5 by Diane Lapp, Barbara Moss, Maria Grant, and Kelly Johnson (#114008)

Common Core State Standards for High School English Language Arts: A Quick-Start Guide by Susan Ryan and Dana Frazee; edited by John Kendall (#113010)

Common Core State Standards for Middle School English Language Arts: A Quick-Start Guide by Susan Ryan and Dana Frazee; edited by John Kendall (#113012)

The Multiple Intelligences of Reading and Writing: Making the Words Come Alive by Thomas Armstrong (#102280)

Teaching Reading in the Content Areas: If Not Me, Then Who? 3rd edition by Vicki Urqhart and Dana Frazee (#112024)

Total Literacy Techniques: Tools to Help Students Analyze Literature and Informational Texts by Pérsida Himmele and William Himmele, with Keely Potter (#114009)

PD Online
The Common Core: Teaching Argumentative Writing and Speaking: Grades 6–12 (#PD14OC018)

Common Core and Literacy Strategies: History/Social Studies, 2nd Edition (#PD14OC005M)

Common Core and Literacy Strategies: Science, 2nd Edition (#PD14OC004M)

Text Complexity: Understanding the Literacy Shifts in the Common Core Standards: Grades 6–12 (#PD13OC007M)

DVD
The Innovators: Integrating Literacy into Curriculum DVD (#613070)

THE WHOLE CHILD The Whole Child Initiative helps schools and communities create learning environments that allow students to be healthy, safe, engaged, supported, and challenged. To learn more about other books and resources that relate to the whole child, visit www.wholechildeducation.org.

For more information: send e-mail to member@ascd.org; call 1-800-933-2723 or 703-578-9600, press 2; send a fax to 703-575-5400; or write to Information Services, ASCD, 1703 N. Beauregard St., Alexandria, VA 22311-1714 USA.